IS THE

GOOD
BOOK
BAD?

MOSAICA PRESS

IS THE

GOOD BOOK BAD?

A Traditional Jewish Response
to the Moral Indictments of the Bible

MICHOEL STERN

Published by Mosaica Press, Inc.
www.mosaicapress.com
info@mosaicapress.com

I would like to dedicate this book to those who have already gone to reap their reward in *Olam Haba* (the World to Come) and were a great influence upon me and my wife in shaping and inspiring us to strive to contribute to the Jewish community and be proud of our heritage.

YAAKOV BEN MORDECHAI TZVI (JACOB GUNZ)

He went through the horrors of the Holocaust and yet stayed steadfast in his faith and commitment to Hashem and His Torah. He suffered immense and lasting trauma from what he endured, yet you would never guess it from his constant positive countenance.

NINA BAS MEIR (NINA MOCTON)

She was a pillar of kindness in her community, and yet even her closest family members were unaware of the complete scope of her kindness, as she was more interested in helping others than receiving recognition for her selfless service.

BLEMA BAS SHMUEL (BLEMA BAER)

She was the matriarch of the family who had the most compassion and pleasant spirit of anyone I know or ever knew. She only knew how to give and constantly had the needs of others on her mind.

MIRIAM BAS SHMUEL (MARIAN STERN)

She was active in the Jewish community and was always proud of her Jewish heritage.

Rabbi Zev Leff   הרב זאב לף

Rabbi of Moshav Matityahu   מרא דאתרא מושב מתתיהו
Rosh HaYeshiva—Yeshiva Gedola Matityahu   ראש הישיבה—ישיבה גדולה מתתיהו

D.N. Modiin 71917   **Tel:** 08-976-1138 טל'   **Fax:** 08-976-5326 פקס'   71917 מודיעין ד.נ.

Dear Friends,

I have read portions of the book "Is the Good Book Bad?" by Michoel Stern.

The book as its subtitle relates is "A traditional Jewish response to the moral indictments of the Bible". Our sages enjoin us "To know how to answer the heretic" many times this is not in order to convince the heretic, as people are often blinded by their subjective positions and not open to discussion, persausion or proofs. Rather the purpose is to strengthen one's own faith and belief by exposing the falseness of the various challenges of the heretics.

The author presents the various challenges that are made that question the morality of the Torah vis a vis the politically correct morality of the secular world and he answers them in an extremely effective manner.

The sources he quotes both in presentation of the challenges and in his presentation of the Torah sources in rebuttal are extremely inpressive and his vast scholarship in both areas is evident.

His responses are not apologetics, as the Torah needs not to apologize as it is G-d's word, but rather instructive, revealing the fallacies and often ignorance that the challenges are based on.

I found this work enlightening, informative and interesting and recommend it to all who are aware of these attacks on the Torah and need strenghening , as well as to those who come in contact and are in a position to influence those who seek answers to these challenges, that sometimes serve as an impediment for them to embrace a Torah lifestyle.

I commend the author for a truly quality presentation. I pray that Hashem bless him and his family with life, health and the wherewithal to continue to merit the community with further Torah works.

Sincerely,
With Torah blessings
Zev Leff
Rabbi Zev Leff

תפארת גדליה

YGW

From the Desk of

RABBI AHRON LOPIANSKY

Rosh HaYeshiva

Menachem Av 5779

B"h there has been a resurgence of Torah learning in our generation. Many people who have begun studying Torah find the study of Navi particularly uplifting. Yet many sections of Navi leaves the student baffled in terms of understanding the moral rectitude of the events.

Rabbi Stern has spent years gathering authentic Torah sources who deal with these issues in particular. This will be helpful both for the teacher who may elaborate on the points noted here, and the student who is capable of using these texts to strike out on his own.

This work fills a great vacuum, and iy"h will prove to be an invaluable aid in making the word of Hashem accessible to all.

Ahron Lopiansky

TABLE OF CONTENTS

FOREWORD. XI

PREFACE XII

ACKNOWLEDGMENTS. XIV

INTRODUCTION 1

The Point and the Premise / Exclusive Focus on the Jewish Scriptures / Mesorah, the Integral Nature of the Oral Tradition / Not All Violence in Scripture Is Endorsed by the Divine / The Importance of Acknowledging a Spiritual Reality / The Verses Covered Are Comprehensive, but Not Totally Exhaustive / An In-Depth Explanation of the Concepts of Peace and Mercy / Explanations and Reasons—a Limited Endeavor

CHAPTER ONE

DO THE SCRIPTURES SUPPORT
UNWARRANTED VIOLENCE?. 17

I: National Violence / II: Individual Violence / III: The Death Penalty and Other Punishments / Summary

CHAPTER TWO

VIOLENCE CARRIED OUT OR ORDERED BY GOD 63

I: The Nature of God / II: God Punishing the Jewish People as a Nation for Disobedience / III: Violence Not Related to Punishment of the Jewish People / Summary

CHAPTER THREE

DOES SCRIPTURE ENCOURAGE BARBARIC
AND BACKWARD PRACTICES? 87

I: Animals / II: Women's Issues / III: Slavery / IV: The Chosen People / Summary

CHAPTER 4

THE SUPERIORITY OF A BIBLICALLY BASED MORALITY . . .155

I: Natural Law according to Judaism / II: Scientific Naturalism / Materialism / III: Individual (Personal) Advantages to Divine Morality / IV: Societal Advantages to Divine Morality / V: Holiness—beyond Ethics / VI: Religious Motivation for Ethics / VII: Conclusion / Summary

EPILOGUE 207

APPENDIX A

A CRITICAL EXAMINATION OF ARGUMENTS
OFFERED BY GAY ACTIVISTS 209

APPENDIX B

PHILOSOPHICAL ADVANTAGES
TO DIVINE-BASED MORALITY 217

The Euthyphro Dilemma / Other Philosophical Objections to Divine Command Theory (DCT) / Secular Attempts at Objective Morality Independent of God

APPENDIX C

LOOSE ENDS 266

Why Non-Biblical Justifications for Violence Are Irrelevant in This Book / A Justification for Biblical Violence, not a Promotion for Post-Biblical Violence / Many Interpretations to Choose From, but Who Has the Advantage? / Is Belief in God Escapism?

FOREWORD

R abbi Michael Stern has produced a very valuable study of
morality in classical Jewish sources. The topics covered are
drawn from a variety of familiar contemporary complaints
against the morality of traditional Judaism. In addition to a very extensive treatment of violence, the book addresses the nature of idolatry,
the nature of sexual morality, the appropriate psychology of Divine service, the role of God in morality, and many more related subjects. In his
treatment of these topics, Rabbi Stern engages a wide variety of secular
sources, including the works of the so-called new atheists and other
philosophers and other social critics. I believe that anyone who cares
about these subjects—and even those who have researched them—will
find an enormous amount of valuable material in this book. Rabbi
Stern has attempted to address very difficult questions on which there
is widespread comment both from within and without the Jewish tradition. His scholarship is far-ranging and very illuminating. The issues
by their very nature are difficult, subtle, and nuanced. Some readers
may prefer approaches other than that of Rabbi Stern, but everyone
will be better informed by his analysis and his wide-ranging sources.
I congratulate him on his valuable contribution to the presentation of
genuine Jewish sources on these difficult topics.

Rabbi Dr. Dovid Gottlieb
Yeshivat Ohr Somayach

PREFACE

This book was written from an outgrowth of my concern for the many people who have the desire to grow in their spirituality but have the impediment of being bombarded by manipulation and those who ridicule the source of their spiritual nourishment, namely the word of God. The impetus for my researching this topic was my own quest to sufficiently address for myself the myriad of moral accusations leveled against the Bible. You, as the reader, are invited to see where that quest has led me.

Many today, merely by living in our Western society, have obtained a worldview that often views Scripture and its value as archaic. Well-meaning secular writers and professors in academia have greatly contributed to this perception. For them, at best, the Bible is a book written for people who lived in a time where that was the best they could do. However, they feel Scripture pales in comparison to the "noble" standard of twenty-first-century "morality." It is my contention that the Bible[1] and absolute ethical behavior (back then as well as now) are not only not in opposition to one another, but that the word of God is the source for absolute ethics.

For people who did not grow up in a religious environment, I am confident that my work will give them food for thought and will provide them with a different and unique perspective from which to view Scripture as never before. For people raised in a religious environment but who were never exposed to an in-depth treatment of this topic,

---

1   Including the Oral Tradition that accompanies it.

I hope this material will provide support for and confidence in what they already know to be true. Even for the most Orthodox among us, much of the violence mentioned in the Bible can come across as barbaric if we are not aware of the meaning, context, and intended application or lesson. In this spirit, by uniting the literal words of God with the beauty of the traditional understanding of those words, we will see that the "Good Book" is truly good.

ACKNOWLEDGMENTS

I would like to thank Rabbi Adland and Rabbi Slaton, both of whom were supportive of my enthusiasm when I was in high school and encouraged my involvement in youth groups and the Jewish community.

I will leave some families out, but I wanted to thank particularly the Litvin, Levy, and Golding families for hosting me for Shabbos in Louisville. I want to especially thank Rabbi Avrohom Litvin, Rabbi Yitzchok Lenefsky, and Rabbi Dr. Joshua Golding for their guidance when I was spending Shabbosim and *Yamim Tovim* in Louisville.

I would like to thank Rabbi Moshe Druin and Rabbi Eli Ginsparg, who helped me along my path to Orthodox Jewish belief; and Rabbi Motty Galinsky—my Partner in Torah—and Asher Israel, who helped me to transition from high school in Frankfort, Kentucky, to yeshiva in Monsey, New York. I want to acknowledge the inspiration Rabbi Tuvia Singer gave me via *ahavas Yisrael* and the importance of *kavod Hashem* through his interaction, outreach, and care for every Jew.

My yeshiva, Yeshiva Kol Yaakov, was instrumental in my formative years of Jewish education and gave me guidance on how to live a fulfilled life as a person who is *machshiv* Torah, its teachers, and its ambassadors—the *Gedolei Yisrael*. This gift is truly precious and beyond my ability to express how it has enhanced my life. I would like to thank the following rabbis who taught me through text and example how to live a Torah life: Rabbi Dovid Stefansky, Rabbi Dovid Wolpin, Rabbi Yaakov Kapelner, Rabbi Eliyahu Berney, Rabbi Pinchos Jung, Rabbi Yehuda Friedland, Rabbi Tzvi Hirschberg, Rabbi Shmuel

Gluck, and Rabbi Dovid Frankel, *zt"l*. Finally, I would like to thank the Rosh Yeshiva, Rabbi Leib Tropper, for providing me with the tools, guidance, and inspiration to lead a life to help and inspire others. I spent so many Shabbos meals in Monsey by so many incredible families that I cannot mention them all here, but I will name those families that I often frequented: Gilbert, Soiefer, Adler, Friedland, Tropper, Hammer, Assovsky, Reznick, Kirzner, Katz, Koneig, Marks, Shaygard, and Stefansky.

I would like to thank Rabbi Yakov Barros for bringing me to South Fallsburg to be part of his shul (SFHA) and the outreach Kollel.

I would like to thank the Cincinnati Kollel for providing me with great learning opportunities, as well as for making me part of the community. I would particularly like to thank the Roshei Kollel, Rabbi Dovid Spetner, Rabbi Meir Minster, and the S'gan Rosh Kollel Rabbi Chaim Heinemann. Many other people in the Kollel have been amazing, but I would like to particularly thank the Kollel's directors of outreach, Rabbi Yitzchok Preis and Rabbi Rafoel Weinschnider, for helping me get involved with the community. I would like to thank Jackie Rabenstein for his excitement and support of this project. I would also like to thank Rabbi Aron Daniel for helping me with this *sefer*, and I can't leave out my *chavrusa*, Rabbi Moshe Fuchs.

I would like to thank Rabbi Avrohom Weinrib, Rav of Congregation Zichron Eliezer (CZE) for his *chizuk*, leadership, and guidance.

I would like to thank the following for reading and/or commenting on my manuscript: Andrew Grossman, Dan Baras, Dr. Eric Littman, Reuven Levine, Dr. William Wainwright (the philosophical section), Dr. Paul Copan, Dr. Phillip Cary, Dr. Keith Ward, Dr. David Novak, Rabbi Bentzion Kokis, and Rabbi Dr. Dovid Gottlieb. I have great appreciation to Rabbi Zev Leff and Rabbi Ahron Lopiansky, who not only read parts of the manuscript but gave me their *haskamos* for the book as well.

I would like to thank the following for answering some of my questions in my research for the book: Rabbi Ari Kahn, Dr. William Wainwright, Dr. Stephen Evens, Dr. John Haught, Dr. Keith Ward, Dr. Richard Swinburne, Peter Williams, Rabbi Moshe Heigh, Rabbi Dr. Shalom Carmy, Rabbi Yosef Reinman, and Rabbi Zecharia Holtzer.

I want to especially thank Dr. Phillip Cary, Dr. Paul Copan, Rabbi Dr. Joshua Golding, and Rabbi Dr. Dovid Gottlieb for being so accessible and generous with their time. It goes without saying that any problematic issues in the material of this book derive from my shortcomings, not any flaws in those who read and/or advised me with certain questions I had.

I want to thank my friends Vlad Seder and Dovid Harrison for assistance with my projects in general. I would like to thank my best friend, Boruch Lazarus, for helping to sharpen my mind and giving me open access to the "Boruch brain" for great advice. My original editor, Preston Frasch, has been extremely helpful and a friend. I want to thank Andrew Shaffer from the Carnegie Center in Lexington, and Milt Toby, who is affiliated with the Center for their guiding hand through the publishing process.

They are too many to list here, but thank you to all donated to my Gofundme drive. The significant donations of Mrs. Rivkah Frankel, Mr. Bret Caller, Mr. Yehudah Wagner, and those who gave anonymously are much appreciated. I would like to thank the Wilheim family for their generous contribution that allowed this book to come into fruition.

Thank you to Rabbi Doron Kornbluth, Rabbi Yehoshua Beckman, and Rabbi Robert Sussman of Mosaica Press for their expertise.

Thank you Colm and Bekah for being excellent and supportive siblings.

Thank you to my dedicated mother (Carol), who has always been supportive of me pursing my dreams.

Dad (Jim), you might have had an idea that I would eventually write a book when I was dictating a book I wanted to write based on my experience of visiting Mammoth Cave as a wee lad in your office (Kentucky Department of Library and Archives). Thank you for always supporting me and instilling in me an appreciation for the acquiring of knowledge.

Thank you to my amazing in-laws, David and Evelyn Mocton, who have been the pinnacle example of how to raise a Torah family with a love of God, His people, and His Torah. I am truly fortunate to be part of this family. The passion you installed in your daughter (as well as all of your children) for the desire to do what is right comes out in her interactions every day and in every way.

To my children, Yaakov Yehudah, Nechoma Miriam, Yosef Meir, and Simcha Refoel: thank you so much for letting Totty spend so much time researching and writing his book. May Hashem as a reward bless you with many years in happiness and health living a lifestyle that will give us all *Yiddishe nachas*.

To my dear wife, Tova: Thank you for not only letting me pursue my dreams but enabling them. I can't thank you enough for letting me dedicate the resources of time and money toward this goal that I have had for years, as well as for giving me the support and inspiration to complete it. You are truly the rock of the spiritual dedication of our family. In the merit of your dedication, may our whole family experience many years in happiness and health in service to the *Borei Olam*.

To Hashem: Thank you for guiding me in life to incredible people who have been, and continue to be, an inspiration; for bringing me into contact with men of wisdom and understanding. Thank you for blessing me with a wife and family who appreciate the importance of service toward others as a manifestation of the Divine mission. I look back in my life and see the Divine providence guiding me every step of the way. My hope and prayer are that my family and I merit many more years in Divine service in happiness and health, and most importantly we should bring glory to Your Name.

INTRODUCTION

THE POINT AND THE PREMISE

This book is very specific in the particular issues it addresses. There is a wide variety of literature regarding the topics of "Is Religion Dangerous?" or "War in Religion," with some defending the enterprise of religion against claims that it leads to violence, and many more attempting to make a direct link between religion, war, and violence.[1] I have seen many articles, essays, and other works put out addressing general issues of war and violence

---

1   For example, the following:

"Okay, so maybe I went a little too far with these quotations. I do not want to offend anyone. If I did, I am sorry. But I do want to show how many passages like these occur in the Bible. Bad moral advice is not just an occasional aberration in the Bible. There's lots of it—lots more than I listed...'You are taking these passages out of context,' say religious believers. Well, look for yourself. I did check the textual and historical context of these passages, and it does not make them look much better" (Walter-Sinnott-Armstrong, *Morality without God*, p. 143).

"There is now a large and growing literature spanning dozens of books and hundred [*sic*] articles—attacking Richard Dawkins, Daniel Dennett, Christopher Hitchens, and me [Sam Harris] (the so-call New Atheists) for our alleged incivility, bias, and ignorance of how 'sophisticated' believers practice their faith. It is often said that we caricature religion, taking its most extreme forms to represent the whole. We do no such thing. We simply do what a paragon of sophisticated faith like Francis Collins does: we take the specific claims of religions seriously." (Sam Harris, *The Moral Landscape*, p. 174)

"...The small amount of the Bible still being used remains a significant problem, especially in justifying violence and oppression. Thus, total abolition of Biblical authority becomes a moral obligation and a key to this world's survival...Abolishing human reliance on sacred texts is imperative when those sacred texts imperil the existence of human civilization as it is currently configured. The letter can kill. That is why the only mission of Biblical

1

in the Jewish Scriptures. I have yet to see, however, an in-depth and comprehensive coverage of the violence mentioned in Scripture in its totality. I have seen books touch on these issues, and I have seen articles focus on isolated instances of violence (and other issues that are hard to digest for the contemporary palate) in Scripture, but I have never seen all of the issues combined and explained thoroughly, at least not from the point of view defending the integrity of Scriptures.[2] It is my conviction that the material covered in this book is unique in its coverage of the varied topics in the Bible that are perceived as unethical and barbaric. The contribution I hope to make in this work is to shed the light of context onto the Scriptures highlighting the fact that the violence and (perceived) injustice contained within them are either justified or non-existent.

I would like to address the reasons why I have omitted a defense of the citations of violence and injustice in the Talmud and post-Biblical writings. While this work is a response to misrepresentation of Jewish

---

studies should be to end Biblical studies as we know it." (Hector Avalos, *The End of Biblical Studies*, p. 342)

2   During the writing of this book, Paul Copan published a book entitled, *Is God a Moral Monster?* To date, Copan is the only person who I have seen attempt a comprehensive defense of the morality of the Old Testament. The major objections I have with his content are twofold: First, while he does cover a lot of ground, he omits many cases that need explanation. Second, and most important, Copan takes a position that the Hebrew Scriptures were a tool for that time period, and hence we should not be surprised to find morally objectionable content, as he says, "...We don't have to explain away or justify such a practice. Such actions reflect a less morally refined condition" (p. 61); or similarly: "Instead of glossing over some of the inferior moral attitudes and practices we encounter in the Old Testament, we should freely acknowledge them" (p. 62); and finally: "Throughout this book, we'll repeat the message: Israel's Old Testament covenant wasn't a universal ideal and was never intended to be so" (p. 64). To suggest it could have been a lot worse and it was the best we had neglects to defend the Scriptures on their own terms. To take this route rather than defend the integrity of the Scriptures as the true light that they are is a copout, as it says in Psalms (19:8): "The law of the Lord is perfect." Also prior to this book's publication, a book entitled *God Behaving Badly* was published by David Lamb. I feel that Lamb did not give as comprehensive a response as the accusations demand. Finally, Copan and Matt Flannagan coauthored a book that is somewhat of a sequel to Copan's book, which they entitled, *Did God Really Command Genocide?* While the new book is more theologically and philosophically sound than Copan's original book, and does have good material, the work in your hands is more comprehensive and its answers are more structured.

Biblical sources, I am aiming to make it appealing on a universal level. Adding a section on the misconstruing of the Oral Law and post-Biblical writings would serve the interest of few, and may mitigate the impact of my overall message. The primary (ethical) criticism of the Talmud and post-Biblical sources comes overwhelmingly from anti-Semitic white supremacist and radical Islamic sources,[3] with which very few people of academic pedigree (or any critic with self-respect for that matter) feel comfortable putting themselves in the same camp regarding their scholarship of religion. This being the case, and because it is rarely a topic on the table to begin with, I do not view it as a necessity to address the citations of such a small group of people devoid of anyone who has upstanding stature in respectable society.

With all this taken into consideration, I would like to acknowledge ahead of time that God's reason for commanding violence (or anything else for that matter) cannot always be understood by us (and certainly not completely). I am not naïve enough to suggest my investigation into the violent parts of Scripture will answer every question regarding violence in the Bible. As John Ruskin said, "How can man understand God, since he does not yet understand his own mind, with which he endeavors to understand Him?" What I do aim to demonstrate is that there is a cohesive logical pattern of justified violence, and when one understands the underlying logic in this pattern, it will pull the rug out from under the moral criticisms of the Bible.

This book is not an effort to demonstrate the reliability of Scripture but begins from the assumption that the picture of history and the nature of God that the Bible gives are accurate. The anticipated question from the skeptic, or any thinking person for that matter, is: How can you say your understanding of God and the Bible is a reflection of reality? This is a valid question, but it is for a different book. The reason establishing the Divinity of the Bible is not necessary here is because the criticisms of Scripture are based on its content, not its bearing on reality. It will behoove us to take into consideration that

---

3   The neo-atheists such as Dawkins, Harris, Hitchens, et al, and academic critics mentioned in my footnotes don't focus their attention on the post-Biblical writings, and thus neither will I.

the critic really only has two valid forms of critique. First is that even if what the Bible recorded is inaccurate, Scripture is still responsible for giving people incentive for committing atrocities in God's name. The alternative criticism is the claim that the accounts the Bible gives are accurate, and the Jewish People and their God should be held accountable for their actions. Given the fact that the criticism aimed at the Bible is taking the Bible's account as factual, which means every Scriptural verse is a valid testimony of the totality of the picture, one cannot blame Jews for killing Amalekites based on Biblical testimony and at the same time reject the Biblical portrait of the Amalekites as a wicked nation. If one is to challenge the morality of the Bible, it is only logical to admit that the Biblical picture of the facts should govern what we are dealing with in order to consider whether the episodes of violence were justifiable. As Rabbi Moshe Meiselman says: "Matters of interpretation must be decided entirely on the basis of the Torah's own internal dynamic. Introducing external factors is as unacceptable here as it would be in any other self-contained system. The Torah is an entirely independent framework and must be recognized and respected as such."[4]

EXCLUSIVE FOCUS ON THE JEWISH SCRIPTURES

While I am fully aware that the Jewish Scriptures are not unique in being taken out of context and misrepresented regarding violence (not to mention numerous other topics), the exclusive focus of this book is criticism of the Jewish Scriptures. It is not my responsibility or desire to defend the texts of belief systems that differ from my own. Even though I am only covering the Jewish Scriptures and providing a defense from a Jewish point of view, it is my contention that even someone not of the Jewish faith (especially traditional Christians) will find the material here useful in responding to the general critique of skeptics regarding matters of religion and Scripture.

---

4   *Torah, Chazal, and Science*, p. XXXII.

MESORAH, THE INTEGRAL NATURE
OF THE ORAL TRADITION

For the person who is truly familiar with the Pentateuch (i.e., the Written Torah) and the Oral Law (i.e., the Oral Torah), the conclusion flows naturally that the Written and Oral Law are so intertwined that one has to accept or reject both of them together. There are too many sources in Scripture that are direct commands that are ambiguous enough that without an Oral Law as an accompaniment they cannot be understood. Still, there are two main objections to the Oral Law. First, the Oral Law often contradicts Scripture, and, second—rather paradoxically in light of the first objection—the two complement each other so precisely that the rabbis must have created the Oral Law in order to fill in the blanks of the Written Law. A short refutation of the second argument is that the entire thrust of it is based on a premise that the Oral Law was invented by the rabbis—a conclusion stemming not from evidence but rather from the critics' refusal to even attempt to address the issue because of a starting point partially objectionable to them. In other words, it is a complaint based on biased, preconceived starting points and not evidence.

While there certainly are other, lengthier responses, we can address both objections with a concise point. It is clear the Bible was created by God in order to give us instructions for how to live. It is also clear that many of those instructions require a more in-depth description of how to fulfill them. Being that the Oral Law as taught by the rabbis is the only body of law that even claims to accompany the Written Law, it behooves us to appreciate this fact and its ramifications. Going back to the time of Moses, there was always an unwritten instruction on how to fulfill certain parts of Scripture that it would be impossible to fulfill otherwise, and at no point in Jewish history has there ever been an attempt to suggest any oral tradition that accompanied the Torah other than the Talmud! We can and should infer from this that the Talmud is the only legitimate body of explanation that is available to us as an explanation of the Written Law. While complete Scriptural evidence for the assertion of the need for an Oral Law is too numerous for me to mention here, I will give a few examples of evidence that show a need for an oral tradition.

1. King David's great-grandmother, Ruth, was a Moabite. According to the Written Law, a Moabite is explicitly prohibited from marrying into the Jewish People.[5] So, how could Ruth have been permitted to marry Boaz and thus play a crucial role as "the mother of kings" in building the Jewish nation? The Talmud explains that the prohibition allowing Moabite converts to marry is only referring to men of Moabite descent and not women.[6]

2. In Deuteronomy 12:21, we are told to slaughter animals "in the manner that I have commanded you." Where is the manner God commanded us mentioned in the Written Torah? Obviously, God had something specific in mind with the word "manner." The answer can only be found in the Talmud, where the laws dealing with *shechitah*, ritual slaughter, are discussed at length in *Masechta* (Tractate) *Chullin*.

3. In Leviticus 16:31, we are told to "afflict your souls" on Yom Kippur. What does this mean? We should walk on hot coals? Where do we know it means fasting (along with other specific practices)? The answer again is: the Oral Law![7]

4. For the holiday of Sukkos, there is a commandment to "take for yourselves the fruit of a beautiful tree."[8] But from which tree and which fruit? Only the Oral Law lets us know it is an esrog, citron.[9] The esrog is universally accepted and used in practice as the fruit mentioned in Leviticus.

We see from these examples and many more that the Talmud so perfectly complements the Written Torah, with so many details being nonetheless completely in sync, which suggests that no other possible tradition could exist, for no fabrication could be that close-to-perfect.

---

5   Deuteronomy 23:3.
6   *Kesubos* 7b.
7   *Yoma* 74b.
8   Leviticus 23:40.
9   *Sukkah* 35a.

NOT ALL VIOLENCE IN SCRIPTURE IS ENDORSED BY THE DIVINE

While the Bible is not merely "a history book," it does contain a lot of history. Not all violence mentioned in the Bible is actually endorsed by God.[10] When the Bible records violence, it is just that—a recording of a people's history, for better and for worse. For a few examples of the many times this occurs, consider: Judges 9:5, 9:45, 11:29–39, 18:27, 19:22–29, II Samuel 20:10–12, II Kings 15:16, II Chronicles 21:4, and Lamentations 4:9–10.

THE IMPORTANCE OF ACKNOWLEDGING A SPIRITUAL REALITY

When addressing the issue of morality in the Bible, it is imperative to acknowledge the working assumption that the portrayal of reality contained in the Bible is Reality with a capital R. Avoiding the discussion of religion and politics is standard advice in social etiquette because it's impossible to discuss such matters without offending someone. Nowadays, talking about religion in pluralistic societies seems not to have the potency it used to have for getting people riled up. I suggest the reason for this is that for many people in Western culture these days, religion consists more of existentialist pragmatism than set and defined theology. Therefore, when a person comes from an existentialist, pragmatic religious perspective, he is not bothered by other perspectives because he does not believe those religious perspectives to reflect reality.

When it comes to politics, however, the same uncombative, relaxed person can metamorphose into a person frothing at the mouth regarding issues on how to run the country. The reason for this is that they know they are affected by the policies of the country, and they are well aware of the cause-and-effect mechanism of the decision-making that

---

10   A great example of the negation of this basic [yet critical] logic is found in Steven Pinker's treatment of the Hebrew Bible in his work *The Better Angels of Our Nature*: "Yet for all of this reverence, the Bible is one long celebration of violence..." (pp. 6–12). He goes on to mention a plethora of cases with violence in the Bible, unaware that many of the cases he mentions are cases the Bible itself chastises!

goes on by policy makers. In order to properly understand Scripture, however, we must be cognizant of the cause-and-effect mechanism that occurs with spiritual reality. The Torah (five books of Moses) is the blueprint of the world, as taught by authoritative Jewish sources: "God looked into the Torah, and created the world."[11] This being the case, we are obliged to take the overall Biblical picture into consideration (in order to understand the reality in its context). We must not isolate verses in a vacuum.

THE VERSES COVERED ARE COMPREHENSIVE, BUT NOT TOTALLY EXHAUSTIVE

I have tried to address every part of the Bible that could be conceivably judged as violent and morally objectionable. Nevertheless, it is not a realistic expectation for this book to address every verse that every person perceives as morally objectionable. What I have done is try to address as many locations in the Bible as I can that are often quoted by critics as being morally unacceptable.

AN IN-DEPTH EXPLANATION OF THE CONCEPTS OF PEACE AND MERCY

It is my contention that authentic *shalom*, peace, is not limited to the peace of the flower-power type, but that peace also means invoking violence and division when necessary. It is true that abstaining from war is a form of peace; however, the root of the Hebrew word *shalom* comes from the word *shaleim*, meaning complete. Many people have the belief that people have to work toward unity at all costs to achieve peace, but Scripture informs us differently. In the episode where Abraham separates from his nephew Lot, the verse reads, "Thus they parted, one from his brother."[12] On this verse, the *Baal HaTurim* commented: "The final letters of the four words…spell peace. This tells you that they parted in order to maintain peace between them." We see from here that separation between people can be used as a means to achieve peace.

---

11   *Zohar, Parashas Terumah* 161:1; *Bereishis Rabbah* 1:1.
12   Genesis 13:11.

Rabbi Zev Leff elaborates on the concept of peace by informing us:

> *Shalom is not merely the absence of strife or disagreement,*
> *but a state of peaceful serenity. It is precisely through the*
> *interaction of opposites, of fire and water, that God is described*
> *as the One who makes peace. Machlokes l'shem Shamayim,*
> *argument for the purpose of reaching truth, is the epitome of*
> *shalom. The Kohanim, priests, who are the representatives*
> *of shalom—servants in the Beis Hamikdash, the Temple, the*
> *place of shalom—were consecrated by killing their relatives*
> *who served the golden calf. And Pinchas was initiated into the*
> *kehunah, priesthood, by Hashem and given the covenant of*
> *shalom as a result of his slaying Zimri and Kosbi. True shalom*
> *is the achievement of perfection—the harmonious functioning*
> *of the world. As long as evil and evildoers destroy this harmony,*
> *there can be no shalom. There is not shalom, says Hashem,*
> *concerning the wicked.*[13] *Hence, true shalom is conditional on*
> *destroying evil.*[14]

When it comes to the Lord having mercy, this does not mean to say that God tolerates or wants us to tolerate evil in the world as an expression of mercy. In fact, mercy applied in the wrong fashion can be detrimental to society, as the Midrash teaches: "Rabbi Elazar said, 'Whoever acts compassionate toward those who are cruel, will act cruelly toward those who [are in need of] compassion.'"[15] Rabbi Mordechai Gifter uses this concept to answer an enigma in the phraseology in a certain verse of the Torah:

> *The name Elokim denotes the Divine attribute of judgment,*
> *while the name Hashem (the four letter, ineffable name)*
> *denotes the Divine attribute of mercy. Since our verse*[16] *focuses*
> *on God's destruction of entire cities, why does it not use Elokim*

---

13   Isaiah 57:21.

14   Rabbi Zev Leff, *Outlooks and Insights*, pp. 180–81.

15   *Midrash Tanchuma, Metzora* 1.

16   Genesis 19:24.

instead of Hashem? Although destruction may seem harsh, Hashem's destruction of the wicked stems from His mercy on behalf of the rest of the world.[17] This concept is expressed by Seforno on Shemos 15:3: "Hashem is a man of war; Hashem is His name." Seforno explains: "Even though He is a Man of war, decimating the wicked with the attribute of justice, nonetheless Hashem is His name—indicating His attribute of mercy. Through destroying the wicked, He grants being and existence to His world. He removes the thorns from the vineyard, for the wicked destroy the world."[18]

We see from the above that according to the Biblical view (not to mention from the vantage point of logic), violence when channeled correctly is good for society; violence can bring us complete and authentic peace through real mercy.

EXPLANATIONS AND REASONS—A LIMITED ENDEAVOR

When I undertook to write this book, one of the most common concerns people expressed was how it could be possible to explain the ways of God in such a way as to satisfy the secular mind. Although a person who rejects the truth of Scripture will not be pacified with answers based on the premises of the Bible, the purpose of this book is to show that actions can be morally justified within the structure of Scripture. So, even if one does not acknowledge the authority of the Bible, he can still admit that his perception of Biblical moral content has been skewed by a misunderstanding of the nature and context of Scripture. I will be forward and acknowledge that on the whole, my book is more persuasive regarding the exposure of false narratives of critics who are unaware of the proper understanding/context of the Jewish Scriptures than forceful in compelling secular people to recognize the authority of Scripture. While I'm sure people could offer better arguments than I on this topic, I think it is only realistic to admit that proper understanding/context

---

17   In a sense, there is mercy on the destroyed as well.
18   Rabbi Mordechai Gifter, *Pirkei Torah*, p. 44.

of the Jewish Scriptures only goes so far (addressing inaccuracies of Scriptural understanding), where even proper understanding of textual context will not bring most secular critics to accept the moral authority of the God of the Bible. A "buy in" into the system is somewhat required to fully appreciate an internal coherent moral logic of Scripture. I need to be clear on this: There are two ways for the Bible-believing Jew to respond to criticism of the Bible. The most effective way is to show that the critique is incompetent even from the point of view of the critics' beliefs and values. The critic has made some mistake in logic or fact. The second, less forceful response is to show that we (Orthodox Jews) with our beliefs and values can defend ourselves against the critique even though from the critics' point of view their critique is still valid. The former is obviously stronger than the latter. There are certainly cases where I accomplish the first approach. However, for a significant portion of the book, I often appeal to the (Jewish) Oral tradition for explanation (i.e., Talmud); it is in these cases where I am only accomplishing the second approach. I think two further points are necessary to take into consideration. First, the flip side of this applies to the critic. In other words, the critic is at a weaker position if they make an argument based only on their values and beliefs. They are under no obligation (logically) to accept the authority of the Oral Jewish tradition; at the same time the Orthodox Jew is logically under no obligation to accept the critics' premise of rejecting the Oral tradition while defending our (Jewish Orthodox) understanding of the texts. The second point is if the critic would accept the interpretation of the Oral Jewish tradition as moral, then the significance of their opposition to its authority would be diminished via their moral critique even if they do not accept the authority of the Talmud, as they would be on the same page with Orthodox Judaism on the ethical understandings of the interpretations.

A different, but almost as prevalent concern is that by trying to give reason and explanation to certain Biblical events and ideas, I am opening up an opportunity for people to try to make their own justifications based on my explanations. I would suggest that my views are not different than anyone else who can have people rip their message out of context. If someone is going to misconstrue a text to validate religious violence, it certainly will not be my book, which focuses on contextualization of past events.

Not unrelated, another charge is that by pursuing a question to unreasonable measures, I am somehow trying to psychoanalyze God. Rebbe Nachman of Breslov said, "If there is a God, there are no questions. If God does not exist, there are no answers." I think this statement has to be understood in context with a deeper statement pertaining to the nature of our ultimate understanding of the ways of God. We will never be able to fathom the great scheme of God, nor should we expect to even come close to such an understanding. The words of Saadia Gaon are unquestionably true: "To know God, is to be God," and we should not even expect to understand all the depths of Torah, the vehicle of the Divine will. After all, it does contain all of the secrets of the universe.[19]

Nevertheless, we are told to delve into the Torah.[20] One reason for this is that the more we understand the Divine will, the more we will appreciate the greatness of God. Furthermore, when *Ramchal* investigated the principles of Divine oversight, he taught us that accepting the existence of things we cannot understand does not undermine the validity of striving to understand what we can.[21] Rabbi Zev Leff articulates this point well:

> We don't speak about the reasons for mitzvos; we speak about
> the taamei ha'mitzvah, tastes of the mitzvah. It is comparable
> to a regular eating. The reason people eat is not because it
> tastes good, or because it looks good, or because it has a good
> aroma. The reason people eat is because that is the way God
> made the world, and the reason we eat foods that are nutritious
> is because that is the way God made the world—that these

---

19   *Pirkei Avos* 5:26.

20   Ibid.

21   Jeremy Kagan, *The Choice to Be*, p. XVII, quoting *Ramchal, Daas Tevunos* 7:11. For an example of this, Rabbi Zalman Sorotzkin wrote: "Although the entire concept of sacrifices and offerings is beyond human comprehension, our Sages, of blessed memory, did not refrain from advancing explanations of certain aspects of the subject, in accordance with our limited understanding." See his *Insights in the Torah*, vol. 3, *Vayikra*, p. 103.

things give nutrition and other things don't. If you ate rocks, you would gain weight much faster, but it has no nutrition to it. So, we eat foods that are nutritional. Why are these things specifically nutritional and not other things? No one knows. We can describe what they are, but why it is like that, why God couldn't have made us to be sustained by other kinds of food, we have no idea. So we really don't need the answer why do we eat these specific foods, because that is the way God made us, and that is the way He made the world, and there is no explanation that we can possibly understand. We can describe the process, but we can't understand the why. But, once we have to eat, God wanted it to be palatable to us. He wanted us to enjoy it. So he gave it a taste, a color, an aroma that makes it palatable and interesting, and enjoyable. So too, God said: "Look, mitzvah is spiritual food, this is the way it has to be, I made you, I made the world, I made these mitzvos. You don't understand the why, it's beyond your comprehension, but I want you to enjoy it too. So in those mitzvos, I am also going to give you intellectual and emotional understandings...that you can have a taste in that mitzvah too, where it can be palatable to you, on your level."[22]

Rabbi Yisroel Miller wrote:

When the Sefer Hachinuch suggests reasons for mitzvos, he writes: "Mi'sharashei ha'mitzvah—Among the roots of this mitzvah," roots rather than reasons, perhaps to underscore the fact that these are not the mitzvah's primary reasons. Even the more common term for mitzvah-reasons, taamei ha'mitzvos, is often translated as a "taste" of the mitzvah, i.e., an insight that gives us a taste for the mitzvah rather than an explanation of the mitzvah's essence.[23]

22 Rabbi Zev Leff, "Reasons for Matzah," lecture.
23 Rabbi Yisroel Miller, *In Search of Torah Wisdom*, p. 254.

Finally, Rabbi Dovid Hofstedter wrote:

> *The details of a mitzvah are indicative of the nature of the mitzvah itself. If the details of a mitzvah are beyond our comprehension, then the mitzvah itself must be far removed from our ability to understand. Even if we sometimes feel that we do understand the rational[e] for certain mitzvos, particularity those categorized as mishpatim, that relates only to the external nature of those mitzvos. In truth, however, each mitzvah has incredible, sublime effects in the Heavenly realm, and each mitzvah in the Torah is based on endlessly profound Divine logic.*[24]

While it is true that we are in no position to understand God based on only our own understanding, we do have something to attach our understanding to: revelation.[25] If one takes a look at Jewish history, the observer should take note that a great many scholars have spent a great deal of time explaining many facets of the Bible based on their understanding of the revealed sources, and they have spent a great amount of time preserving those explanations in order to ensure we have the opportunity to gain from them. This point becomes even stronger when taken into consideration that many of these men took an accounting of every minute that they wasted. It is unconceivable that these men would have exerted so much time and effort into these matters if they were not worthy of great contemplation.

The reason I pestered others and even myself to come up with such in-depth analysis on the topics included in this book was not to psychoanalyze God, but because my limited experience with Jewish learning has been that, in most cases, the "satisfactory answer" does eventually arrive with perseverance. That being said, I would like to conclude with the insightful words of Rabbi Meiselman: "Reasons and rationales are

---

24   Rabbi Dovid Hofstedter, *Dorash Dovid*, Moadim (Shavuos), Series 1, p. 103.

25   I mean revelation in that Hashem revealed His will via Torah. The scholars passed down our understanding of said revelation.

needed only for a deepened understanding of the Divine will, not for motivation."[26] And, I should add, acceptance.

To sum up the introduction, the point of the book is to evaluate Scripture cited as being indicative of immorality and examine the various variables based on a traditional position of Jewish scholarship. The premise is that skeptics should reserve their doubts on Divine authorship of the Bible, and learn the insider's approach to how to understand troubling passages. This is because it is disingenuous to judge a system's internal merits based on an external value system. The key, we have learned, is to learn the Bible through the lens of the Oral Tradition that has always accompanied the Written Law (i.e., Torah). I have also demonstrated through numerous verses that not all violence recorded in the Bible was endorsed or condoned by God. I mentioned that while coverage of the Biblical concerns would be comprehensive, it will not be exhaustive. We have seen a deeper understanding into the concepts of "peace" and "mercy." Finally, I have tried to convey that even though there is nothing wrong with learning explanations and "reasons" for different parts of Scripture and the commandments, ultimately, the human mind is not capable of understanding everything in the Bible. However, neither should that be the expectation. While Galileo said, "I do not feel obligated to believe that the same God who has endowed us with sense, reason, and intellect has intended us to forego their use," we need also keep the words of Charles Caleb Colton in mind: "He that will believe only what he can fully comprehend must have a very long head, or a very short creed." We can also gain strength from the insight of Ralph Waldo Emerson: "All I have seen teaches me to trust the Creator for all I have not seen."

---

26   Rabbi Moshe Meiselman, *Jewish Women in Jewish Law*, p. 157.

Chapter One

DO THE SCRIPTURES SUPPORT UNWARRANTED VIOLENCE?

T
he verses in this chapter are divided into three sections. The first part addresses violence on a national level; the second part focuses on violence on an individual level, excluding death penalties; and the final part deals with the death penalty. Again, the blanket criticism of violence in the Bible stems from an incomplete knowledge and context of what Scripture is addressing. In examining the verses cited below, details and context will be provided for the violence mentioned so as to help us better understand whether the violence was warranted or not.

I: NATIONAL VIOLENCE

Genesis 34:1–29: Dinah, Jacob's daughter, was abducted and violated by Shechem. Shechem then decided that he wanted to marry Dinah, so he had his father Chamor propose to Jacob (and his sons) that the people of their city and Israel intermarry and reside in Shechem. The sons of Jacob told Shechem that no uncircumcised male could marry the daughter of Jacob and that only after circumcision would Chamor's proposal be accepted.

17

Chamor and Shechem convince the people of their city to undergo circumcision by promising them great material benefits. On the third day after the people were circumcised, Simon and Levi avenged the injustice done to Dinah by killing all of the male inhabitants of the town and rescuing Dinah. When the other sons of Jacob came upon the slain, they "plundered the city that had defiled their sister…all their wealth, all their children, and wives they took captive, and they plundered."

Response: Regarding the slaying of all the males of Shechem's city, the Bible attests to the fact that Jacob did not approve of Simon and Levi's actions.[1] This seems strange, because the brothers were in Jacob's presence when they made an offer that Jacob knew full well was disingenuous (i.e., offering of the daughters of Jacob if they would only circumcise themselves), yet he did not protest. The *Ramban* explains this is because Jacob thought the demand of circumcision would be a deterrent to the people of the city of Shechem regarding the proposal of intermarriage. Furthermore, the *Ramban* adds that Jacob thought that even if the people of Shechem would acquiesce, then on the third day Jacob's sons would come and rescue their sister rather than killing the whole city.[2] It should be noted that Dinah was being held captive, and the sons of Jacob were vastly outnumbered. Jacob was opposed to killing the town's people, but considering the circumstances, he was not opposed to the trickery to rescue Dinah.

Exodus 17:13, Deuteronomy 25:19 (also I Samuel 14:48, 15:3, 7–8, 30:17): The commandment to wipe out Amalek.

---

1   See Genesis 49:5–7, as well as the *Ramban* on ibid. 34:13.

2   Genesis 34:13.

Response: What makes Amalek unique from other nations is that they were the first people to institutionalize atheism, standing in complete opposition to the Jewish People. In fact, their goal was to eradicate the Jewish People[3] and the belief in God from the world.[4] Amalek attacked the fledging Jewish nation fresh after the exodus from Egypt by targeting the weak and straggling at the rear. Amalek attacked Israel, Israel fought back, and the battle ended. There was no truce.

Importantly, the commanded destruction of the nation of Amalek is not unwarranted violence; rather, it is a preemptive strike to preserve and improve the existence of humanity. Irving Bunim made an excellent observation about the extent of Amalek's rebellion against the Divine plan: "Amalek attacked the Israelites not because they threatened its land, nor even from a desire for booty and spoils, nor yet for vengeance. Amalek simply wished to thwart the Divine plan. Amalek 'did not fear God.' Amalek set himself in rebellion against the Almighty Himself: hence his special punishment."[5] When one takes into account that there was no truce between Amalek and the Jewish People, and that the raison d'etre of Amalek is the destruction of the Jewish People, it should not come as a surprise that the Jewish People are commanded to take preemptive measures of self-defense. It is true that eradication is an extreme; it is also true that when the enemy envisions your eradication and will stop at nothing until they achieve it, taking preemptive measures for self-protection is morally justified when trying to avoid your own extinction. Destroying the men would not be enough, because the

---

3   *Me'am Loez*, Exodus 17:16.

4   Rabbi Zev Leff, *Festivals of Life*, pp. 155–56: "In this respect, the *Maharal* says, Amalek is the antithesis of Klal Yisrael. We are at one end of the spectrum and hence called '*reishis*,' the beginning, and Amalek is at the other end of the spectrum, also called '*reishis*,' as it says, '*Reishis goyim Amalek*—Amalek is the first among nations' (Numbers 24:20). All the other nations are in the middle, and there is a struggle that is taking place on an ongoing basis, a tug of war. We strive to influence the world to abandon their idolatry and believe in the one God. Amalek strives to influence the world to abandon their idolatry and become non-believers, atheists."

5   *Ethics from Sinai*, vol. 1, p. 349.

women and children of that diabolical nation will simply breed more generations of those filled with that evil hatred.[6]

Two more important points: The *Rambam* says that part of the Torah's law on waging war is that the war cannot be waged unless peace is offered first, he later infers that this applies to Amalek as well.[7] Finally, it should also be noted that we are not able to racially identify who are Amalekites today. Therefore, this question is more of a philosophical inquiry than a concern that the Jewish People are going on a hunt for Amalekites. This point is elaborated upon below.

> Numbers 31:9, 17–19, 31–40; Deuteronomy 2:33–34, 3:6, 7:2, 20:16; Joshua 1:1–7, 6:21–22, 8:22–25, 10:10–40, 11:8–15, 20–23; Judges 1:4, 6, 8, 17, 3:29, 21:11–12, 14–23: The commandment to wage a war of expulsion against the Seven Nations.

Response: Due to the magnitude of the various issues that need to be addressed in this chapter of Jewish history, I think that it is necessary to lay a few fundamental ideas down in order to give a comprehensive and adequate answer to the difficulties that arise within the aforementioned texts. Also, I think this is a good juncture in the book to bring up some points that will not only address the immediate concerns, but will help us with other concerns further on in the book.

For What Purpose Did God Create Humanity?

What is the purpose of man? Why we are on this earth? The answer to these questions is essential for understanding the common thread and underlying theme that is the basis to the majority of responses to violence in the Bible that this book contains. The world was created for the specific purpose of being a vehicle for God to bestow His goodness.[8]

---

6   For more treatment on this topic, listen to Rabbi Akiva Tatz, "Purim and the Sin of Man," accessed https://bit.ly/3q04x9h.

7   *Mishneh Torah, Hilchos Melachim* 6:1, then 6:6.

8   *Sanhedrin* 39b; *Menachos* 53b.

To fulfill this goal, God created the world as an environment for a creature capable of partaking of this goodness.[9] This creature is man.[10] This means that the goal of any person, whether the person is Jewish or gentile, is to bask in the goodness of God. How do we obtain this goodness? Obedience to God's will brings fulfillment to the purpose of creation.[11]

Now, what if part of humanity conducted their God-given lives with practices that eliminated Godliness from the world? We would have to assess what value the Torah assigns to their lives. According to the Torah, the actions of each individual are of such immense importance; the world was worth creating for their (actions of people using their free will) implementation.[12] If that is the case, how can that same Torah require the wholesale slaughter of a whole group of people? The answer is: When people degrade their spiritually to a certain degree, they lose that infinite value due to the fact that they eradicated the Infinite from their lives. In effect, if a group of people are dragging humanity down into a path of destruction, then it is imperative to take action in a way that will best implement the necessary means to accomplish an atmosphere conducive to preserving humanity and helping it flourish in the way it was meant to.

This can be illustrated by way of analogy: If a person had an infection in his leg that required amputation, it is self-evident that this procedure was performed in order to protect the rest of the body from the spread of infection. When the infection is so bad that it is threatening the rest of the body, it is imperative to take extreme measures to protect the body from a much worse potential catastrophe. If the infection of a wicked nation was threatening the well-being of humanity, the only resort is to amputate it.

---

9   I.e., obtaining knowledge of the Creator.

10   *Derech Hashem* 1:2:5. The *Ramban* said: "If man would not at all know [Who] created him, moreover, if he would not realize that his Creator has considered certain deeds of man more acceptable to Himself and preferable to other deeds He rejected and despised, then man is like cattle, and the purpose of the Creation [of the world] is void" (*Writings of the Ramban*, vol. 1, pp. 176–77).

11   *Shabbos* 30b.

12   *Sanhedrin* 37a.

Why Eretz Yisrael (the Land of Israel)?

Psalms 104:24 says: *"Mal'ah ha'aretz kinyanecha*—The whole world is Your [God's] possession."* Rabbi Simchah Bunim of Peshischa points out that the verse can also mean: "The world is full of ways to acquire God."[13] It is important to recognize that the earth was created as a vehicle to serve God, and when God created the world, He invested certain spiritual potential greater in Eretz Yisrael than any other land.[14] The Midrash explains that the Jewish People and Eretz Yisrael were tailor-made for each other.[15] What makes Eretz Yisrael a unique and a desired land for spiritual growth is that it is under God's constant supervision more than any other land,[16] and due to these conditions, the Jewish People are under more pressure to fulfill their Divine expectations and are given more adequate resources. As the *Ramban* wrote:

> *You may therefore infer from the [spiritual] proximity of Israel to the Holy One, blessed be He, that this is also the cause that brings about their distance [from God]. This is all the more [so] true of all those who are privileged to dwell before the Holy One, blessed be He, in His Land, for they are as those who "see the King's face." If they are heedful of His honor, it is beneficial to them, and they are happy. However, if they rebel against Him, woe to them more so than to the [other] people, for they make war and provoke the King in His own palace.*[17]

The Requirement to Live (Remain) in the Land

Now that we have established some of the background for labeling Eretz Yisrael as *"Eretz HaKodesh,"* the Holy Land, we need to recognize the ramifications for living in such a land. It should go without saying that this land was designated to be utilized for holy purposes, i.e., living lifestyles dedicated to attaining a relationship with God. This being the

---

13 I.e., ways to connect with Hashem.

14 See *Tanna d'Bei Eliyahu Zuta*, chap. 2.

15 *Bamidbar Rabbah* 23:7.

16 See Deuteronomy 11:10–12; *Taanis* 10a.

17 *Writings of the Ramban*, vol. 1, pp. 128–29.

case, it is imperative to appreciate the reality that practicing lifestyles antithetical to holiness, i.e., going against the very purpose of the land in the first place, will lead to, in the language of the Bible, "vomit[ing] them out for their abominable practices."[18]

Rabbi Avigdor Miller writes:

> *In addition to these perils, was the liability imposed merely by residing in the sacred land. This land had always put great responsibility upon its inhabitants. Sodom and its sister cities, wicked as they were (Genesis 13:13, 18:20; Ezekiel 16:49–50), were probably not worse than many cities outside of Canaan. They were not accused of brigandage or warfare, in which other peoples engaged (Genesis 14:1). Yet they were utterly destroyed, as were in less measure the Refaim, Zuzim, and Emim (ibid. 14:5), and as were the progeny of Shem who had dwelt in this land and were afterward disinherited by the Canaani invaders. These invaders were permitted to remain in the land until their own sinfulness accumulated (ibid. 15:16), and now the land was about to vomit them out for their abominable practices (Leviticus 18:25). Had the Canaani dwelt elsewhere, they would not have been sentenced to destruction, despite their depravity...Even the most righteous of nations [i.e., Israel], when after 850 years it sank below the tremendously exalted standards required of it, was to be forced into exile to be able to exist. "You came and defiled my land" (Jeremiah 2:7).[19]*

---

18 Leviticus 18:25.

19 It should be noted that secular Biblical scholars, such as J. Harold Ellens, professor of Near Eastern Studies at the University of Michigan, seemingly ignore Scriptural context when they accuse "the Biblical writers" of only wanting to justify the takeover of Canaan and claiming it was the Divine will: "It seems to have been clearly the case of the ancient Biblical Israelites who confused their own acquisitive prejudices with the Divine will when it came to extermination of the Canaanites 'because the cup of their iniquity was filled.' Few readers notice that the cup was filled with exactly the idolatrous and abusive behavior to which the Israelites were forever inclined themselves, given half a chance to diverge from the 'call of [G-d]' to be a distinctive people of grace" (*The Destructive Power of Religion*, vol. 2, p. 95). Professor Ellens seems to forget that it was the influence of idolatry that the Divine was concerned about that merited the commandment to eradicate them from the land in the first place!

It was indeed "a land which devours its inhabitants" (Numbers 13:32) and was so known among the nations (Ezekiel 36:13).[20]

Why Must the Seven Nations Leave?

So what did the Seven Nations do to merit being forced out of Israel? In short, they displayed moral corruption of the highest magnitude, including: practicing human sacrifice, even with their children;[21] incest, even with their closest relatives; bestiality;[22] and molesting and murdering travelers.[23] The Canaanites were expelled from the land not only because they were morally corrupt but also because of their ability to influence the Jewish People with their wickedness,[24] as God unequivocally warned the Jewish nation: "They (Canaanites) should not dwell in your land, lest they cause you to sin against me,"[25] and "You must destroy them...in order that they should not teach you to do according to their abominations."[26]

In the end, the Canaanite nations were not totally eradicated from the land.[27] As a result, the Canaanite influence eventually took hold,[28] and it resulted in the Jewish nation being exiled from their land.[29] Paul Copan and Matthew Flannagan have a very good articulation of the concern with the Israelites assimilating with the seven nations:

The main concern, then, is that the small embryonic Israelite nation, which is called to be a people of God and the vehicle through which God will redeem the world, will be assimilated into the corrupt religious practices of the surrounding nations

---

20 *Behold a People*, p. 157.
21 Deuteronomy 12:31.
22 Leviticus 18:3–28, 20:1–23.
23 Genesis 19:5.
24 "One who leads another person to sin is worse than one who kills him," see *Rashi*, Deuteronomy 23:9.
25 Exodus 23:33.
26 Deuteronomy 20:17–18.
27 See Judges 1:27 until the end of the chapter.
28 II Kings 17:7–8.
29 Ibid., v. 23.

living in the land. To establish and sustain Israel's own national identity and mission to be a channel of blessing to the entire world is no trivial matter. Indeed, the Hebrew Scriptures take seriously this life-and-death struggle for Israel's own national and spiritual integrity.[30]

Options Other than War

The Canaanites were only to be fought by the Israelites if they were going to continue to contaminate the land and threaten to drag Israel into their evil practices. Therefore, they had two options in front of them to avoid conflict with the children of Israel: They could either evacuate the land on their own volition,[31] or they could live in their land but reject their previous idolatry and wicked practices by adhering to

---

30   *Did God Really Command Genocide?*, p. 69.

31   As was done by the Girgashites when Joshua warned them, as well as every other place he was about to conquer: "Whoever seeks peace with us, let him come and make peace; and whoever seeks to leave his land, let him leave; and whoever seeks to make war against us, let him make war." This was Joshua's fulfillment of Deuteronomy 20:10 (see Jerusalem Talmud, *Sheviis* 6:1). Despite the clear reference in Deuteronomy, Robert Eisen, professor of Judaic Studies at George Washington University, projects his flawed understanding of the workings of Jewish texts by claiming that the Talmud and Maimonides invented concepts in that Scripture in order to mitigate the harshness of the Biblical texts:

> *No example better illustrates the dilemma here than the Midrashic source that retells the story of the Canaanite conquest and informs us that Joshua had to offer terms of peace to the Canaanites...This source was later canonized into law in Maimonides' legal code. The viewpoint that insisted on a benevolent reading of Judaism cited scholars who saw the Midrashic source and its use by Maimonides as remarkable instances of interpretation in which violent biblical sources were boldly and creatively reread by later interpreters because of moral considerations. In the biblical text, the Canaanites were not given the choices spelled out by the Midrash and Maimonides, and these later interpretations were therefore rereading the text because of objections to the notion that the Canaanites would be killed without first being given the option to flee or surrender" (The Peace and Violence of Judaism, p. 212).*

This is a pristine example of how some secular scholars are not free from building entirely flawed theories based on a premise that stems from their lack of familiarity with the entire picture of Scripture due to their lack of overall Biblical knowledge.

the Noahide covenant[32] and paying tribute and service to Israel.[33] One perspective that may help to understand this concept is the expression: "Lead, follow, or get out of the way." They had the option to convert to Judaism and become leaders. If they did not want the responsibility, they could have chosen to help the Jewish nation in its quest for spiritual greatness (hence the servitude; more on this later under slavery). Finally, if they were not going to contribute to the pursuit of spiritual greatness, they could, at the very least, avoid influencing and dragging down the people who were active in this noble ideal by leaving. Because the Canaanites did not exercise any of the aforementioned options, Israel was forced to defeat them in battle in order to preserve the Jewish People's likelihood of achieving spiritual success.

Whose Decision Was It to Expel the Seven Nations?

It should be clear by now that the destruction of the seven nations was not an act of conquest, but rather was only done because God wanted to prevent the Canaanites from influencing the Jewish People with their depraved practices. A good illustration of this point can be found in Joshua 6:17–19, where the Jewish nation was instructed to refrain from partaking of the spoils of war. If this was a materialistic conquest, this restriction would be absurd. This is not a small point; the norm for this time period was to engage in conquest specifically for spoils of war. The uniqueness of this conquest and the unlikelihood

---

32 The Gibeonites chose to follow this road (see Joshua 9:9); see *Ramban* (Deuteronomy 20:10) to find out how we deduce that they were responsible to observe the Noahide covenant. In the pre-Abraham period, humanity was given seven basic laws (which branch out into more laws, about a third of the 613 commandments that Jews are obliged to keep) known as the "*sheva mitzvos B'nei Noach,*" seven commandments for the children of Noah, a.k.a. the Noahide covenant. They are the positive commandment of establishing courts of justice and the prohibitions of idolatry, blasphemy, murder, forbidden relations, stealing, and eating a limb from a live animal; see *Sanhedrin* 56a.

33 See Deuteronomy 20:11; this is referring to a service the nations would perform for the Jewish People in order to help them (the Jewish People) dedicate more of their (the Jewish People's) resources toward serving God. This will be explained further in Chapter Three where I will explain Canaanite servitude.

of materialistic motivation is highlighted by the fact that someone did take spoils, and the entire nation was punished for it.[34]

How Does This Apply to the Present Situation?

Taking the above into account, many may wonder when they can expect to see the "Jewish Jihad" coming to their neighborhood to obliterate the heretical and influential infidels. This is not an issue in our current state of affairs for two reasons. First, the commanded wars of aggression were exclusively aimed at the Seven Nations and Amalek. This is a non-issue nowadays because we cannot identify the Seven Nations or Amalek due to Sennacherib's policy of forced resettlement.[35] Secondly, regarding everyone else, the traditional Jewish position has been to be isolated from outside influences (as best as possible) in a non-combative manner. One of the great sages in recent Jewish history, Rabbi Elazar Menachem Mann Shach, observed: "The Torah way is to try not to make our presence felt, but rather to be 'a people that dwells apart and that is not reckoned with the nations.' This has been our strategy throughout the generations. Review our history in your mind and see whether you can come up with an example to the contrary. If not, then it follows that all other approaches must derive from alien sources."[36]

Another question arises: If the land (of Israel) vomits out sinners,[37] how in the world is the modern state, which lives as a whole in a constant state of sin,[38] still a state? In truth, the sensitivity of the Land remains as it was in Biblical times.[39] In terms of Jewish history, the modern state of Israel has been in existence a short time, but the process of being expelled from the land is not an overnight occurrence. It is still possible for the Jewish People to be forced out of Israel (God

---

34   Joshua 7:1, 11.

35   See *Berachos* 28a; *Rambam, Mishneh Torah, Melachim* 5:4; and *Minchas Chinuch* 604:5 regarding Amalek.

36   *Rav Shach Speaks*, p. 14.

37   Leviticus 18:25.

38   In this regard, I refer to public Sabbath desecration, immodest behavior, and celebration of lifestyles antithetical to Torah—to name a few.

39   See *Kol Bo*, vol. 2, #127.

forbid!). Let us hope and pray that the spiritual awakening in Israel only grows stronger, and may we never see the day where the Jewish People are again rejected from the Holy Land due to their sins.

> Numbers 31 (also Judges 7:19–25 and 8:15–21): God commanded Israel to take vengeance on the Midianites. The Israelite armies killed all (adult) males and took the young children and women captive. Moses demanded the armies finish off the male children and also the women old enough to have had relations with a man. As for the young female captives, the armies were allowed to keep them for themselves. Subsequently, Judges (6, 7, and 8) relates how the Midianites were defeated in battle by the Israelites.[40]

Response: As opposed to most wars fought in the *Tanach*, it was specifically the wars against Amalek and Midian that the sole purpose of the attack was to destroy the connection between the Jewish people and God. Rabbi S. Binyomin Ginsberg comments on this connection: "Balak and Bilaam were central figures and drivers in Yisrael's struggle with Midian. The *Zohar* (*Parashas Balak*) reveals that they served as the manifestation of Amalek, as alluded to by the final letters of their names, Balak and Bilaam, which together form the word Amalek."[41] Furthermore, if one looks at the verses in *Tanach* in context, we see that Midian was always the one to provoke animosity between the two nations. Midian went on the offensive against the Jewish nation in Numbers (chap. 22) by hiring the prophet Balaam to curse them; failing that attempt to destroy the Jewish nation, they (with Moab) implemented a plan to bring Israel to sin (and thereby have God punish Israel for their immorality). And it worked![42] For the gravity of seducing

---

40   This was a different battle that was many years after the battle in Numbers.

41   *Gems from the Nesivos Sholom, Bamidbar*, p. 427, based on *Nesivos Sholom*, vol. 3, pp. 169–71.

42   See 25:1–3 for a more in-depth explanation of what happened; see *Sanhedrin* 106a.

people into idol worship, the Midianites deserved death.[43] Regarding the reference to female captives, it should be noted that they were taken as slaves (see comments on slavery later on), and when the verse says, "you may keep them for yourselves," there was no sexual connotation or incidents resulting from it.[44] Regarding the male children, it seems the male children shared the same element that Amalek had where a proclivity for wanting to destroy the connection between the Jewish people and God was ingrained. In regard to the killing of the male children, Rabbi Samson Raphael Hirsch writes: "As the purpose of this act was the prevention of heathen immoral elements becoming implanted in Israel, we must take it that the national degeneration had its roots essentially in the male sex, but that the female sex, if removed from impure influences and impressions at an early age, remained fully able to absorb and adopt all the ideas of pure morality."[45] Tragic as war is, the casualties Midian suffered were due to their unprovoked acts of aggression.

> Joshua 1:18: "Any man who will rebel against your utterance or will not listen to your words, in whatever you may command him, will be put to death." The army assures Joshua they will obey his direction as they had done for Moses.

Response: The context of this verse is when the Jewish People are about to go into battle.[46] To contradict the prophet is tantamount to treason against the king. Rabbi Mordechai Gifter observes how the tribes of Gad, Reuben, and Menashe are reaffirming Joshua's leadership.[47] The timing of this is immediately after Moses' passing, and they are saying they will be as loyal to Joshua as they were to Moses.

---

43   See above comments on the Seven Nations.
44   See *Shabbos* 64a.
45   Rabbi Samson Raphael Hirsch on Numbers 31:17–18.
46   See Joshua 1:10–11.
47   See *ArtScroll Tanach Series, Yehoshua*, p. 108.

Judges 3:31 (also see 14:19, 15:15; I Samuel 7:7–11, 14:31, 18:27; II Samuel 5:25, 8:1–18): The myriad of battles between the Jewish People and the Philistines.

Response: The Israelites had a treaty of peace with the Philistines from the agreement Abraham had made with Abimelech.[48] However, the Philistines broke this treaty during the period of the Judges when they violently oppressed the Jewish People.[49] The back-and-forth violence between the Philistines and the Jewish People is the result of the breach of covenant that the Philistines triggered when they afflicted the Israelites with unwarranted violence.

Judges chaps. 19–21: The concubine at Givah. In this episode, a Levite man has a fight with his concubine. She left his house and went to her father's house. The man went to his father-in-law's house to regain favor of his concubine. On the trip back, they stayed overnight in the town of Givah, located in the territory of Benjamin. They had a hard time finding someone to house them, and when someone finally offered them shelter, they were set upon by a group of men who surrounded the house, demanding the Levite so they could molest him. The Levite took his concubine and gave her to the crowd. The wicked men abused her sexually and otherwise all night long, letting her go at dawn. She arrived to the host house and perished on the doorstep. In the morning, the Levite opened the door to the house to find his concubine dead. The man took her body, cut it into twelve pieces, and sent the pieces throughout Israel to different leaders in different communities. The leaders of the other tribes in Israel were shocked and furious over what happened in Givah.

---

48   Genesis 21:23, for an example of how the Israelites refrained from attacking the Philistines because of the oath; see Joshua 15:63 with the commentary of *Rashi* and *Radak*.

49   *Sotah* 10a.

The leaders of the tribes called a meeting to discuss what happened in Givah and what should be the response, without inviting the leaders of Benjamin. The other tribes felt that since the tribe of Benjamin didn't take action on the wicked men, it was up to them to go to Givah and carry out justice for what was done to the concubine. The tribe of Benjamin essentially became territorial, and instead of addressing what happened in Givah, they decided to battle the other tribes. There was a giant battle between the tribes of Benjamin and everyone else that claimed thousands and nearly wiped out Benjamin.

Response: In the words of Rabbi Michael Hattin: "It begins as a personal tragedy but quickly becomes a national catastrophe."[50] The question is what elicited the severe response from the other tribes on Benjamin. The answer is that the abomination that was allowed in Givah was not viewed as a mere random (granted awful) occurrence but rather something indicative of the moral rot of behavior similar to the actions of the Canaanites that contributed to their expulsion from the land of Israel, as well as a string of events that were reminiscent of what previously had occurred in Sodom, which led to the Divine evisceration of the city. In the words of Rabbi Avigdor Miller: "That a person had been so maltreated was hitherto unknown in Israel; and it was an alarm signal that the evil practices of Canaan were beginning to seep in as forewarned in the Torah" (Exodus 23:33; Deuteronomy 20:17–18).[51]

It is worthwhile to give a little backdrop on how failed Givah and its inhabitants had become. First, the whole reason they (Levite and concubine) stayed in Givah as opposed to a different town was the Levite man calculated (incorrectly) they would be better treated in the Jewish town of Givah.[52] The Levite sought shelter for the night for a long time

---

50   *Judges: Perils of Possession*, p. 187.
51   *Behold a People*, p. 194.
52   Judges 19:11–12.

in the town to no avail,[53] until finally an old man who was not originally from the town (i.e., not of the tribe of Benjamin) offered some hospitality.[54] The *Yalkut Me'am Loez* observes that the Levite man pointed out that the people who killed his concubine and attacked the house were not isolated citizens but instead respected members of the town.[55]

As Rabbi Avigdor Miller points out, the verse (Judges 19:30) says: "Nothing like this has been seen (in Israel) from the time the children of Israel went up from Egypt from this day."[56] This is the context for the justification the other tribes felt they had in going to war against the tribe of Benjamin. Their calculation was that the moral failing of Givah (and by extension the tribe of Benjamin, who refused to bring the perpetrators to justice) was of such magnitude that if left unchecked by a devastating response, the moral rot could spread and ultimately cause the long-term effects of expulsion from the land (the fate of Canaan due to its practices) or worse (utter destruction as in the case of Sodom). Rabbi Miller says elsewhere that the intention of the leaders of the tribes was to extract this horrible Canaanite influence as one would find it necessary to get rid of cancer—even by means of amputation to save the rest of the body.[57]

I Samuel 11:11: "And they struck down Ammon by the time the day became hot."

Response: What happened in the above verse was an Israelite response to an earlier attack by the Ammonites (see v. 1).

II Samuel 10:18, I Kings 20:29: "And the children of Israel struck down Aram..."

---

53   Ibid., v. 13–15.
54   Ibid., v. 16–20.
55   *The Torah Anthology*, p. 392.
56   *Behold a People*, p. 194.
57   "The Concubine at Givah," lecture 011.

Response: In both instances of violence mentioned in the above verses, the context shows that they were based on retaliation for previous Aramite aggression.[58]

> II Kings 10:7 (also II Kings 9:24, 27; 10:14, 17, 19–27): Jehu wages war against idolaters in Israel: "And so it happened, when the scroll reached them, they took the king's sons and slaughtered seventy men; they put their heads in kettles and sent them to [Jehu], to Jezreel."

Response: The image of severed heads elicits imagery of tribal headhunters, but the reason that Jehu was sent the heads was for identification, not as an act of cruel barbarism. Like chemotherapy is required to eradicate cancer, the violence in Jehu's quest to eradicate idolatry in Israel needs to be understood as necessary. The reason for why idolatry should be understood as the grave offence that it is will be explained in the third section of this chapter.

II: INDIVIDUAL VIOLENCE

> Exodus 2:11–12: "It happened in those days that Moses grew up and went out to his brethren and observed their burdens; and he saw an Egyptian man striking a Hebrew man, of his brethren. He turned this way and that and saw that there was no man, so he struck down the Egyptian and hid him in the sand." Moses defends an Israelite being abused by an Egyptian man.

Response: Professor Hector Avalos[59] uses this verse as evidence of the Bible condoning unwarranted violence: "By any modern American legal standard, this qualifies as murder, as it was premeditated murder

---

58   See II Samuel 10:1–8 and I Kings 20:26.

59   Professor Avalos may be controversial, but he is highly regarded in university Bible studies.

and not an act of self-defense."[60] This reference really belongs with the other neglected verses that people cite out of context (hence, my ignoring them due to their being obviously taken out of context). However, I feel it is imperative to highlight the often-neglected truth that poor textual scholarship is not relegated to the uninformed masses. We have here a university level, high-caliber Bible scholar who, blinded by the zeal for his agenda, commits an elementary error in textual study. The truth is that by any modern legal standard, Moses did not commit premeditated murder; he merely defended another person who was being attacked. What happened (as is explicit in the verse) is that Moses saw a Hebrew being beaten (likely to death) and defended the Hebrew. In the process, he killed the Egyptian. By any legal system, this would be a justified homicide.

II Samuel 2:23: "But he refused to turn aside, and Abner struck him with the back of his spear, into his fifth rib; and the spear came out of his back, and he fell there and died in his place." In the midst of battle (civil war), Abner defends himself from Asahel.

Response: It should be noted that this incident happened when the Jewish People were engaged in a civil war for the claim of the throne; it was not a random act of violence but rather a scenario that happened in the midst of battle. Abner was being pursued by Asahel and killed him in self-defense. Abner was critiqued for killing him rather than wounding him (see next response), but this is a far cry from cold-blooded murder. Furthermore, Abner tried to dissuade Asahel from pursuing him so that he would not have to kill him. Asahel persisted, though, and so Abner had no choice other than to kill him in self-defense.

---

60   Hector Avalos, *The End of Biblical Studies*, p. 332.

> II Samuel 3:30: "Joab and his brother Abishai had killed Abner because he had killed their brother Asahel in Gibeon." This is a response to some of the fighting that transpired in the civil war.

Response: The Talmud provides an account of what transpired when Joab was brought to trial for killing Abner. Rabbi Yochanan explains that when Abner hit Asahel in the fifth rib, he was aiming for a spot sure to have the direct result of certain death (in other words, he could have defended himself without killing Asahel, but he didn't, so it is considered murder, being that Abner killed him unnecessarily). Benaiah (the head of the court) conceded that Joab was exempt from killing Abner due to the fact that Abner was in some way guilty of killing the brother of Joab, Asahel.[61]

> II Samuel 4:7–8: "After they had entered the house while he was asleep in his bed in his bedroom, and struck him, they had severed his head. They then took his head and traveled through the Arabah all night. They brought the head of Ish-Bosheth to David in Hebron, and said to the king, 'Here is the head of Ish-Bosheth, son of Saul your enemy, who sought [to take] your life! Hashem granted my lord the king revenge from Saul and his offspring this day." Rechab and Baanah murder Ish-Bosheth.

Response: Rechab and Baanah tried to ingratiate themselves to King David by killing Ish-Bosheth and bringing David his head. We see a few verses later how well their "gift" was received by David (vs. 9–12)—they were executed for their act, which was murder in its clearest form.

---

61   *Sanhedrin* 49a.

> II Samuel 4:12: "David then commanded the soldiers and they killed them. They cut off their hands and feet, and hung them over the pool in Hebron." Rechab and Baanah are executed for murder of Ish-Bosheth.

Response: This was a case of men being executed for murdering someone in cold blood. The reason they were executed in such a brutal manner was that King David wanted to establish clearly that not only did he have absolutely nothing to do with actions of Rechab and Baanah, but he was, in fact, extremely opposed to what they did.[62] The *Abarbanel* (on this verse) adds an important historical observation: This happened during a turbulent time when the leadership of the nation was in flux; David wanted to forcefully demonstrate that assassination was neither accepted nor tolerated.[63]

> II Samuel 11:14–27: David's "sin" with Bathsheba. It is portrayed that David saw a beautiful woman, took her to have relations with her, then sent her husband out in battle so he could marry her.

Response: This issue is one of the most enigmatic and often misunderstood parts of Scripture. According to a superficial reading of the verses contained in chapters 11 and 12, it seems that "God's anointed" saw a beautiful woman, who happened to be married. He decided to take her for himself, and then he had her husband sent to his death so she could be all his. Yet, the Talmud proclaims: "Whoever says David sinned is simply mistaken."[64] How do we understand this?

Some detailed observations regarding the relevant verses are in order. One point that needs to be stressed is that if David's relationship with

---

62   See *Radak* on the verse.
63   See ArtScroll Samuel, p. 226.
64   *Shabbos* 56a.

Bathsheba prior to Uriah's death was really considered adulterous according to Jewish law, then David would not have been able to marry her after Uriah died.[65] Another proof is offered as indication that it was not really adultery: "Additional proof in support of the Talmudic contention that David did not sin can be discerned from Nathan's reproach of David in the following chapter. Here Nathan reprimands David for marrying Bathsheba after causing her husband's death, but fails to accuse him of the prior act of having relations with her while she was still married to Uriah."[66] The reason why this was not considered an adulterous act (at least in law if not in spirit as well) was that it was standard practice for a soldier to give his wife a bill of divorce before going into battle,[67] so Bathsheba was not really married at the time.

What about sending Uriah to his death? What was David's culpability in this aspect of the incident? The Talmud informs us that Uriah was already guilty of a crime that is punishable by death, namely rebelling against the king in a time of war,[68] so David did not murder Uriah. Nevertheless, the Talmud does say further that David did wrong to Uriah by having him sent to the front lines instead of having a trial by means of the Sanhedrin.[69] For this reason, Scripture later relates: "David did that which was just in the eyes of Hashem, and did not swerve from all that He commanded him, all the days of his life, except for the matter of Uriah the Hittite."[70]

There is a question that still remains: How could King David, who is often given as a textbook example of what a great Jewish leader is supposed to be, be tripped up even on a minute level? The Talmud teaches us that David knew Bathsheba was destined to be his wife since the Six Days of Creation.[71] But still, even though David knew Bathsheba was his soul mate, why—in the language of the Talmud—did he take her

---

65   *Sotah* 27a.

66   From the Judaica Press series on the Books of the Prophets, pp. 318–19.

67   *Kesubos* 9b.

68   See II Samuel 11:11, and *Megillah* 14b.

69   *Shabbos* 56a.

70   I Kings 15:5.

71   *Sanhedrin* 107a.

before the time was ripe? Jewish tradition provides two answers to this question. First, David challenged God to test him,[72] which was a grave mistake that brought suffering upon him. ArtScroll's commentary on the book of Samuel articulates the second reason.[73] It is true that David did not sin in action. The consensus of the commentators, however, is that in some shape or form, he had a serious shortcoming regarding his intentions for someone on his level. Because of his failure to stay consistent with what was expected of him (with regard to this incident with Uriah), the Scriptures condemned him in such a harsh manner (not to mention the punishment meted out to him in Chapter 12).

We must make two observations regarding how this text plays into the justice scheme of the Bible. (1) The Biblical verses were reprimanding him not for what he literally did, but rather for the gravity of what he did do as a person on his spiritual level. (2) David was punished for the shortcomings that he was guilty of. In contrast to many other cultures of his day (not to mention a few today), the king was held accountable, like any other man, for whatever transgressions of which he was guilty.

> I Kings 2:24–25: "'And now, as Hashem lives, Who has established me and has set me upon the throne of my father David, and Who has made a dynasty for me as He had spoken—[I swear] that today Adonijah shall be put to death.' So King Solomon dispatched Benaiah son of Jehoiada, and he struck him, killing him." Adonijah tries to usurp the kingdom of Solomon.

Response: The background regarding the death sentence placed on Adonijah stems from his attempt to usurp the kingdom from Solomon.[74] It was prophesied by the prophet Nathan that Solomon would take the

---

72 Ibid.

73 ArtScroll Samuel I-II, p. 269; see also *Avodah Zarah* 4b; *Michtav Me'Eliyahu*, vol. 3, p. 82.

74 I Kings 1:5–7, 9–10.

reins from David over Israel,[75] yet Adonijah challenged the Divine plan by trying to replace David as king of Israel. We should take note that Adonijah cleverly recruited Joab and Abiathar, who were both popular with the people and had stakes in Adonijah ruling Israel rather than Solomon. When Nathan and Bathsheba foiled his plan,[76] Adonijah begged Solomon for mercy and pledged to be a loyal servant of the king,[77] and King Solomon told him that if he would remain loyal, he would remain safe.[78] Despite his close brush with death, Adonijah was not deterred from his mission to be the king of Israel. Later, Adonijah concocted a new scheme to undermine King Solomon's leadership by asking King Solomon's mother to request of her son that he give Abishag (King David's servant) to Adonijah as a wife.[79] The problem with this request was that because Abishag had been King David's servant, she was prohibited from a person who was not the king, so Adonijah would only be allowed to marry her if he was king. Therefore, Adonijah's request was tantamount to claiming he should have the status of a king.[80] King Solomon saw right through Adonijah's traitorous plan and sentenced him to death for continuously attempting to overthrow the Divinely appointed monarchy.

I Kings 2:29–34: "It was told to King Solomon that Joab had fled to the tent of Hashem and said to [Joab], 'Thus said the king: "Go out!"' But he replied, 'No; for I shall die here.' Benaiah sent back word to the king, saying, 'Thus spoke Joab, and thus did he answer me.' The king then said to him, 'Do as he said—strike him down [there], and bury him; eliminate the innocent blood that Joab spilled, from me and from my father's house.

---

75   I Chronicles 22:9–10.
76   I Kings 1:11–48.
77   Ibid., v. 50–51.
78   Ibid., v. 52–53.
79   I Kings 2:13–22.
80   See *Rashi* and *Radak*, I Kings 2:22.

'Hashem will thus return him blood upon his head because he struck two men who were more righteous and good than he, and he killed them by the sword, yet my father David did not know—Abner son of Ner, commander of the army of Israel, and Amasa son of Jether, commander of the army of Judah. Let their blood return upon the head of Joab and the head of his offspring forever, while [to] David and his offspring and his house and his throne there should be peace forever from Hashem.' So Benaiah son of Jehoiada went up and struck him and killed him, and he was buried at his house in the desert." King David wanted to have Joab killed because his murder of Abner.

Response: King David wanted King Solomon to have Joab killed because Joab murdered Abner. Joab not only murdered Abner, but he murdered him by deceiving him that he was interested in peace.[81] This threatened to reignite the civil war that was taking place in the house of Israel at a time when King David was trying to establish unity.[82]

I Kings 2:46: "The king then commanded Benaiah son of Jehoiada, and he went out and struck him and he died." Shimi has a death penalty carried out against him (eventually) because of subservience in battle.

Response: The verse is talking about Shimi, who cursed King David, which deserves the death penalty, as will be explained further below. David spared his life, but then before he (David) died, he instructed Solomon to kill him (Shimi). The Midrash says that King David initially spared Shimi because Mordechai (from the book of Esther) was going to descend from him.[83] The *Metzudas David* suggests another reason why

---

81   See *Rashi*, I Kings 2:5–6.
82   See *Sanhedrin* 20a, explaining II Samuel 3:31.
83   *Targum Sheni*, Esther 2:5.

King David spared Shimi: The people as a whole would be overly afraid of his vengeance against him and would not accept him as king.[84]

The Talmud derives from the verse in Deuteronomy (17:15) that we are commanded to fear the king.[85] Why is this necessary? The *B'nei Yissachar* explains that through fear of the king, people learn fear of God. The Talmud teaches that to curse a Torah scholar (like King David) is tantamount to cursing the Torah.[86] The actions of Shimi caused both fear of God and the honor of Torah to be diminished. This is one of the reasons why rebellion against the king carries such a heavy punishment; rebellion against a righteous king ultimately is a rebellion against God and His authority. Another reason for the gravity of the punishment for rebellion against the king is that when the Jewish kingdom is unified with the king, there is predominantly peace. When a person rebels against the king, it threatens the stability of the kingdom and puts all the citizens at risk. Therefore, the king has a right to execute the rebel because the rebel is putting all the citizens in the kingdom at risk—just like a person must defend his life from an attack, so too in this instance the people (represented by the king) have a right to defend themselves.[87]

> II Kings 2:23–24: "He went up from Beth-el. As he was going up on the road, some young lads came out of the city and mocked him, saying to him, 'Go on up, Baldhead! Go on up, Baldhead!' He turned around and saw them and cursed them in the name of Hashem. Two bears then came out of the forest and tore apart forty-two of the lads."

Response: The term "young lads" could also be translated as "little lads." The Talmud comments "little" is representative of people with "little faith." Another explanation in the Talmud is that they were

---

84   *Metzudas David*, II Samuel 19:23.
85   *Kiddushin* 32b.
86   *Sanhedrin* 99b.
87   See *Maharitz Chiyus, Toras Neviim*.

grown-up youths who behaved contemptibly like children.[88] The *Ralbag* notes that the verse says, "He turned around and saw them and cursed them," meaning that he (Elisha) saw prophetically that they were bad apples and that nothing good would come from them. Rabbi Yaakov Yisroel Kanievsky gives us a crucial perspective in understanding this incident:

> *"In the Name of Hashem." By invoking the name of God, Elisha was placing the final decision in God's hands, as if to say that it was for Him to determine whether and how the impudent lads should be punished. Clearly, God's holy prophet would not have transgressed the prohibition against taking revenge, especially for such a relatively trivial offense. Rather, by ridiculing him and his miracle of curing the water, these youths were ridiculing God Who had designated Elisha as His prophet and Who had performed the miracle. Also, as mentioned above, they were undermining Elisha's ability to influence the people and their leaders to repent. By calling for Divine punishment, Elisha was proving to the nation that their criticism had no basis.[89]*

II Kings 5:27: "Naaman's leprosy shall therefore cleave to you and to your children forever! When [Gechazi] left his presence, he was [white] as snow with leprosy." Gechazi, the attendant of Elisha, took advantage of Naaman due to his greed, and then lied to Elisha regarding what he was doing.

Response: The first thing to understand is that the English term for what Naaman had is misleading. The Hebrew term *tzaraas* is often translated as "leprosy" because its physical manifestation closely resembles that affliction. Nevertheless, it is important to understand

---

88   *Sotah* 46b.
89   ArtScroll I-ll Kings, p. 245.

this as a malaise with spiritual roots, inflicted upon people who engage in certain anti-social sins (a proof for this is that it affects not only people but also their possessions, i.e., clothing, homes[90]). The Talmud informs us that Gechazi earned his punishment because of his false oath to Naaman.[91] Still, the longevity of the punishment seems harsh.

A reason for the severity of the punishment can be understood from a contextual understanding of the verses. The entire reason Elisha refused payment for healing Naaman was to glorify God's name.[92] In fact, his goal was accomplished; Naaman renounced his idolatry[93] as a result of Elisha's pure intentions not to benefit from the miracle.[94] This sheds light on the words of the Midrash: "Whoever profanes the name of Heaven is stricken with *tzaraas*, as in the case of Gechazi, who pursued Naaman to take money from him...Elisha sanctified the Name of the Holy One, blessed be He, by not accepting anything from Naaman, but Gechazi pursued him and swore falsely that Elisha had sent him for money. Thus, he profaned the Name of Heaven that Elisha had sanctified."[95] The *Radak* points out that his children were punished because of their being accomplices to the deception.[96]

> Psalms 137:9: "Praiseworthy is He who will clutch and dash your infants against the rock." A prophetic lament over the exiles.

Response: This verse is referring to a warning of retribution that the Babylonians had coming due to their treatment of the Jewish People.[97] King David was telling them that not only will they be conquered, but their conquerors will inflict them with the same vicious violence

---

90   See *Rambam, Nega'im* 12:5.
91   *Arachin* 16a.
92   See *Abarbanel*, II Kings 5:8.
93   *Gittin* 57b.
94   See *Ralbag*, II Kings 12:18, sect. 28.
95   *Bamidbar Rabbah* 7:5.
96   Clearly, any subsequent children were not affected by the punishment.
97   See *Malbim*, Psalms 137:8.

that they meted out to the Jewish People.[98] The praise is directed to God, and the point is that God is praised when He metes out justice in this world. This was not praising the actual act of revenge, but the system of justice that ensures that great wrongs will receive a just response from God.

III: THE DEATH PENALTY AND OTHER PUNISHMENTS

The death penalty is perhaps one of the most misunderstood and abused concepts in the whole of Scripture. Many are at best mystified how it is possible that a religious document can not only condone but even prescribe death as a punishment for transgressions that many perceive as a mere difference in choice of lifestyle. More troubling are the people at the other end who relish the opportunity to "expose" the Bible as a barbaric group of tribal warriors who, stones in hand, are looking for the chance to enforce the word of God. A good illustration of the misconceptions held by both groups is articulated by the pen of a passionate disbeliever who highlights the easy confusion regarding understanding what warrants the death penalty:

> *This is clear: don't pick up sticks on Saturday. If you pick up sticks God's followers will pick up stones. Is this a good guide for morality? When I was a child, each year my family would spend weeks camping in the mountains of California. My brothers and I had the job of picking up and kindling wood for the fire. This often happened on the weekend. Didn't my born-again parents read the bible?...The man who was stoned to death was likely gathering firewood to cook food to feed his family. He was the one acting morally.[99]*

---

98   See *Gittin* 58a for the reference of the Babylonians smashing Jewish infants against a rock.

99   Dan Barker, *Godless*, p. 164. As a sidenote: Observe how the end part of his account reflects his agenda; notice how he accepts the account of the stoning as factual, but steps outside of the Biblical text and ignores Biblical context to vilify the people who keep the Sabbath. Was he collecting wood to kindle a fire to feed his family? This was certainly not mentioned in the text (Numbers 15:32–36) he quoted that precedes his moral indictments. Where do the grounds to make this assertion stem from? Even if we were to ignore Barker's lack of evidence in support of his claim, his suggestion is still logically flawed because there is

It is true that the Biblical justice system's death penalty will not necessarily resonate well with the twenty-first-century mindset, even after it has been explained thoroughly. Nevertheless, it is crucial to understand that it has been grossly misconstrued in the perception of many people, and it needs to be understood in the context of what the actual requirements are for its implementation.

When the Talmud proclaims that a rabbinical court that puts one person to death in seventy years is labeled a "destroyer,"[100] it is not as unfathomable as it seems. Especially when one considers what must have transpired in order to carry the death penalty out. The transgression must have been

- in defiance of and immediately proceeded by a warning given just before the transgressor acts;[101]
- undertaken in a mentally stable state;[102]
- committed in the presence of at least two witnesses.[103]

If that is the case, why were the penalties prescribed in the first place? Even though the punishments were almost never invoked, the penalties served the purpose of being a deterrent. They were also used as a guide to indicate the seriousness of the sins for which they were prescribed.

(Biblical) counter-evidence to his claim. Could it really have been the case that this family would starve if they did not cook food on the Sabbath? Not very likely, especially when one considers that the Israelites were sustained by the manna (see Numbers 11:7 and Exodus 16:35) while in the desert, which included Sabbath provisions (Exodus 16:29). To rely on the Bible's account of the stoning, he does gladly, but to rely the other part of the Bible's historicity (the manna) he omits. This is a perfect example of the intellectual dishonesty that I mentioned in the introduction regarding how people accept the Bible's historicity when it is convenient for them, yet, at the same time, reject the Bible's historicity when it conflicts with their agenda. One cannot have his cake and eat it too.

100   *Makkos* 7a.
101   *Sanhedrin* 40b.
102   *Rashi, Chagigah* 3b, s.v. *Aizehu*.
103   Numbers 35:30, Deuteronomy 17:6, see also *Sanhedrin* 32a, 40a. It should also be noted that the requirements for who can qualify as valid witnesses also is limited with the knowledge that they can receive the punishment of death if found to be lying; *Makkos* 6b, see also *Sanhedrin* 8b, 41a, and 72b.

Rabbi Yisroel Miller explains:

> *Capital punishment transgressions are those that undermine our entire status as covenant-keepers and a holy nation (e.g., Shabbos-desecrators and various forms of immorality), and a willful transgressor should feel that his life is forfeited. While in practice, the Oral law is more lenient, the Chumash [five books of Moses] teaches us the attitude of full responsibility.*[104]

Furthermore, Rabbi Shubert Spero wrote:

> *In the words of Dr. Belkin…"The only state the Rabbis were conscious of was the Divine state of God as revealed in the Torah and interpreted and transmitted by the oral traditions. Any crime committed by an individual was never thought of as an offense against the community or state. It was looked upon as an offence against an individual who suffered by the act and as a serious sin against the theocracy of Judaism which united all Israelites in the 'religious nationality' of Judaism."…We do have instances in the Book of Deuteronomy where punishments were given for a certain group of transgressors and the explanation offered seems to suggest not so much retributive or expiatory considerations as primarily utilitarian or deterrent ones. Thus, we find, "And thou shalt stone him…and all Israel shall hear, and fear, and shall do no more such wickedness;" "And all the people shall hear, and fear, and do no more presumptuously;" "…so that thou shall put evil away from you, and all Israel shall hear, and fear." Nachmanides makes it clear that these locutions indicate that the harshness of the penalty in these cases is not generated by the mere grievousness of the sin, but by the need to have the punishments act as a deterrent against future occurrences.*[105]

---

104   Rabbi Yisroel Miller, *In Search of Torah Wisdom*, p. 304.
105   Shubert Spero, *Morality, Halakha, and the Jewish Tradition*, pp. 233–34.

If it is the case that the death penalty was hardly ever implemented, and the judicial court system is not functioning anyway, why bother to mention some of the reasons why certain sins merited it? The answer lies in one of the reasons that the possibility existed in the first place: to help us understand the gravity of certain transgressions.[106] My goal then is not to explain every occurrence in the Bible where the death penalty is mentioned; rather, what I hope to accomplish is to illustrate the philosophical underpinnings of certain Biblical sections that condone in the strongest terms what contemporary society views either as insignificant or as a matter of personal expression.

Lashes were administered only when the same list of the requirements for the death penalty were fulfilled, so they were also a rare occurrence.[107] Their function was basically the same as that of the death penalty: to stress the severity of the transgression and to atone for the sin. The function of atonement (via punishment) for sin in the Torah is a method of removing harsher (spiritual) consequences of sin. In contrast to other religions, atonement is not merely affliction but also the process of avoiding a worse fate spiritually.

"Eye for an Eye"

One of the most misunderstood verses of the Bible is found in Exodus 21:24, though even the Biblically illiterate will be familiar with it: "...an eye for an eye, a tooth for a tooth..." This Scriptural passage has often been criticized as a brutal form of revenge practiced by uncivilized people, which creates a circle of violence. As the famous quote from Gandhi goes, "An eye for an eye leaves the world blind." The truth, however, is that this verse is referring to monetary compensation for damage inflicted upon the victim's body. This is not an apologetic answer invented to deflect moral critiques of the law; rather, this understanding

---

106 The *Rambam* suggests that the severity of the offense can be inferred from the kind of penalty that applies. In other words, the most serious transgressions are punishable by a form of execution, while the less severe transgressions are punishable by lesser consequences, for examples, lashes. See *Rambam*'s Commentary on the Mishnah, *Pirkei Avos* 2:1.

107 *Rambam, Mishneh Torah, Sanhedrin* 16:4; *Pesachim* 63b; *Makkos* 15b, 17a; *Shevous* 28b; *Temurah* 3b.

was always within the structure of Jewish law.[108] In fact, this interpretation is alluded to in Scripture itself, as Rabbi Samson Raphael Hirsch points out in his commentary on the topic,[109] since the Hebrew word "*tachas*," in place of, is used in other Scriptural references referring to expression of compensation not retribution.[110] Furthermore, the Vilna Gaon points out: "If we arrange the letters of the *alef-beis*, alphabet, we find that underneath the letters of the word '*ayin*,' the letters *pey-kuf-samach* appear.[111] The letters *pey-kuf-samach*, rearranged, form the word *kesef*, money. The phrase '*ayin tachas ayin*' can thus be rendered as follows: *ayin*, for an injury to an eye, one must pay *tachas ayin*, that which is *tachas*, underneath, the letters *ayin*, namely *kesef*, money."[112]

Idolatry, the Most Severe Sin in the Bible

The *Rambam* wrote of idolatry: "Know that when you will look through the Torah and all the Books of the Prophets, you will not find the expression of fury or anger or vengeful jealousy [ascribed to the Almighty] except in connection with idolatry; nor will you find anyone called an enemy of the Lord…except someone who worships idols."[113] In fact, idol worship is equivalent to breaking all of the Torah.[114]

The reason for this is articulated well in the Taryag Legacy Foundation's book, *The Ten Commandments*:

> *Inasmuch as the mitzvah [commandment] to reject the other deities serves to complement the mitzvah of emunah [faith], it becomes part of the foundation of faith on which the entire body of Torah and mitzvos [commandments] must rest. Unqualified acceptance of the mitzvos hinges on a fully developed belief in the Unity of God. So long as there is room in one's mind for*

---

108   *Bava Kama* 83b–84a.
109   Rabbi Samson Raphael Hirsch on Numbers 31:17–18.
110   Habakuk 3:16, Genesis 2:26, Isaiah 60:17, Deuteronomy 22:29, and Numbers 25:15.
111   The Hebrew term *tachas* also means "under." The word for "money" (after its letters are rearranged) is under the word "eye" in the Torah scroll.
112   *Torah Treasures*, vol. 1, p. 181.
113   *Rambam, Guide for the Perplexed* 1:36.
114   *Horayos* 8a, *Nedarim* 25a, *Kiddushin* 40a, *Shevuos* 29a, and *Chullin* 5a.

a deity other than God, the compelling nature of the Torah is lost, for the dictates of God are bound to conflict with those of the other. Therefore, say Chazal (Sifri, Devarim 540), anyone who gives legitimacy to the worship of idols has, in effect, denied the entire Torah (Sefer Hachinuch #26).[115]

However, more insight is required to appreciate the roots of this sin that makes it so severe. Rabbi Akiva Tatz articulates well the fundamental issue at stake in his book, *Letters to a Buddhist Jew*:

Idolatry, in essence, is the idea of relating not to the supernal Source of all existence, the ultimate Oneness, but to the channels that bring down energy into the world, the "openings and pipelines." An idolater focuses on the zodiac ("the worship of stars and zodiac" is the common Torah terminology) or on the various forces of nature: the sun, the wind, the rain. His graven images are tangible representatives of these energies (an idolater who literally worships his piece of wood or stone as Divine has transgressed the prohibition of foolishness long before the prohibition of idolatry). Of course, one who relates only to the ineffable Source could never create a physical representation; one whose perception goes no deeper than a source of the natural can.

Maimonides says that originally, close to the beginning of history, people acknowledged God alone. Then there came a stage when they reasoned since He uses agencies such as the sun and moon to accomplish His will, surely it would be fitting to give honor to these as His emissaries, His viceroys. They began to accord honor to the intermediaries as well as to God. And eventually, they ignored Him and remained focused on the channels only. Such was the development of idolatry. What needs further study, though, is this: what was the underlying motivation in this error? Such slips are not casual.

---

115   Introductory volume of the Taryag Legacy Foundation, *The Ten Commandments*, p. 78.

The underlying reason for forgetting the Source and remembering the intermediate levels is the most basic of all vested interests: the focus on self.

The real difference between worship of the Source and worship of intermediaries is this: one who serves the Source is concerned about what his obligations are; what does He demand of me?[116] How do I give myself to Him? One who serves the intermediaries is concerned about what they can do for him. The intermediaries are, after all, the proximate source of all human needs, all natural functions of the world. The idolater looks to the immediate source of power, love, wealth—in fact, of all his needs—and asks: How can they serve me? He does not need to look further.[117]

(A) False Prophet and Enticer to Go Astray (Deuteronomy 13:2–6, 7–12)

It is obligatory to understand the ramifications for the worship of idols: One does not only lose his life for this transgression in this world (under the right circumstances), but he also forfeits his existence in the World to Come[118] unless he repents. While people have different opinions regarding the use of the death penalty generally, even opponents of the death penalty will often acknowledge that the idea of killing someone who murdered another person is not a barbaric idea. It is self-understood that ending another person's existence in this world is one of the most heinous things that someone can do, especially when the victim is a youth. To take a life full of potential and to deprive it of the

---

116   This point is highlighted by an observation Robert R. Reilly makes in his book, *America on Trial* (pp. 37–38): "Even when the Jews were defeated in battle or conquered by Assyrians, Babylonians, Persians, Greeks, and Romans, they quit[e] extraordinarily did not consider their God defeated. There was no other god to defeat Him. If the Hebrews were overcome by the Babylonians and taken as their captives, it was not because their God had failed them but because they had failed their God. Jewish Scripture reveals the Israelites' dawning consciousness that their God is not the god of their city or tribe, but is wholly transcendent, omniscient, omnipotent God."

117   Rabbi Akiva Tatz, *Letters to a Buddhist Jew*, pp. 58–59.

118   *Sanhedrin* 90a; *Rosh Hashanah* 17a.

privilege of enjoying life is a great evil. How much more, then, is the sin evil that robs a person of an eternity basking in the goodness of God? When the gravity of this crime is put into proper context, opponents clearly should judge the punishment not as vicious but rather as virtuous in the system of Divine justice. In other words, removing a threat to people losing their afterlife is an act of virtue, not viciousness. The false prophet is attempting to ruin this life and life in the World to Come for the Jewish People.

(B) The Destruction of the Wayward City (Deuteronomy 13:13–19)

The Torah commands the wholesale destruction of a city (in Israel) where the majority of its (Jewish) residents are idol worshipers.[119] The Talmud stipulates (according to Rabbi Eliezer) that it is impossible for such a city to have existed.[120] The Talmud asks why, if this is the case, is it even mentioned in the Torah? The answer given is that it was given to be expounded and to receive reward for doing so.

Breaking the Sabbath: A Denial of God's Supervision over the World

From the outset, it should be mentioned that only the Jewish People are required to keep the laws of the Sabbath; this is because the Sabbath (in Hebrew, *Shabbos* or *Shabbat*) is a gift God specifically gave to the Jewish People as a sign of His covenant.[121] The Sabbath is not just a mere day of rest; it is a testimony to God's active role in the creation of the world. The Taryag Legacy Foundation's book, *The Ten Commandments*, articulates this well:

---

119 Deuteronomy 13:13–19.

120 *Sanhedrin* 71a. Rabbi Yonasan disagrees, but the fact that there is an opinion that it is impossible for such a situation to occur is a good indication about how often this law was enforced. Also, according to Rabbi Shimon Schwab (*Maayan Beis Hashoevah*, p. 427), the differing views can be reconciled where the court didn't carry out the penalty, even according to Rabbi Yonasan.

121 Exodus 31:16–17. Incidentally, this is another mistake on Dan Barker's part. Given that his background was Christian, i.e., not Jewish, neither he nor his family are capable of being guilty of Sabbath desecration.

In what arrangement were the Ten Commandments given? Five were on one tablet and five on the other...The fourth commandment inscribed on the first tablet was, Remember the Shabbos day to sanctify it. Directly opposite, on the second tablet, appeared the words, You shall not bear false witness. The Torah thus teaches that one who desecrates Shabbos in effect testifies in God's presence that He did not create the world in six days and then rest on the seventh. Conversely, one who observes Shabbos bears witness before God that He created the world in six days and then rested on the seventh. As we are told by the prophet (Isaiah 43:12): You are My witnesses; so declares God (Mechilta, Yisro par. 8; Pesikta Zutrasa, Exodus 20:13).

When a person desecrates the Sabbath, he is, in effect, denying God's supervision over the world. Therefore, it should not come as a surprise that Shabbos desecration is compared to idol worship.[122]

Rebellions

(A) One Who Curses His Mother and/or Father
(Exodus 21:17, Leviticus 20:9)

Rabbi Samson Raphael Hirsch writes:

The Exodus from Egypt and the Revelation of the Torah are the two foundations in fact on which the nation of Israel is built. It is they that serve as the basis for our submission to Hashem as the Ruler and Master of our destinies and lives. These two events are historical facts, and we know them and recognize them to be historical truths. However, the only guarantor of their truth is Tradition, and the basis for Tradition is a faithful transmission to children by their fathers, and a willing acceptance of it by the children from their fathers. The foundations of the great edifice established by God in Israel have survived the many long years

---

122   *Shabbos* 118b.

only through the intellectual and practical obedience of children to their fathers and mothers. It emerges from this that respect for one's father and mother is the basic precondition for the eternity of the Jewish People. Through the father and mother, God imparts to the child not only his basic existence, but the link to his Jewish past that enables him to be a Jew. From the parents, the child receives the tradition of the Jewish mission in knowledge, way of life, and education. They transmit to him the lessons of Jewish history and the teachings of the Torah, so that he too will bequeath them to his children when the time comes. In the same way that a child looks up to his parent, so too will his children look upon him. Without this bond the chain of generations is broken, the hopes of the Jewish future are lost, and the faith of the Jews would cease to exist. Indeed, the role of parents in Jewish life is pivotal, and for this reason the Torah assigned them a place in the Ten Commandments, Honor your father and your mother.[123]

We see from Rabbi Hirsch's comments that by showing such blatant disregard for one's parents, a person is capable of undermining the system for the transmission of God's teachings. It should be noted that the only "curse" that makes one liable for the death penalty is one that invokes the Name of God. Rabbi Yonasan Eibeshitz explains what makes this such an exceeding great sin: "When he curses his parents, he is obliviously not oblivious to God's presence, since he actually invokes His Name in his curse. Nevertheless, with full awareness of God's presence, he has the audacity to curse his parents and even to draw God into his iniquity."[124]

(B) The Rebellious Elder (Deuteronomy 17:8–13)

The death penalty for a rebellious elder (read: sage, not just a plain elderly person) serves to protect the authoritative dignity and demand

---

123 Rabbi Samson Raphael Hirsch, Exodus 20:12.
124 See *Talelei Oros*, vol. 2, Exodus 21:15, 17.

for the process of implementing what the Torah demands of the Jewish People. The reasoning behind this command is clear: The only way we can fulfill God's will is by following the Torah. When a person challenges the Sanhedrin, High Jewish Court, he is in essence challenging God's will. The danger is increased when it is a Torah sage who challenges the Sanhedrin because it is likely such a person will drag others down with him, and this will cause confusion regarding what the Torah (i.e., God) wants from us. Therefore, one should understand the Torah is preventing a severing of our relationship with God because of confusion about what God expects of us. Finally, the matter is debated first and the penalty is imposed only if the elder refuses to accept the ruling of the majority.

(C) The Rebellious Son (Deuteronomy 21:18–21)

This happens to be one of the most often-quoted Scriptural texts people use to try to suggest that the Bible advocates vicious punishments for the unfortunate person who falls into human nature and betrays the Law. The Talmud informs us that there is an opinion that such an occurrence is impossible,[125] and an opinion that mentioned such a person existed.[126] It should be noted that the Talmud says that the reason we kill him is because if he[127] fulfills all of the criteria for being a "rebellious son," he will eventually down the road certainly (this becomes apparent after seeing the required behaviors) become a murderous thief, so we take away this world from him in order to preserve his place in the World to Come.[128] The *Maharsha* explains that the boy's parents are not capable of appreciating a preemptive death for their son and will delude themselves that he will change his ways. The Torah therefore teaches them that he will inevitably degenerate into a murderer and

---

125 *Sanhedrin* 72a.

126 Ibid.

127 He, and not she, is correct. The Talmud says that this law does not apply to females; *Sanhedrin* 68b.

128 *Sanhedrin* 72a.

be deserving of death. This will motivate the parents to discipline this errant child, and they will be rewarded by properly training him.[129]

This section of Scripture is not recommending that **any** childhood rebellion be handled by killing the child. It is specifically limited to a very precise set of conditions that must be met; in fact, one opinion in the Talmud maintains that it is impossible that these conditions will ever be met, and the entire episode exists purely for the sake of studying it and receiving reward for doing so. Finally, Dennis Prager gives a unique insight into a great benefit of the law: "The greatness of the Deuteronomy law is that it takes away the parents' ability to murder their child."[130] Even today, where in some cultures "honor killings" still exist, as well as other instances of parental marshal law, we can appreciate the deterrent (of parents taking justice into their own hands) that the Bible prescribes.

Homosexuality

A book defending the moral integrity of the Bible does not have the option of ignoring the topic of homosexuality. The Bible is the source of morality, and it is therefore necessary to explain why the Torah condemns homosexual activity. I have separated this topic into two sections. The first section, which follows below, is an explanation of how the Torah directly addresses homosexuality. The other section can be found in Appendix A at the end of the book, because it does not directly address the Biblical view of homosexuality but rather takes a critical look at the arguments people espouse for mainstreaming homosexual behavior in society. The reason for including this current section in the book is that the arguments given for accepting the homosexual lifestyle relate to the moral arguments against the Biblical opposition to homosexual actions.

I am not under the illusion that my arguments here will convince the person of secular persuasion that they should adopt the Torah's view on homosexual activity. My goal in this section is threefold: First, to explain that there is a difference between the Torah's treatment of activity vs.

---

129 *Maharsha* ad loc. See Rabbi Mendel Weinbach, OhrSomayach/Talmudigest *Sanhedrin* 65–71, week ending April 17, 2010, http://orh.edu/yhiy/article.php/4252.

130 "Prager deals with three misconceptions Obama and liberals have with the Bible," *Dennis Prager Show*, YouTube, posted 02/09/2013.

how the Torah judges the individual; second, to explain the Torah's view of why gay male intercourse is treated with such seriousness; and finally, in the appendix, to explain why arguments for mainstreaming homosexual acts/lifestyles fail on a rational level.

Before we begin the topic, it is important to bear in mind that the Torah speaks about homosexual actions,[131] not about people who, for whatever reason, identify as homosexual in their sexual orientation. Rabbi Aharon Soloveitchik incorporated this point when giving a class on Torah and homosexuality. He started by saying that before he would start the topic, his audience should keep a fundamental verse from Leviticus in mind. His students automatically assumed he was referring to the prohibition of a man sleeping with a man as he would a woman,[132] but he said, "Love your fellow as you love yourself."[133] It is important that, when discussing this topic, we not judge the people who have homosexual inclinations but instead focus on why there is a Biblical prohibition for them to act on their desires. It cannot be over-emphasized: When dealing with marginalized people, there needs to be **more** acceptance, not **less**.

Dennis Prager correctly observed: "It is impossible for Judaism to make peace with homosexuality, because homosexuality denies many of Judaism's most fundamental values. It denies life; it denies God's expressed desire that men and women cohabit; and it denies the root structure that Judaism wishes for all mankind, the family."[134] Rabbi Yosef Reinman explains: "Sexual sin rejects God's design for the world and humanity in particular. They [the sinners] hijack an important tool that God instilled in nature for a specific purpose and divert it to something else."[135] Rabbi Aryeh Kaplan articulates how this happens:

---

131 The verse in Leviticus 18:22 specifically refers to the prohibition of male gay intercourse. There is Rabbinic disagreement as to whether there is a Biblical- or only a Rabbinic-level prohibition on lesbian sexual activity. Suffice it to say, though it is not punishable by death and is not as severe as male gay intercourse, it is unquestionably forbidden.

132 Leviticus 18:22.

133 Ibid., 19:18; Rabbi Soloveitchik anecdote culled from Dr. David Luchins, "Gay Marriage Has Arrived," Aish audio (LD885B).

134 Dennis Prager, *Ultimate Issues*—Special Edition: Judaism, Homosexuality, and Civilization, p. 10.

135 Through an e-mail exchange with this author.

> *The Hebrew word for marriage is Kiddushin, which literally means "sanctification" or "holiness." When a man marries a woman, the words he declares to her are, "Behold you become holy to me with this ring."...Interestingly, the opposite of marriage is prostitution and one of the words for a prostitute is kadeshah—literally a woman who had defiled her holiness, indicating the "other side" of this holiness, which is its perversion [Rashi commenting on the word "kodesh" on Sanhedrin 82a].*
>
> *In other words, God provided sexual relations as a tool to enhance the relationship between a husband and a wife for the sake of the institution of marriage—and only that relationship. I am not comparing the gay relationship to the immorality of prostitution; I am asserting that sexual intimacy was designed specifically for the Divine intention of marriage. Therefore, any other use of this "tool," i.e., its misuse, is unauthorized in the same sense—regardless of the intentions or nature of the unsanctioned relationship (be it homosexuality, sex outside of marriage, or any other of the prohibited relationships mentioned in Leviticus). One reason that marital relations are so holy (special) is that it has the ability to accomplish something that is beyond the power of any other human function—namely, to draw a soul down to the world and to produce a living human being.[136]*

If a person was to take that potential and waste it on an act for the exclusive purpose of pleasure, then that would be a pristine example of its misappropriation.

The family structure is such that the male and female personalities combine to make different but equally essential traits (strengths and weaknesses) that work as one to create a family. Homosexuality obliterates the understanding of the reality of gender distinction and claims that the male and female format is unnecessary for a healthy

---

136   Rabbi Aryeh Kaplan, *The Rabbi Aryeh Kaplan Anthology*, vol. 2, pp. 354–55.

and wholesome family life. A piece by Rabbi Benjamin Hecht further illustrates the components of this point:

> *Rabbi Steven Greenberg [a self-proclaimed gay Orthodox apologist] uses the verse of Bereishis (Genesis) 2:24 to argue for the need for the human being to have a romantic relationship. The verse, however, does not simply discuss two human beings. A man is to leave his parents and cleave specifically unto his wife—and thereby become one being. It is not merely coincidence that T.B. Sanhedrin 58a (and, interestingly, in a slightly different manner, Rambam, Mishneh Torah, Melachim 9:5) presents this verse as the source for the prohibition of homosexual behavior within the Noachide code....This is the basic Torah parameter of marriage, and it is from this basis that the Torah view of family emerges. In a certain way, marriage and family are the basic building blocks of the Torah society because it is at this point that man and women meet. The same-sex relationship, by definition, is outside this realm.*[137]

The Bible demands that we accept the notion that God desires a certain family structure, even if we do not always see the wisdom and necessity in that structure. As Daniel Fridman put it: "Torah is neither Democratic nor Republican, progressive nor conservative, any more than the laws of physics and mathematics have a partisan affiliation. Torah is a set of decidedly a priori Divine non-utilitarian truths that, much like the laws of mathematics and physics, are immutable, universal, and contentiously autonomous. They need not be, and should not be, held up to any other ideological, ethical, or political system."[138]

---

137   Rabbi Benjamin Hecht, "Trembling before God"—Part 7: The Parameters of Marriage. Rabbi Hecht's series of online articles deals with a documentary entitled, "Trembling before God," which was produced to highlight the emotional plight of the Orthodox homosexual to appeal for acceptance of homosexuals in the Orthodox community.

138   "Eternal Truth in the Age of Unrestricted Autonomy: A Halakhic Approach to Homosexuality," YUTorah.org, May 03, 2013.

One of the main qualms people have with the Torah's restriction on homosexual behavior is that it excludes the possibility of a gay person having an intimate relationship with a person to whom he is attracted. This is a legitimate objection to make, and there is no answer I can give outside of a Torah framework (in other words, the acceptance of people who have challenging situations in life that various explanations based in Jewish theology account for). While such a reaction is understandable, it is an emotional reaction and not a rational objection (taking a Torah framework into account). On the one hand, as Rabbi Chaim Rapoport put it, "Gay men and women cannot be blamed or censored for having the feelings and desires that they naturally have. To do so would be a violation of basic morality and would be antithetical to Jewish values."[139] On the other hand, the Torah places incredible, if not ultimate, value on desiring only what the Torah desires, over people's natural, albeit sometimes very strong, desires—even in this case where the outcome is that people are deprived of a fulfilling partnership they can only achieve with someone that they are attracted to.

The reason why marriage is relegated to a man and a woman is because that is the structure God implanted in the world to help us achieve what would be most beneficial to humanity. Rabbi Benjamin Hecht articulates this point more in-depth:

> *Fundamentally, the Halachic [Jewish law] system is intended to direct behavior. It is a call upon the human being to act in a certain manner...Halacha is thus seen as, inherently, causing one to act in a manner that is contrary to the natural outcome of one's drives and perceptions. Such a view would not see the dilemma of the gay individual as any different than the dilemma of any other human being. One wishes to do something and Halacha says no. Does this not sometimes cause anxiety and pain? The answer is yes, but this is the call of Halacha....But we must also recognize that sometimes the Divine command is to defeat a drive regardless of the*

---

139   Rabbi Chaim Rapoport, *Judaism and Homosexuality*, p. 47.

pain. *"Who is a hero? The one who defeats his inclination."*[140]
Sometimes pain in the performance of a commandment is to be
expected. The braiding of the Torah relationship with human
nature is complex not just simply because we value human
nature and drives. It is complex because, as Torah demands us
sometimes to use the energy of our drives in the performance
of a mitzvah, it also at times demands us to thwart a drive and,
painfully, ignore its call. It is not homosexuality that is at issue.
It is the very understanding of Torah's relationship to human
nature that is at issue and demands study...we thus can feel
for the gay individual's struggle with his homosexuality drive
and the pain in its non-satisfaction. We can ask why God
would create such a drive and put individuals in the morass of
attempting to deal with this drive. But the questions cannot be
used as daggers to attempt to cause reform in the structure of
Halacha without the proper investigation of the law within the
parameters of halachic reasoning.[141]

This is not to suggest that the marriage of any given man and woman
will produce a well-balanced family. The point is that God is clearly
articulating the centrality and importance of marriage as the only relationship that will potentially produce the family that the Divine plan
intends. Dennis Prager makes the point: All this being equal, most people agree the best family unit is a mother and a father. The acceptance
of gay marriage (which includes children) is essentially saying either
the father or mother is irrelevant. Common sense dictates that the
best upbringing for children includes the interplay of male and female
role models. In other words, the mainstreaming of gay marriage is in
essence mainstreaming motherless and fatherless homes.

As mentioned above, the death penalty was rarely carried out. The
understanding is God is teaching us a lesson of the magnitude of what

---

140   *Avos* 4:1.
141   Hecht, Part 5: Drives and the Homosexual Drive.

we are dealing with.[142] The focus should not be on the death penalty for homosexual relations. Rather the lesson we should be taking away from the "relations" section of Leviticus is the premium that God put on having a family structure in accordance to His plan.

SUMMARY

In summary of Chapter One, we were reminded that some violence in the Bible is actually itself condemned by the Bible (for example, the brothers' retaliation against Shechem and his people for what he did to Dinah [Genesis 34:1–19]). Many acts of violence were preemptive strikes, self-defense, or retaliation in war (for example, Exodus 17:13, Numbers, chap. 31, Judges 3:31, I Samuel 11:11, II Samuel 2:23, 4:7–8, 10:18). In many other cases, the person who was killed was a murderer himself, so the execution was justified on the grounds of carrying out justice (for example, II Samuel 3:30, 4:12, I Kings 2:29–34). A different cause for incurring death was the various instances where the crime committed was the undermining and challenging of the leadership in war, which is equivalent to treason (for example, Joshua 1:18, I Kings 2:24–25, 46). Therefore, those instances where the Torah appears to be condoning violence are all justified based on their context, and are not examples of a barbaric, violent theme running through the Torah.

The last category in Sections I and II (Numbers 21:2, II Kings 2:23–24, 5:27, 10:7) discussed the punishment of death prescribed for people who actively or by example take away God's influence through causing other people to commit grave sins (which is worse than killing them) or who diminish God's authority in people's eyes (an act of spiritual treason). Finally, in Section III, we covered the death penalty as administered by the courts. We learned that it was incredibly rare for the death penalty to actually be enforced, and that it was primarily there as a deterrent and barometer to gauge the severity of the sin.

---

142   The *Rambam* suggests that the severity of the offence can be inferred from the kind of penalty that applies. In other words, the most serious transgressions are punishable by a form of execution, while the less severe infractions comport lesser consequences—for examples, lashes. See *Rambam*, Commentary on the Mishnah, *Avos* 2:1.

Chapter Two

VIOLENCE CARRIED OUT OR ORDERED BY GOD

This chapter will cover violence that was ordered by God as well as God's more direct involvement in implementing punishments to a group of people or individuals.[1] In this chapter, we will have three sections; Section I will deal with the nature of God; Section II will deal with God punishing the Jewish People for their disobedience; and Section III will deal with miscellaneous passages that are not related to punishing the Jewish People for their disobedience.

I: THE NATURE OF GOD

When the Bible speaks of God in physical, anthropomorphic terms, it is imperative to understand that this is only a method of expressing information that would otherwise be unable to be conveyed. It is clear that we will not be able to understand God in "His terms," hence we must understand how God relates to the world in our terms. Thus, the rabbis teach: "Torah speaks in the language of man."[2]

This basic and fundamental theological premise is ignored by many, as demonstrated in the New York Times bestseller, *Breaking the Spell, Religion as a Natural Phenomenon*, by Tufts University philosophy

---

1 Some of the God-ordered violence was covered already in Chapter One due to the nature of the violence being more related to violence between people.

2 *Bava Metzia* 31b.

professor Daniel Dennett: "I can see Jeh-vah might be really peeved if He found lots of people oblivious to His power and greatness. Part of what makes Jeh-vah such a fascinating participant in stories of the Old Testament is His kinglike jealousy and pride, and His great appetite for praise and sacrifice."[3]

The Scriptures never intended to convey that God has actual feelings of jealousy and pride, but rather, as Rabbi Yehudah Halevi explains: "God's attributes and descriptions are based on the effects upon His creations, which occur according to His decrees and deeds."[4] When a passage refers to God "wanting" or "desiring" something, this is not addressing a lack in God; it is referring to God's plan or will[5] for the world requiring certain things to be done or abstained from in order for humanity to make the best use of this world by exercising free will in a way that brings their potential into fruition. Rabbi Aryeh Kaplan gives a good illustration of this in his writings:

> *God is the Creator and Giver, and there is no one who can give Him anything. God thus speaks through the Psalmist and says, "Even if I were hungry, I would not tell you, for the earth and everything in it are mine" (Psalms 50:10). The Midrash tells us that God is saying, "Can you give oil to the olive or wine to the grape? If not, how can you give anything to me?" [Pesikta 6 (57b)]. God is saying that the olive and the grape are the givers of oil and wine; therefore, one cannot give these products to them. Furthermore, even these are creations of God. God is the*

---

3   Daniel Dennett, *Breaking the Spell, Religion as a Natural Phenomenon*, p. 265. This perception is not relegated only to the average Joe and the New Atheists, but it is also prevalent in academia: e.g., see Susan Niditch, *War in the Hebrew Bible*, where she dedicates a whole chapter, "The Ban as Sacrifice," to the assertion that at least part of the Bible implies God desires different things from people as a need. My response to Dennett can be found on my webpage, www.michoelstern.com, under the article entitled, "The Headless Horsemen—What needs to be known about what the New Atheists do not know."

4   *Kuzari* 2:2.

5   "Desire." In fact, the Hebrew word "*ratzon*" means both desire and will.

Giver of everything; and therefore, one can certainly not give Him anything.[6]

Accordingly, we are taught that God only gave the commandments in order to help creation.[7] Thus we are informed that Elihu told Job: "If you sin, how does it touch Him? If you do much evil, how can you harm Him? If you do good, what do you give Him? What does He gain from your deeds? Your evil is only against man, and your good is only for mortals."[8]

II: GOD PUNISHING THE JEWISH PEOPLE AS A NATION FOR DISOBEDIENCE

(1) God Using Punishment to Bring Atonement for the People

In order to gain a proper perspective of the importance of atonement, it is essential to first understand how the soul (spiritual life) in the Biblical perspective supersedes the importance of life. Therefore, as much as the Bible values life on this planet (which it does), it values life in the World to Come on an immensely greater scale. The reason for this is that life in this world is a means (which is why life is so important) to achieve the end of closeness to God in the Next World. It is also because life in this world is temporary, whereas life in the World to Come is forever.

God created two levels of existence. God created the present world (*Olam Hazeh*), the first level, as an environment for challenge and accomplishment, where we can earn our ultimate reward. God also created the World to Come (*Olam Haba*), a second level, as a world of ultimate reward. Furthermore, Rabbi Moshe Chaim Luzzatto explains:

> *We have stated earlier that the purpose of the creation of the human species is that man should become worthy of attaining true good, namely, being drawn close to Him (God) in the World to Come. The highest wisdom decreed, however, that this would be best attained if man would first exist in the*

---

6   *The Rabbi Aryeh Kaplan Anthology*, vol. 1, p. 144.

7   See *Ramban*, Deuteronomy 22:6; *Sefer Hachinuch* #545.

8   Job 35:6–8.

present world, bound and limited by its laws. This is actually the true and proper preparation necessary for the desired goal, and everything in this world was therefore arranged so that it should serve as a means of preparing and readying man for this ultimate purpose.[9]

In the *Ethics of our Fathers*, it is taught: "Rabbi Yaakov says: This world is like a corridor before the World to Come; prepare yourself in the corridor so that you may enter the banquet hall."[10] Therefore, the difficult and painful experiences—in addition to the pleasurable and ecstatic ones—that one endures while in this world are not granted to a person by God for their own sake but as part of the preparation for the person's real existence in the World to Come. Rabbi Eliyahu Dessler expounds upon this quote from the Sages:

The whole essence of this world lies in its being a preparatory stage for Olam Haba. It is not a world in its own right. Anyone who builds a corridor without the mansion to which it is supposed to lead has not built anything. So it is with this world and all that occurs in it. All this bears a precise relationship to our spiritual needs. Everything that affects us, everything that impinges on our senses, is planned and apportioned with the utmost precision towards that single goal—our ultimate destiny, Olam Haba.[11]

Now that I have laid the foundations for the premise that we endure suffering in this world in order to have a better future in the World to Come,[12] I will explain how suffering improves our relationship with God. Rabbi Yitzchok Kirzner makes an essential point we can use as a springboard point into our discussion:

---

9   *Derech Hashem* 2:2:1.

10   *Pirkei Avos* 4:21.

11   Rabbi Aryeh Carmell, *Strive for Truth*, vol. 1, p. 83, based on *Michtav Me'Eliyahu*, the writings of Rabbi Eliyahu Dessler.

12   There are other reasons for suffering, but for the purpose of the point I am about to make I am limiting the discussion to what is germane to the topic at hand.

We are used to thinking of the physical universe as operating on fixed rules. Certain chemicals, for instance, mixed together under the proper conditions will inevitably explode. And certain poisons when drunk will inevitably lead to death or very serious illness. But when we think about the spiritual universe, if we do so at all, we tend not to think in terms of such causal links between our deeds and the spiritual consequences they entail. When we do something forbidden by the Torah, we acknowledge that we have transgressed God's Will, but we do not assume that any consequences follow automatically from that transgression in the same way that they follow from swallowing poison. Rather we attribute any adverse consequences that flow from our transgressions to God's independent decision to be strict with us. This is a fundamental misunderstanding of the spiritual world.[13] ... The Hebrew word for punishment, onesh, conveys the sense of punishment as the removal of a blockage. It derives from the same root as nashah, which means to move from its place. Onesh, then, is designed to remove the blockage that follows from transgression.[14]

It is written in the book of Proverbs (3:12): "The Lord chastises the ones He loves, and as a father placates his son." Rabbi Yonah of Gerona comments on this verse: "He (God) chastens him so that no trace of his sin should remain, lest it lessen His love for him." What Rabbi Yonah is referring to is the concept that God wants to give us good things (that flow from His love), but when a person has sinned, as mentioned above, the sin causes distance from God (i.e., blockage), which limits the love God can give us due to our distancing ourselves in the form of our transgressions.[15]

Therefore, due to the gravity of the sins the Jewish People committed (see the verses below), it was at times essential for God to purge that

---

13   Rabbi Yitzchok Kirzner, *Making Sense of Suffering*, p. 66.
14   Ibid., p. 70.
15   See *Avodah Zarah* 4a.

poison from our collective system, thereby removing any blockages and enabling us to return to our relationship and ultimately be able to partake of the closeness that will take place in the World to Come. As Rabbi Kirzner puts it, "When we distance ourselves from God, we have to draw close once again. When the lines of communication have been blocked, they must become cleared to allow for free flow of relationship once again."[16]

(2) God Using Punishment as a Way to Keep the Jewish People in Check

Rabbi Jeremy Kagan has an interesting insight regarding the nature of the covenant between God and the Jewish People:

> *The word for covenant in Hebrew is brit. It is related to the word briah (creation) [Ramban, Genesis 6:18]. This conveys the idea that a covenant is not merely a contractual argument. Rather, it is the creation of a new entity composed of two parties. This can only happen if one loses his identity as an individual unit—meaning they each come to be defined by, and only exist through, the new union. After a covenant has been made, two individuals that were originally wholes unto themselves become incomplete halves outside the union. Forming a covenant is therefore understood to be cutting, because both parties effectively cut themselves and become individually incomplete in order to fully join in the larger whole. Because we made a covenant with God, we have no existence outside of our relationship with Him—hence the destruction that follows our turning away from God. It is less a punishment than the reality of what we are without the relationship. It does not show God's domination so much as measure the depth to which the relationship is constitutive of who we are [as heard from Rav Moshe Shapiro]. When we move away from God, we are actually losing ourselves. Effectively, it is a slow-acting*

---

16   *Making Sense of Suffering*, p. 76.

suicide. Through our suffering, we realize this in time to turn back and regain ourselves and our existence.[17]

The Jewish People (i.e., Israelites) have been charged with a special mission by none other than the Creator of the Universe. This is what the whole concept of "the Chosen Nation" stems from.[18] The Jewish People are referred to as "a kingdom of priests"[19] because we are supposed to render a service to the other nations. We are supposed to be a light unto the nations[20] by being witnesses[21] to the greatness of God and by proclaiming the purpose of Creation.[22] It is said, "The Torah is like the oil in a lamp, and Israel is its wick, causing the light of God to shine forth on all of Creation."[23]

The Sages[24] teach us on the verse in Deuteronomy:[25] "Do not read 'they will overtake you,' but rather, 'they shall preserve you'…If not for your suffering, which causes you to return to the Lord and atones for your sins, you would not continue to exist." In the words of Rabbi Avigdor Miller: "Israel (the Jewish People) is eternal, because Hashem constantly corrects them."[26] The truth is when the Jewish People commit a sin that is so severe that it threatens their relationship with God, the order requires a punishment of such severity that the Jewish nation is forced to acknowledge their betrayal of the relationship and return to their Creator.

(3) How the Verses Fall into the Aforementioned Categories

As we see from the verses below, the Israelites were not perfect in their observance of Torah. God is more demanding upon the Jewish People because of the high level of expectation stemming from our

---

17   Rabbi Jeremy Kagan, *The Intellect and the Exodus*, pp. 48–49.
18   More to be said on this in the following chapter.
19   Exodus 19:6.
20   Isaiah 42:6.
21   Ibid., 43:10.
22   See *Vayikra Rabbah* 6:5 [end].
23   *Tikkunei Zohar* 21 [60b].
24   *The Midrash Says* (*Devarim*), p. 310.
25   Deuteronomy 28:15.
26   Rabbi Avigdor Miller, *Fortunate Nation*, p. 121.

close relationship with Him.[27] Nevertheless, God uses punishment for the improvement of the Jewish People whether it is to keep us going as the "eternal nation" or whether it is used as a means to give us an "eternal reward."

Exodus 32:27–35: Levites kill their kinsmen and the plague following the golden calf

The reason they killed their kinsmen was because a portion of the nation worshiped an idol.[28] The plague was used by God as a means to impress upon the people the severity of their actions.

Numbers 11:33: Complaints mourning their departure from Egypt are a response to dissatisfaction with the manna

Here, the Israelites expressed a desire to be removed from God's presence. In Numbers 11:20, God points out that the Israelites rejected "Hashem who is in your midst." *Rashi* comments that when the Jewish People said, "We remember the fish that we ate in Egypt free of charge," he says what they meant by "free of charge" was that they were not expected to keep the commandments in order to get their ration of food (i.e., the manna in the wilderness).[29] The punishment was in response to the Jewish People rejecting God and the commandments.

Numbers 16:31–35: Korach challenges Moses's authority that represents God

Here, Korach and his supporters are swallowed up by the ground (or incinerated, depending on which role they had in the rebellion). The severity of the punishment is the result of their rebellion and its ramifications. The *Akeidas Yitzchak* gives evidence that Korach's rebellion was not relegated to Moses but rather was against God as well. He says, "In his second statement, Moses addressed himself to the underlying motive of Korach's complaint in a more subtle manner. '*Ha'me'at mikem*

---

27   See Amos 3:2, with the commentary of *Ibn Ezra* and *Radak*.
28   For the background of the severity of idolatry and how it severs a connection with God, see Chapter One.
29   *Rashi*, Numbers 11:5.

ki hivdil'—are you not sufficiently aggrieved that the elevated position the Torah has granted you as Levites prevents you from effective land-ownership of Canaan that you want to assume the even heavier burden of the priesthood?' Besides, since you challenge the validity of priestly functions per se, your specific complaint against Aharon surely must hide a personal motive? Why else bother with this detail? Therefore, Moses continued, 'I am convinced that you are in effect rebelling against God,' i.e., *"ha'noadim al Hashem,"* (16:11) not against us. Though you pretend to challenge our authority, you are challenging God's authority."[30] This is the reason for the harsh punishment; Korach was attempting to seduce the Jewish People to rebel against the authority of God Almighty!

Numbers 21:6: A complaint of "Why did we leave Egypt?" results in a plague of serpents

Here again, we have an episode where many Israelites desired to be removed from God's presence. The *Akeidas Yitzchak* writes: "The displeasure of the people was occasioned through the tedious detour around Edom, a march away from the direction of their eventual destination. The general dissatisfaction also led to the search for complaints against the manner of God's providence. Their complaint was that their provisions, both bread and water, were due only to miraculous, super-natural means. They did not feel assured of the continuance of these supplies and longed for an existence based on natural law. The appearance of snakes reminded the people that an existence based on natural law would be perilous indeed, and that they, therefore, had no reason to quarrel with God's providence. They realized this when they begged Moses to pray for renewed *hashgachah pratis* (Divine Providence)."[31]

Rabbi Samson R. Hirsch explains how the punishment of the snakes was a punishment *middah k'neged middah* [measure for measure; in traditional Jewish thought,[32] there is a concept that God rewards and

---

30   See *Akeidas Yitzchak* (trans. Eliyahu Munk), vol. 2, p. 731.
31   Ibid., p. 761.
32   *Shabbos* 105b, *Sanhedrin* 90a, *Nedarim* 32a, to name a few sources out of many.

punishes in ways linked to the respective actions or inactions] for the Israelites' desire to rid themselves of the Divine providence: "...Here too, God did not send the serpents, but let them go and did not hold them back...[33] Hence not 'poisonous serpents' but 'the poisonous serpents'; they had always been there in the wilderness, but hitherto they had been kept back by God's protecting Power with the clouds of glory. Now, God withdraws this restraining power and the serpents of the wilderness follow their natural traits to which the people succumbed.[34] He writes further: "The serpents' bite had the sole purpose of letting the people see the dangers that dog a person's steps when he goes through a wilderness, and that it was only the miraculous power of God that had hitherto kept them far from them, so far indeed that they did not even have an idea of their existence."[35]

Numbers 25:4–9: Moab and Midyan get the Jewish People to do acts of promiscuity and acts of idol worship; also Pinchas kills Zimri and Kozbi[36]

The list of severe transgressions is long, and each of them on its own merits one suffering because of transgression. One of the worst sins a person can do is cause a public desecration of God's name.[37] When the men (and many of them were leaders no less!) succumbed to acts of promiscuity and acts of idol worship with the Moabite women, they caused a desecration of God's name on a national level.

Deuteronomy 28:15–69 (also Leviticus 26:14–46): Curses for not keeping the Torah in Eretz Yisrael / rebellion against God

The following sections of the Torah are known as the "*tochachah*," the admonition. The horrible punishments listed are not a form of Divine revenge but are God's way of making sure that the Jewish People

---

33   Rabbi Hirsch spent the first paragraph proving from Hebrew grammar [supported by other verses] that the verse does not say, "then God sent the poisonous serpents" but rather "then God let the poisonous serpents loose against the people."

34   Rabbi Samson Raphael Hirsch, Numbers 21:6.

35   Ibid., v. 8.

36   Zimri had challenged Moses' leadership and publicly fornicated with a Midianite princess.

37   Jerusalem Talmud, *Nedarim* 3:9, 12b; *Rambam, Mishneh Torah, Teshuvah* 1:4.

repent and do not deviate from the teachings of the Torah (which would cause them to cease from their function as the "nation of priests"). The evidence for this is that the punishments are inflicted in stages of increasing severity (hence where the Torah says over and over, "If despite this you do not heed Me..."). The fact that God puts such a premium on the Jewish People not deviating from their mission is a strong indication of their essential role in bringing the Divine plan to fruition. An excellent example of how this is not a punishment on the people, but is rather a cleansing, which can be found in the end of the curses in Leviticus: "But despite all this, while they will be in the land of their enemies, I will not have been revolted by them nor will I have rejected them to obliterate them, to annul My covenant with them, for I am the Lord their God. I will remember for them the covenant of the ancients, those whom I have taken out of the land of Egypt before the eyes of the nations, to be God unto them; I am the Lord."[38]

II Samuel 24:1–25: David's wrongful census and the pestilence

In this section of the Bible, King David takes a census that leads to a pestilence that wipes out many of the Israelites. What is odd is that the first verse of the chapter states: "The anger of Hashem again flared against Israel, and He incited David because of them, to say, 'Go count the people of Israel and Judah.'" It is clear from the verse that God wanted to punish the Israelites for a previous sin, and the pestilence was not brought on by the wrongful census, but rather that the census was a channel for a punishment previously deserved.

Referring to (the book of) Numbers, the *Ramban* makes a convincing and Scriptural case that the reason the Jewish People received God's wrath at that time was due to their procrastination in requesting that the Temple (Beis Hamikdash) be built.[39]

What was inherently so wrong with the Jewish People delaying the building of the Temple that God saw fit to punish them on such

---

38   Leviticus 26:44–45.
39   *Ramban*, Numbers 16:21.

a massive scale? We can get a glimmer of an understanding as we try to understand why the Temple was destroyed. ArtScroll's book on Tishah B'Av gives us some insight into the problem:

> *Why did God not reveal in the Torah precisely where the Temple would stand? Malbim explains this in light of the command to erect a permanent dwelling for God's presence: "For only to the place that Hashem will choose from among all our tribes to place his name there—(a place for) the manifestation of His presence you shall seek and there you will come."*[40] *David understood the term, "the manifestation of His presence you shall seek," to mean that to be worthy of God's presence, one must actively seek it...For God to continue to manifest His presence among His people, it was necessary that they live their lives in a manner that reflected a yearning for His closeness. When the Jews' yearning waned and they became overtaken by sinful desires, the Divine presence ceased to dwell among them. The Temple was transformed into a hollow structure, and their fate was sealed.*[41]

We see here that the delay in building the Temple is tied into the same flaws that the people had when the Temple was destroyed. The common denominator is apathy for what is missing when one is not relying on God and fails to strive for a better relationship with God. This apathy is implied when Scriptures record the Divine reprimand: "For I have not dwelled in a house from the day I brought Israel up until this very day, but I have moved from tent to tent and from tabernacle to tabernacle."[42] Even in Shiloh, where the Tabernacle stood for a number of centuries, only the walls were of stone; they were covered with a ceiling made of curtains.[43]

---

40   Deuteronomy 12:5.
41   P. 44.
42   I Chronicles 17:5.
43   See *Zevachim* 112b.

Rabbi Yaakov Kamenetsky[44] makes a correlation between the censuses in Numbers and the one with King David having to do with lack of trust in God:

> *"However, the tribe of Levi do not count."*
>
> *And, therefore, the tribe of Levi was not counted, because it was unable to stumble in the sin of the spies. Because the cause of the sin of the golden calf was also a lack of faith, for the fear that they remained in the wilderness without bread and water caused them to seek a replacement for Moses. But the tribe of Levi that did not stumble in the sin of the golden calf, also did not join in the sin of the spies, and therefore was not counted with all of Israel. It is explained with this that which was told to David (II Samuel 24:13) to choose one of three punishments after he counted Israel: Seven years of famine, or to flee before an enemy, or plague. Because, with the counting of the children of Israel, it is possible that David wanted to know how many "working hands" were to be found in the Jewish People. And the work of the Israelite nation was the work of the fields, and they would sell the bounty of the land to their neighbors, as we find in Ezekiel 27:17 that Judah and the land of Israel would sell their wheat, honey, and oil to Tzur. Therefore, measure for measure, there would be famine in the land for seven years. And if the count was to know how great was his strength in war against the enemy, in equal proportion he will punish him to flee before his enemies. And if, in general, for arrogance, to know how many men are subjugated before him—then there will be plague that they will be decreased, and his arrogance will be lowered.*

Also, God did not randomly use King David as a way to implement His punishment. King David made himself susceptible to the test of

---

44   Rabbi Yaakov Kamenetsky, *Emes L'Yaakov*, Numbers 1:49, pp. 414–15. Thank you to Rabbis Yehudah Friedland and Refoel Weinshnider for their time and effort helping me with this piece.

the census previously when he elicited God's retribution for pardoning Saul from his malice and blaming God as it were for Saul's behavior.[45] The Talmud says: "At that time, God said, as it were, 'You have accused me of being an inciter. I will incite you to do something even schoolchildren know is forbidden (i.e., taking a head count).'"[46] God allowed David to choose from three punishments,[47] and of the three, the Jewish king chose pestilence because only God will decide who is affected by the plague.[48]

Ezekiel 6:12–13 (also see 9:4–7, and 21:3–4):
God says Jewish idol worshipers will be eradicated

This is referring to the *tochachah* (admonition); see above.

III: VIOLENCE NOT RELATED TO PUNISHMENT OF THE JEWISH PEOPLE

(1) Genesis 19:26

Lot's wife turned into a pillar of salt. If one were to only make a cursory reading of this section, as Steven Pinker did, it is easy to see how a person could arrive at Pinker's conclusion: "Lot's wife, for the crime of turning around to look at the inferno, is to be put to death as well."[49]

The Rabbinic background to this text, however, gives us a completely different picture from Pinker. Lot's wife was receiving a punishment *middah k'neged middah* for her behavior. Lot's wife disapproved of having guests, as according to the laws of Sodom, feeding guests was a capital offense.[50] When Lot brought guests to his home, his wife went to the neighbors to "borrow salt for our guests."[51] Essentially, what she did was alert the townsfolk so that they could judge her husband and subsequently rob/maltreat the strangers in accordance with official

---

45   See I Samuel 26:19.

46   *Berachos* 62b.

47   See II Samuel 24:12–13.

48   Ibid., v. 14.

49   Steven Pinker, *The Better Angels of Our Nature*, p. 6.

50   *Yalkut Shimoni, Vayeira* 83; *Pirkei D'Rabi Eliezer*, Genesis 25:13.

51   *Yalkut Shimoni, Vayeira* 85.

Sodom policy.[52] So we can see, Lot's wife was not turned into a pillar of salt merely because she could not resist the urge to turn around and see the Divine wrath, for which she was not on a high enough level to behold. Rather, her disregard for the angels' advice was just the final straw that brought to fruition a punishment she provided for herself though the pretense of asking her neighbors for salt. In the words of the *Malbim*: "She looked back to see the upheaval, and the affliction adhered to her, her body turning into a pillar of salt—a monument to her wickedness, for her deeds were like those of the Sodomites, as our Sages (*Bereishis Rabbah* 51:5) explain."[53]

(2) Genesis 22:1–18

Akeidas Yitzchak, the binding of Isaac. What coverage of the violence in Scripture would be complete without addressing the binding of Isaac? Though much as been written on this topic, in truth, I don't have much to say about it for a reason that seems to elude many: In the end, Abraham did not sacrifice Isaac! God was only testing Abraham to make sure that he would follow orders unquestioningly.

Regarding this episode in the Bible, former associate director of the Harvard Center for the Study of World Religions, Carol Delaney, writes: "Rather than putting God first, I think we need to love our children and one another first…Rather than focus on authority and obedience, I think that we need to think more about responsibility—to and for each other…Finally, I ask you to consider how our world would look had protection of the child been at the foundation of faith instead of the willingness to sacrifice him."[54]

First of all, Professor Delaney is reading the scripture without the benefit of the Jewish oral tradition that accompanies it. Isaac was thirty-seven at the time, hardly a child; also, once he realized that he was the one to be "brought up," he willingly went through with it,[55] even

---

52   *Bereishis Rabbah* 50:8.
53   *Malbim*, Genesis 19:26.
54   Carol Delaney in *The Just War and Jihad*, p. 228, ed. R. Joseph Hoffman.
55   See *Rashi*, Genesis 22:8, who notes that Isaac "goes together" with Abraham even after he found out that he was to be "the sheep."

to the extent that he requested his elderly father to bind him tightly so that he would not flinch and cause a blemish, thereby making him unfit to be sacrificed.[56]

However, even when we overlook Delaney's misreading of Scripture, we are still in a position to critique her conclusion. The major question is whether the continued life of an individual is the highest virtue. If we take a hedonistic and materialist approach, then yes, to continue living on this earth is the most virtuous goal there is. Yet, we see in many arenas of life that this is not the highest virtue, even in the secular world. If a person neglected to save the life of a child to spare his own, he would be shunned by a majority of the world. But why should this be? After all, if longevity is the pinnacle of virtue in our earthly existence, he was doing the right thing. But, depending on the conviction or the cause, everyone on this earth believes it is worthwhile to forfeit his individual existence for something so dear to him that it transcends his desire for self-preservation. This being the case, understanding the Biblical worldview that God desires what is best for us all, being willing to do what is for the betterment of humanity cannot be viewed as immoral.

How would the world look like if Abraham refused to obey the Creator of the world due to his love for his child and "protected him" instead? I imagine that it would look a lot like the instances we see today where many people suffer because others are unwilling to sacrifice what they love in order to create a better society. On the other hand, if more people internalized the message of the *Akeidah*—that we should be willing to sacrifice what we care about in order to serve a higher purpose[57]—it would be a better world indeed! We have life as a gift from God. If we are directed to use it in a way that is difficult for us, it may be unpleasant to cope with, but it is not immoral. God does not owe us anything.

---

56 See *Bereishis Rabbah* 56:8; *Pirkei D'Rabi Eliezer*, chap. 30.

57 There are other messages as well. A different message is that God does not want human sacrifice. The emphasis is put on Abraham's willingness to give up what was important to him for God's service and trust in God.

(3) Leviticus 10:1–3

"And Nadab and Abihu, the sons of Aaron, took each his censer, put fire on them, and put incense thereon, and offered strange fire before God, which He had not commanded them. Then there went a fire from God and consumed them, and they died before God. Then Moses said to Aaron: 'This is what God spoke, saying: "By them that are close to me will I be sanctified and so will I be honored before all people"'; and Aaron was silent."

This text is confusing by itself; it is also confusing to the classic Torah commentators. Steven Pinker adds a layer of a different kind of confusion: "Aaron and his two sons prepare the Tabernacle for the first service, but the sons slip up and use the wrong incense. So God burns them."[58] Even though he claims that he is just reviewing the literal context of the Hebrew Bible,[59] a glance at the verses indicates that he managed to mislead himself and his readers regarding how the events transpired.

According to Pinker, Aaron's sons were trying to do business as usual, slipped up, and used one incense instead of another. God decided they should have been more careful and were deserving of death by fire. However, with the aid of the Oral Tradition, we get a much keener insight into the events that led up to the tragedy.[60] In order to understand the magnitude of the sin, a little bit of background is in order. Nadab and Abihu were very righteous,[61] and therefore the expectations placed upon them were very high. The mistake they made, as I will describe, would not have been punished similarly if it were committed by someone of lesser stature.[62]

---

58   *Better Angels*, p. 7.

59   Ibid., p. 11.

60   Also, nowhere is it stated in Leviticus, chap. 8, the portion of the Bible devoted to the inaugural service, that they were to bring *ketores*, so their infraction was tantamount to performing a rite that they were not commanded to do.

61   *Yalkut Shimoni*, Ecclesiastes 7:15; *Zevachim* 115b.

62   The *Nefesh Hachaim* teaches that the severity of the punishment meted out to the very righteous for a seemingly small transgression in this world is really based upon the damage caused by the effects of the sin in the spiritual realm. Because of the greatness of the people involved, their small failures in this world actually cause catastrophic havoc in the spiritual

Another thing to keep in mind is the importance of the day (the inauguration of the Tabernacle) combined with the importance of the location (the first service in the most important structure on earth). Finally, what needs to be taken into consideration is the root of the sin. The sin might have been "small," but the ramifications of the misguided intentions that led to it are severe. Rabbi Yissachar Dov Rubin explains:

> The Sefas Emes points out that despite their pure motives, the desire to enhance the Divine service was the root of their sin. The Kohen acts as an agent of God in performing the Divine service and is therefore required to act precisely according to the instructions that he receives without attempting to enhance the service by introducing foreign or external elements...Thus, they were punished because they acted in a manner that He had not commanded them, i.e., they did not fulfill the commandments of God as given, but tried to improve upon them with their own ideas.[63]

Rabbi Samson Raphael Hirsch helps us build upon this idea:

> For Kirvas Elokim, the proximity and getting near to God, which is the purpose of every offering, is to be found by the way of obedience, by compliance with God's will and subordination to it. This is one of the points in which Judaism and Paganism go in diametrically opposite directions. The Pagan brings his offering in attempt to make the god subservient to his wishes. The Jew, with his offering, wishes to place himself in the service of God, which the bringer, by his offering, undertakes to make the normal routine for his future life. So that self-devised offerings would be a killing of just those very truths which our offerings are meant to impress and dominate the bringers, would be placing a pedestal on which to glorify one's own ideas,

---

world, and for this reason we see them being severely punished for even a seemingly small infraction.

63   *Talelei Oros*, Leviticus, p. 92.

where the throne was meant to be built for obedience and obedience only. We can understand the deaths of these priestly youths, and their death in the first moment of the consecration of the Sanctuary of God, is solemn warning for all future priests of this Sanctuary of God—which was to be nothing else but the Sanctuary of His Torah—every expression, of caprice, and every subjective idea of what is right and becoming! Not by fresh innovations even God-serving novices, but by carrying out that which is ordained by God has the Jewish priest to establish the authenticity of his activities.[64]

Rabbi Zev Leff drives the point home:

"[Moses] said to B'nei Yisrael, 'remove the yetzer hara [evil urge] from your hearts so that you will be inspired with a common awe and service of Hashem. As He is One, so too should your service to Him be one" (Yalkut Shimoni 521). Already in the time of [Moses], says the Netziv, there were those who sought to experience religious ecstasy and draw near to the Divine through means other than those delineated by the Torah. It was from this yetzer hara that [Moses] exhorted people to distance themselves, for the desire to draw close to Hashem in ways not prescribed is not holiness; it is the work of the yetzer hara. As Chazal [Rabbis of the Talmud] say on the verse, "This is the thing that God commanded for you to do and the Glory of God will appear to you" (Leviticus 9:6): When on his emotions alone in determining his path to Hashem, then each person creates his own path and the service of Hashem is fragmented into many diverse molds, which is a contradiction to God's Oneness. Therefore, the paths must be guided by the Torah so that the resultant unity of expression reflects God's unity. Avodas Hashem [Divine Service] must be a blend of emotion with meticulous care to express the emotion in the manner prescribed

---

64   Rav Hirsch, Leviticus 1, vol. 3, p. 253.

*by Hashem Himself, i.e., the Torah's framework must be infused
with one's own unique emotions and sensitivities. To ignore the
framework that the Torah provides and seek to create paths to
Hashem based on subjective emotions and intuition is to echo
the sin of the Golden Calf. That too was an attempt to create
a bond with Hashem through a non-prescribed intermediary.[65]*

To recap: The major sin of Nadab and Abihu was not merely taking the
wrong ingredients; it was following an alien approach to Divine service
on the day that the Tabernacle was consecrated and the foundation for
all further service to God established. As the *Netziv* explains, the full
force of God's trait of judgment struck them immediately because the
sin had been committed "before God," i.e., in the palace of the King of
kings.[66] The *Chasam Sofer* points out that the punishment of *middah
k'neged middah* is reflected in a Divine fire taking their lives after they
brought up a strange fire.[67] Nevertheless, the punishment was quick
as a sign of their righteousness,[68] and their souls were burned and
not their bodies or clothing.[69] The *Ramban* explains Moses' words of
comfort to his brother Aaron: Thus, Moses was saying as follows, "This
incident that has just occurred is what God has decreed to happen,
saying to Himself, 'I will be sanctified among those nearest Me, for
through these deaths they will not "break through My sacred place,"
and furthermore I will be honored before the entire people, as they will
treat My Tabernacle respectfully.'"[70]

(4) I Samuel 6:19

Hashem kills people who look at the Ark of Hashem. The background
to this episode in the Bible is that the Philistines had captured the Ark
of the Covenant and were subsequently punished with severe physical

---

65 Rabbi Zev Leff, *Outlooks and Insights*, p. 136.
66 *Netziv, Haamek Davar*, Leviticus 16:1.
67 *Toras Moshe* 51 (paragraph beginning *vav, nun, lamed*), quoted in ArtScroll *Chasam Sofer*, *Vayikra*, p. 133.
68 *The Midrash Says*, Leviticus, p. 79.
69 *Sanhedrin* 52a.
70 *Ramban*, Leviticus 10:3.

ailments to the extent that, to alleviate their suffering, they decided to return the Ark to the Israelites and appease them (and their God).[71] As they returned the Ark to the Israelites, the Israelites of Beth Shemesh looked at the Ark and rejoiced.[72] According to *Rashi*, the people lost their sense of awe in their rejoicing, a failing that was especially egregious in that it so starkly contrasted with the respect that the Philistines had afforded the Ark.[73] In other words, the desecration of God's name (through the lack of respect to the Ark) was amplified by the fact that a group of people who were the antithesis of what the Ark of the Covenant represented (Philistines) were more reverent to it than the people of Beth Shemesh, who are supposed to be the ambassadors for what the Ark of the covenant carried.[74]

Another observation that must be made here is the counting of the people of Beth Shemesh that died in the plague. I Samuel 6:19 states that, "He struck among them seventy men, fifty thousand men." The verse is worded in a somewhat strange fashion. The Talmud states that only seventy men died, however, each one of them was so extraordinary that they were the equivalent of fifty thousand men.[75] This fits well with our explanation of the magnitude of the sin; not only were the Philistines more respectful of the Ark, but they were more reverent than the extraordinary people of Beth Shemesh!

(5) II Samuel 12

David's child from Bathsheba dies. This was a punishment for King David's actions with Bathsheba (regarding Uriah).[76] The prophet Nathan reprimanded David by telling him a story of a rich man and a poor man, where the rich man took the one ewe of the poor man and fed it to his guest. When David heard the story, he was incensed and said that

---

71   I Samuel 4:11–6:12.

72   Ibid., v. 13.

73   ArtScroll I Samuel, p. 109.

74   The commentators have some varied explanations for the sin of the people of Beth Shemesh, but they all boil down to a lack of respect for the Ark. See *Sotah* 35a and *Bereishis Rabbah* 54:4.

75   *Sotah* 35b.

76   See above, Chapter 1, Part II.

the rich man deserved to pay four times over for the ewe. Nathan then informed David that he was that rich man, and God would thus pay him fourfold for his deed.[77] The Talmud teaches that God punished David fourfold through his children, and David's newborn through Bathsheba was part of the equation.[78] Two points should be kept in mind when evaluating this passage:

1. Just as there are consequences in the physical reality when a parent does something wrong that affects an innocent child (e.g., drinking alcohol during pregnancy), so too there are consequences in the spiritual reality that the "natural" cause and effect of certain actions will result in innocent parties being affected negatively.

2. Unlike the workings of the physical world, in the spiritual reality innocent people are compensated for their undue suffering.[79] In other words, people are compensated in the World to Come (primarily, it happens in this world also) for suffering they experience while on earth.

(6) I Kings 13:15–24

A false prophet gets the "man of God" to fall for a trap, and God kills a true prophet. The Talmud explains that the "man of God" deserved death because he violated his own prophecy.[80] For a person who is on the level of being an intermediary between God and the people to transgress his own words, even if he was tricked into doing so, it shows a supreme lack of vigilance. The gravity of the situation is that this event was with a person of such stature disregarding direct communication from God, which cheapens the reliability of Hashem's transmission of His will through the prophets.

---

77   See II Samuel 12:1–7.
78   *Yoma* 22b.
79   See *Kuzari* 3:19:3.
80   *Sanhedrin* 89b.

(7) Isaiah 13:15

The downfall of Babylonia. While it is very unfortunate that innocent civilians are slaughtered in a hostile takeover of Babylon, it must be kept in mind that this is their punishment—measure for measure—for having inflicted such on the Jewish People (with it being carried out by Media). Rabbi Yehudah Halevi teaches us regarding matters of Divine judgment where innocent people suffer because of living in an over-whelmingly wicked land: "These are the judgments of the Blessed One of the universe, and He takes care of compensation for these individuals (the righteous minority) in the World to Come."[81]

SUMMARY

In summary of Chapter Two: We discussed the nature of God and learned that the Bible was written "in the language of man," and there-fore actual emotions (like anger and jealousy) don't apply to Him. We also learned that God has no needs. Therefore, any punishment given by God is a benefit or act of justice for the sake humanity (God does not get offended and seek vengeance).

It was also pointed out that when God punishes the Jewish People as a whole, two main reasons are given: First, Israel should have atone-ment for their collective transgressions; and second, God uses collective punishment to keep the nation intact and prevent it from destroying itself. As far as individual punishment from God, some cases were jus-tice being carried out on an evil person (Lot's wife), others were cases in which the action caused a cheapening of God's rulership (Nadab and Abihu; I Samuel 6:19, I Kings 13:15–24). Finally, some cases involve the consequences of cause and effect in the spiritual realm (II Samuel, chap. 12; Isaiah 13:15).

---

81   *Kuzari* 3:19:3.

Chapter Three

DOES SCRIPTURE ENCOURAGE BARBARIC AND BACKWARD PRACTICES?

I: ANIMALS

A Basic Overview of the Jewish (i.e., Biblical) View of Animals

The Biblical principle that God gave the earth and everything in it to humanity is explicitly mentioned in Genesis: "...And God said to them [Adam and Eve], 'Be fruitful and multiply, fill the earth and subdue it; and rule over the fish of the sea, the bird of the sky, and everything that moves on earth.'"[1] The Talmud teaches us that man is superior to the animals because humanity was created to serve God, and animals were created to serve humanity.[2] Therefore, the idea that animals are on the same level as humans is anathema to the Biblical description of the value of humanity.

Often when people question the Bible's system of animal sacrifices with moral indignation, the response is given: Do you like to barbecue and eat meat? Yes? Then you agree that it is acceptable to kill animals to

---

1   *Bereishis* 1:28; see also *Koheles Rabbah* 7:113, where God tells Adam the entire creation was created for his sake.
2   *Kiddushin* 82a.

serve your stomach. If you wear leather, then it is OK to kill animals to serve the comfort of your feet. It's not the killing of animals that bothers you; it's the reason behind it. The killing of animals for sacrifices enables one to serve God and grow spiritually.[3]

But what about vegetarians who argue that it is morally reprehensible to eat meat? Rabbi Zev Leff writes:

> *Rav Yosef Albo explains why, after the flood, God permitted man to kill animals and eat their flesh in his sefer Ha'ikarim. The root of the depraved behavior that led to man's downfall and ultimately to the flood began with Kayin [Cain], who refused to be a shepherd like his brother Hevel [Abel] because he felt it was wrong to exploit animal life. However, this attitude does not serve to elevate animal life to the sanctity of human life, but rather reduces human life to the level of animals. Since this ideology views man as just another animal, albeit more intelligent, it eventually led mankind to act like animals and resulted in the flood…Therefore, after the flood, says the sefer Ha'ikarim, Hashem [God] permitted man to kill and eat animals. This would decisively show mankind that human beings are not on par with animals.[4]*

It is scary to imagine, but there is a not-too-small segment of the population that believes that there is no significant difference between animals and humans other than evolutionary advantages. If this philosophy is taken to its logical conclusion, then the animal-rights activists who take this position cannot really blame the human carnivores for doing "what comes naturally." After all, do the same people get upset at a bear when it feasts on an innocent salmon swimming in the stream?

Furthermore, when vegetarians and vegans abstain from eating or benefiting from animals, they are still benefiting from a different life form, namely vegetation. As Rabbi Dovid Orlofsky has pointed out in numerous lectures: "Who are you to take out your human aggression on

---

3   This process will be explained below.
4   Rabbi Zev Leff, *Shemoneh Esreh*, p. 400.

the vegetable kingdom? The only reason you feel more OK with killing a tomato is that it doesn't have the little brown eyes." Rabbi Orlofsky is not the only one to make this point. Professor J. Harold Ellens writes:

> *Those vegetarians who also avoid chicken, fish, and dairy, vegans, with only a strict vegetarian diet, are usually mystified when I ask them how they can possibly tolerate killing these living things they eat, the poor lettuce leaf, celery stalks, beautiful carrots and the like. They tend to respond that these are short-lived forms of life anyway, are planted for harvesting, and have no consciousness or feelings. Of course, there is a significant debate about whether the last claim is true. There seems to be adequate evidence that plants respond to what seems comparable to our central nervous system stimulation. However, when all is said and done, the argument boils down to the fact that plants are so far down the evolutionary tree as not to be worth considering as a life-form in the sense that humans are life-forms.[5]*

In the grand scheme of things, the justification for killing subspecies for food (or other uses) based on evolutionary considerations or Biblical teachings comes out morally the same. Humans are superior and therefore may utilize (within reason) other life forms—whether they are animal or vegetation.

Because humans are given superiority over animals and vegetation, it does not mean we have permission to destroy them at will. The Torah has specific regulations in order to ensure that animals and the environment are protected (excluding extenuating circumstances). In fact, David Sears quotes Rabbi Avraham Kook: "The Torah's mandate that humankind subdue the earth 'does not mean the domination of a harsh ruler, who afflicts his people and servants merely to fulfill his personal whim and desire, according to the crookedness of his heart.'

---

5   J. Harold Ellens, *The Destructive Power of Religion*, vol. 2, p. 95.

Rather, it compares a form of stewardship for which humanity is answerable to God."[6]

As derived from the Talmud and codified in the Code of Jewish Law, it is forbidden to make an animal suffer unnecessarily.[7] Rabbi Zalman Sorotzkin brings out this lesson from the Torah nicely: "The word *chayah*, animal, is related to the word *chai*, alive. It tells us that all creatures included in this term have feelings; and man, the pinnacle of Creation, should not pain them needlessly. Therefore, in the same place where the Torah says, 'You may eat from among all the animals,' it says, 'These are the creatures (*chayah*)'—they are alive, they feel. 'Causing [needless] suffering to living things is forbidden by the Torah' (*Shabbos* 128)."[8]

It is also forbidden to engage in wanton destruction of the earth's resources.[9] One of the main differences between how secular movements approach animal welfare and the Biblical method of protecting the environment is summed up nicely by David Sears: "As a rule, the Torah does not speak of rights, whether concerning Jews or non-Jews, men or women, employers or employees, masters or slaves, or animals. In truth, all 'rights' belong to the Master of the Universe: 'The earth and all that fills it belongs to the Lord, the world and all those that dwell within.'[10] Rather, the Torah imposes on the Jewish People, as well as humanity as a whole, duties and responsibilities toward God, and toward one another."[11]

The difference accomplishes the same goal, but instead of focusing on the animals and environment, it puts the obligation on humanity. Animals even take precedence over humans when the Bible dictates it; for example, in Deuteronomy 11:15, where the feeding of the cattle is mentioned before the filling of the person's stomach. From this verse,

---

6   David Sears, *The Vision of Eden*, p. 69.
7   *Bava Metzia* 32a; *Shulchan Aruch, Choshen Mishpat* 272:9.
8   Rabbi Zalman Sorotzkin, *Insights in the Torah*, vol. 3, *Vayikra*, p. 150.
9   See Deuteronomy 20:19–20; *Berachos* 52b; *Shabbos* 67b; and *Kiddushin* 32a.
10   Psalms 24:1.
11   *Vision of Eden*, p. 61.

it was codified in Jewish law that a person's animals are to be fed before the owner may eat his own food.[12]

(1) Hamstringing the Horses

Joshua 11:6: "Hashem said to Joshua…'You shall hamstring their horses and burn their chariots in fire.'"

The consensus of the commentaries is that this was a rare situation where the Jewish People encountered an army consisting of horse-drawn chariots for the first time.[13] The purpose of the command was twofold. First, the horses were disabled for battle and chariots were burned as a demonstration of this advanced weaponry's failure to help the nation attacking the Jews.[14] Second, it was a maneuver to ensure that the Jewish army would not be tempted to use this great advantage over its enemies. This was due to the high likelihood that the newly acquired power could cause the Jewish army to trust in its military strength, and not in Hashem.[15] The very fact that the commentators of the Middle Ages were even concerned by the question of why the animals suffered is an indication of their moral sensitivity to the pain of animals. How many other cultures at that time were questioning not only whether their lead general should kill animals, but even if he should inflict pain in them at all?[16]

(2) Sacrifices

In the first part of the chapter, we touched on issues relating to animal sacrifices. Now we will cover the subject more in-depth. A cursory read of the verses pertaining to sacrifices could lead one to erroneously liken Judaism's concept of sacrifices to how other cultures/religions viewed sacrifices, i.e., as ways to appease and placate their gods. Although this could not be further from the truth, without further clarification

---

12 See *Kitzur Shulchan Aruch* 42:1; *Berachos* 40a.

13 See *Radak, Ralbag*, et al., loc cit., v. 9. These commentaries were written in the Middle Ages, and thus it is unique of that era to find such sensitivity.

14 See *Me'am Loez*, Joshua 11:9.

15 See *Radak* ibid.

16 See *Avodah Zarah* 13a.

and explanation, one could arrive at this mistaken conclusion. Daniel Dennett captures the perspective of a person who reads the verses at face value without the benefit of further investigation when he observes that the God of the Bible has "a great 'appetite' for praise and sacrifices."[17]

The truth, however, is that God does not have a great "'appetite' for praise and sacrifices." Regarding praise, the claim of theists was never that God needed our prayers but that prayer is for the improvement of the person.[18] When a person praises God, he enhances his relationship with his Creator by verbalizing (even if mentally) what God has done for him. Praise was instituted in order to help humanity appreciate, show gratitude, and form a stronger bond with God, and not in order to fulfill some sort of need of God to be appreciated. So too, sacrifices were instituted for the benefit of humanity, not for the benefit of God.[19]

Rabbi Shneur Zalman of Liadi points out that the verse in Leviticus says: "Speak to the children of Israel and say to them: '*When one of you offers a sacrifice to Hashem*, the sacrifice must be taken from the cattle, sheep, or goats.'"[20] The grammar of the verse is irregular, causing the verse to more accurately mean: "When one offers a sacrifice of you." This teaches us that the essence of sacrifice is that we actually sacrifice ourselves.[21] The Hebrew word for sacrifice, *korban*, is from the root word to draw close. Rabbi Jonathan Sacks explains:

> *The result of such "coming close" is that, after it, we return to the world changed. Renouncing our ownership of something (an animal, or part of the harvest), we acknowledge God's ownership of the world. We are not alone in the universe. We are trusties or guardians on behalf of God. For this reason, when the Temple was destroyed, other forms of reunification could be*

---

17   Daniel Dennett, *Breaking the Spell...Religion as a Natural Phenomenon*, p. 265.

18   The Hebrew, *le'hispallel*, is reflexive, clearly demonstrating that it is the one doing the praying who is being influenced.

19   As it says in Psalms 50:13, "Do I eat the flesh of bulls...?"

20   Leviticus 1:2.

21   *Likkutei Torah, Vayikra* 2a ff.

substituted: of will (in case of prayer), or the mind (learning), or of property (tzedakah and hospitality to strangers). When we give, we come close to the Soul of Being...The noun korban, "sacrifice," and the verb le'hakriv, "to offer something as a sacrifice," actually mean "that which is brought close" and "the act of bringing close." The key element is not so much giving something up (the usual meaning of sacrifice), but rather bringing something close to God. Le'hakriv is to bring the animal element within us to be transformed through the Divine fire that once burned on the Altar, and still burns at the heart of prayer if we truly seek closeness to God...No animal is capable of self-transformation, but we are...By bringing that which is animal within us close to God, we allow the material to be suffused with the spiritual and we become something else: no longer slaves of nature but servants of the living God.[22]

In fact, contrary to Dennett's grotesque caricature of a barbaric and bloodthirsty God, a complete reading of the Bible informs us that God does not desire sacrifices. To mention but a couple of sources: Hosea tells us, "For I desire kindness, and not sacrifice; and knowledge of God more than burnt offerings."[23] Furthermore, it is written: "And Samuel said, has the Lord as much desire in the burnt offerings, as in obeying the voice of the Lord? Behold, to obey is better than peace-offerings; to hearken is better than the fat of rams."[24] These passages clearly indicate that the sacrifices were instituted as a way to help a person, not to satisfy some need of God. Was God ever understood to have any needs? Not only were they not instituted because God desired them, but they have no intrinsic value in of themselves, as Rabbi Shubert Spero explains:

It is generally acknowledged that the prophets did not come to repudiate the Temple and its sacrifices or to deny the value of feasts and assemblies or to replace Temple worship with

---

22 Rabbi Jonathan Sacks, *Covenant and Conversation: Leviticus*, pp. 68, 82–83.
23 Hosea 6:6.
24 I Samuel 15:22.

moral living. Precisely because the sacrificial cult was so highly regarded as the way to the Divine, the prophet used it to shock the people into a realization that the truly supreme act was morality and not sacrifice. The prophet is denigrating only the worth of a cult that is not morally informed. Indeed, only sacrifices performed by immoral individuals and burnt-offerings brought by unrepentant evildoers are "despised" and a burden to God. Nevertheless, these statements choosing morality rather than sacrifices do seem to imply that the ritual commands are of instrumental value only, whereas morality possesses intrinsic and absolute value. If sacrifices were of intrinsic value, it would not make sense to reject them simply because they were brought by individuals who were not fulfilling their obligations to their fellow men, even as we would not reject moral behavior on the part of agents who did not worship God. Belief in the intrinsic value of morality is consistent with the teachings in Exodus, already alluded to, that moral values are somehow of the essence of God Himself.[25]

Before we get started with the individual offerings, we need to gain a deeper understanding of the word *kaparah*. Rabbi Jeremy Kagan explains: "Though this is the way the word "atone"—*kaparah*—is used in common parlance, both Torah and Rabbinic literature give the term a broader meaning of "cleansing" or "removal." In fact, the commentaries explain that this is its meaning even when used in relation to sin. Atonement is not a process of making up with an offended God. Rather, sin creates a lack in the transgressor—lack is the true meaning of *cheit*, which we translate as "sin." Atonement is removing that lack."[26] Rabbi Zalman Sorotzkin gives us an interesting insight into many of the offerings: "Although the entire concept of sacrifices and offerings is beyond human comprehension, our Sages, of blessed memory, did not refrain from advancing explanations of certain aspects of the subject,

---

25   Shubert Spero, *Morality, Halakha, and the Jewish Tradition*, pp. 38–39.
26   Jeremy Kagan, *The Choice to Be*, p. 111.

in accordance with our limited understanding. *Abarbanel* quotes other commentaries who attempt to explain why Hashem chose blood and *chelev*, fat, to be placed upon the Altar. Blood, which is red, symbolizes sin, while *chelev*, which is white, symbolizes atonement, as it is said: 'Though your sins be like scarlet, they will turn white as snow; though they have become red as crimson thread, they will be like wool.'[27] Throwing the blood on the Altar symbolizes abandoning the sin, and making the *chelev* go up in smoke symbolizes atonement."[28] This being the case, let us now examine the different sacrifices and how they functioned as a stepping stone to bring people closer to the Divine.[29]

(A) Korban Chatas and Korban Asham

The *Sefer Hachinuch* explains some of the reasoning behind sacrifices for sins:

> *Now, we said that the main ways of the heart depend on [a person's] actions. Therefore, should a man sin, he will not cleanse his heart well by way of lips alone, i.e., that he should say, between himself and the wall, "I have sinned; I will not do so anymore." But when he does some important deed on account of his sin, taking "he-goats out of his fold" and toiling to bring them to the Temple, to the Kohen—and so all the activity written about the offerings of sinners—out of that entire immense act, the evil of sin will be impressed on his spirit, and he will refrain from it another time. I found something similar to this reason [written] by the Ramban of blessed memory, in the way of simple, direct explanation, which he wrote in the name of others. These are his words (on Leviticus 1:9): Because human deeds are carried to completion by thought, speech, and action, the Eternal Lord (blessed be He) ordained that when a person sins, he is to bring an offering and rest his hands upon*

---

27 Isaiah 1:18.

28 Rabbi Zalman Sorotzkin, *Insights in the Torah*, vol. 3, *Vayikra*, p. 103.

29 The root of the Hebrew word *korban*, sacrifice, is the same root as to draw near, thus enforcing the understanding of their function to bring us close to God.

it—which corresponds to action; he is to confess [his sin] with his mouth—which corresponds to speech; and he is to burn on the [Altar] fire the entrails and the kidneys, which are the vessels of thought and desire, and the legs which correspond to man's head and feet, that do all his work. The blood is to be sprinkled on the Altar, corresponding to his blood, which gives him life—so that a man will consider, as he does all these [acts], that he sinned toward God with his body and his spirit, and he deserves that his blood should be spilled and his body burned—if not for the kindness of the Creator, that He has taken from the offering as exchange and ransom, that its blood should be instead of his blood, one life in lieu of another... There is yet another way in which the heart is bestirred by an animal offering: through that of similarity—since the bodies of man and animal resemble one another in all their features, being differentiated only by the fact that intelligence was given to one and not the other. Now, since the body of man leaves the boundary of intelligence at the time of the sin [based on Sotah 3a: "A man does not commit a sin unless a spirit of lunacy has possessed him"], he ought to know that then he enters the boundary of the animals, as this alone sets them apart. For this reason, he was commanded to take a body of flesh like himself and bring it to the site chosen for the ennobling exaltation of the intelligence; and there he is to burn it—to eradicate its memory it is burnt completely; "it shall not come to mind or be remembered" (Jeremiah 3:16)—in place of his body; this, in order to form a strong conception in his heart that the entire business of a body without intelligence must perish and become completely void.[30]

---

30   *Sefer Hachinuch* 95, the mitzvah of building the Holy Temple. Written many years ago (by an anonymous author), *Sefer Hachinuch* deals with the reasoning behind the commandments. This book is universally accepted and is often the first place people look for understanding different commandments.

In other words, the vivid experience of sacrificing the animal will help the person to understand the damage he has done through his sin and how he neglected his intellect and acted on his base desires. This strong emotional experience will help propel the person toward repentance and help as a safeguard to prevent him from ignoring his intellect in the future.

(B) Korban Olah

The *Olah* offering, translated as an Elevation or Burnt offering, has a few different functions. The first is to mark the desire of a person to "elevate" himself. Also, it is an offering to mark certain occasions and situations. The author of *Akeidas Yitzchak* writes: "The various paragraphs seem to follow one another in a natural order. The Torah starts with the *Olah*, representing man, as his noblest, altruistic intention wishes to offer, i.e., himself. The Torah emphasizes 'from you an offering,' not 'an offering from you.' This alluded to the underlying intention that although the actual sacrifice consists of sheep or cattle, it will be considered as if you had offered yourself."[31] Rabbi Avigdor Miller comments on the deep meaning of the offering:

> *The Olah is a korban that "goes up" in the fire of the Mizbei'ach, Altar. Just as the offering ascends in the form of smoke heavenward, so also does the soul of the Israelite eventually ascend to Hashem: "And the spirit returns to God that gave it."[32] The innermost desire of the soul is to join Hashem in eternal life, and because this longing is not fulfilled during a man's lifetime, he can never gain total happiness no matter how fortunate his life is. The Olah goes upward to symbolize this longing to be united forever with Hashem, and Hashem grants His favor for those who earnestly seek it...And thus the Olah is a symbol and a foretaste of the unequaled existence in the afterlife. The fire of the Mizbei'ach symbolizes the presence*

---

31   Chap. 57.
32   Ecclesiastes 12:7.

of Hashem; when the Olah and the fire become one and ascend
upward, it is a prayer, and also a portent of the fulfillment of
the purpose of our lives to join Hashem in the Afterlife.[33]

The *Ramban* quotes the teaching of the Midrash that the *Olah* was specifically used for atonement for improper musings of the heart.[34] He explains that the reason for this is that because having improper thoughts is a sin of which only God is aware, it is appropriate to achieve atonement through a sacrifice that is in its entirety wholly consumed (i.e., burnt offering).[35] Rabbi A.L. Scheinbaum writes of an interesting connection between the offerings and the patriarchs: "Yitzchak [Isaac] was prepared to give up his life—an act which corresponds to overcoming idolatry, an intellectual deficiency which causes one to falsely attribute power to an idol. We atone for the sin brought about by intellectual corruption by offering a *Korban Olah*, burnt offering."[36] Yitzchak exemplified the highest level of desiring to be close to Hashem by offering himself completely, his own life, like a *Korban Olah*. He, as the *Olah*, was prepared to become one with the fire and ascend upward to unite with Hashem.

(C) Korban Shelamim

The outstanding characteristic of the peace offering is that the majority of its meat may be partaken of by the owner and his guests. For this reason, it is an offering brought for communal celebrations. The *ArtScroll Tanach Series* sheds some light on the deeper meaning of this sacrifice:

According to the Korban Aharon,[37] *the peace expressed by the*
name (of the offering) is the harmony between the Heavenly
world of the spirit and the earthly world of materialism. One
who brings a peace offering seeks to unite the two worlds. The

---

33   *Kingdom of Kohanim*, pp. 20–21.
34   *Vayikra Rabbah* 7:3.
35   Leviticus 1:4.
36   *Peninim on the Torah*, vol. 11, p. 171.
37   A commentator.

> *Panim Yafos comments that it is axiomatic that God created the world in order to shower His benefits upon man. Unlike the elevation offering that only represents man's yearning to be united with God, because the entire offering is burned on the Altar, the peace-offering serves two purposes. Part of it is an offering to God that is consumed on the Altar, while the rest goes to the Kohanim and the owner, thus symbolizing God's yearning, as it were, to provide for His creatures.[38]*

On a practical level, the idea is that this offering serves the function of bringing people together for a feast in honor of the relationship between God and humanity.

(D) Korban Todah

The *Korban Todah*, thanksgiving offering, is brought to give thanks to God. While a person may perform this offering on any occasion when he is motivated, the Talmud mentions four specific situations that warrant a thanksgiving offering: recovery from a grave illness; safe return from a voyage across the desert; return from a sea voyage; and release from prison (it was not uncommon for Jews to be imprisoned for keeping the Torah).[39] The *ArtScroll Tanach Series* offers some intriguing insight behind this particular offering:

> *On the subject of the thanksgiving offering, the Midrash cites the verse, "one who offers a thanks-giving offering honors Me" (Psalms 50:23). The word "honors Me" is spelled with two nuns, upon which the Midrash comments that one should render God honor after honor (Vaykira Rabbah 9:2). The person who thanks God should have two honors in mind: He should be grateful for the miracle that saved him, and he should be grateful for the danger as well, because his plight influenced him to repent or at least recognize his dependence on God. This is the idea behind the Talmudic dictum quoted above that, in*

---

38   ArtScroll Leviticus, pp. 66–67.
39   *Berachos* 54b.

future times, people will bless God even for the seemingly bad
(Kesav Sofer).[40]

In his book *Penimim on the Torah*, Rabbi A.L. Scheinbaum quotes the
commentary *Haamek Davar* by the *Netziv*, who explains that, "the extra
'food' that must be consumed with the *Korban Todah*, coupled together
with the decreased amount of time allotted for consumption,[41] is by
design. In order to complete eating this huge amount of food in the
allotted timeframe, one must invite friends and associates to join in
the thanksgiving celebration, thereby publicizing Hashem's miraculous
deed."[42] In the observant community, Jews who survived against incredible odds give thanks to God by inviting family and friends to a *"seudas
hodaah,"* a meal of thanksgiving. Using the medium of food is a very
common way to bring people together and heighten their awareness of
what is important in their lives; what could possibly be more important
than acknowledging our dependence on God?

(E) Korban Bechor

If the first offspring of a cow, sheep, or goat is a male, it is automatically sanctified as an offering. This offspring is known as a *Korban
Bechor*, firstborn offering. It acquires sanctity at birth and must be
given to a Kohen, who in turn brings it as an offering.[43] The *Sefer
Hachinuch* gives some insight into a way that the Israelites used this
offering to internalize a very important lesson by quoting his reason for
the mitzvah of the offering of the first fruits:

> *At the root of the precept lies the fact that the Eternal Lord
> wished to grant us the merit to perform a mitzvah with "the
> first of our fruit," in order to know that everything is His and
> that a man has nothing in the world but what the Eternal Lord
> allots to him in His kindness. This will be understood when,*

---

40   ArtScroll Leviticus, p. 113.
41   A *korban Todah* is unique in that one must bring many loaves of bread with it, and it can only
      be eaten on the day of its offering and the subsequent night.
42   *Peninim on the Torah*, vol. 12, p. 178.
43   *ArtScroll Tanach Series*, Leviticus, p. 600.

*after a man has toiled through many labors and gone through
many troubles in this world, and the time has come when the
fruit is yielded—and the first of his fruit is beloved to him
as the apple of his eye—he gives it at once to the Holy One,
blessed be He; he deprives himself of his possession, making it
the possession of the Creator.*[44]

By giving up prized possessions, one is brought closer to God by
acknowledging that God is really the source for all that is yielded.

(F) Korban Maaser

Every year, a person must tithe from all the newborn offspring of
his cattle, sheep, and goats. He puts them in a pen and leads them out
one by one, marking off every tenth animal, later to be brought up as
a *maaser*, tithe, offering. The animals remain the property of the owner,
who must take them up to Jerusalem and offer them in the Temple.[45]
Whether one is tithing produce or animals for sacrifices, the objective is
the same. One of the major purposes for tithing is that it forces a person
to recognize that the tithe that he is giving up for God is symbolic of the
fact that really all of his crop and flocks belong to the Master of the
Universe. It is out of Divine kindness that a person is allowed to keep
and utilize most it for his livelihood. It's human nature to be proud of
one's handiwork. When one spends months planting, sowing, plowing,
harvesting, etc., one can't help but look forward to enjoying the fruits
of one's labor. We may be tempted to think that our first fruits came
about solely because of our own efforts, but *maaser* forces us to recognize that Hashem is working "behind the scenes" to provide us with our
sustenance. By giving *maaser*, we acknowledge that everything is a gift
from Hashem, even the most seemingly mundane and materialistic
things, which, in turn, brings us closer to Hashem.

---

44   *Sefer Hachinuch* #393, citing #18, from which the same lesson applies to animals as well.
45   Leviticus 27:32.

(G) Korban Pesach

The Bible commands that the exodus from Egypt be commemorated each year on the festival of Passover with a *Korban Pesach*, Passover offering. The word *"pesach"* means "pass over,"[46] and it commemorates God's mercy toward the Jewish People on the night of their exodus from Egypt, for he took the lives of the Egyptian firstborn, but passed over the homes where the Jews had eaten the Pesach offering. Rabbi Avigdor Miller explains some further symbolism behind the annual offering:

> *The significance of this symbolism is one of the miracles of history: the eternity of Israel as a nation in this world. The destroyer eventually brings destruction to every nation, one after the other. No nation has survived the inexorable fate of eventual downfall: Egypt (today Egypt is merely a name, but the people and culture of Egypt's original greatness have vanished entirely), Assyria, Babylon, Persia, Greece, and Rome have all disappeared from the face of the earth. But Israel, that accepted God's service forever, is passed over by the destroyer; and they shall continue as a nation forever.[47]*

The Jewish People are the only ones to survive for more than three thousand years without their own country while still maintaining their national identity. The Passover offering was a great way for the Jewish People to relive a foundational moment in their past, and an opportunity to contemplate the impact of its meaning for the future.

It's so easy to get caught up in the day-to-day minutiae and lose sight of the bigger picture. This is especially true when "times are good," e.g., when the nation is prosperous, healthy, successful, etc. The further away we get from the redemption from Egypt, the less tangible and the less painful it is in our minds. It's easy to become complacent with everyday life, especially when everything is going well. It's also easy to lose sight of the struggles and trials that we had to undergo. The *Korban*

---

46   *Rashi*, Exodus 12:11.
47   Rabbi Avigdor Miller, *A Nation Is Born*, p. 129.

Pesach served as an annual reminder of where we came from and what we had to endure to get "here." It also served to provide inspiration and motivation toward our future religious observance. Thus, even if we were to get caught up in the day-to-day minutiae, the *Korban Pesach*, by uniting past, present, and future, ensured that at least once a year we would come closer to Hashem; we would strengthen our relationship with Hashem and our commitment to observing His Torah.

Final Thoughts

I have tried to present different rationales and benefits for the various offerings, and there is much that could be discussed and much more out there in terms of in-depth explanations offered by the commentators. Nevertheless, it is imperative for us to appreciate our vast limitations understanding the complete picture regarding sacrifices.

I have tried to present different examples of how the various *korbanos* served, each in its own way, as stepping stones for us to come closer to Hashem. One should note, however, that I have only begun to touch on the depth of the importance and meaning of the *korbanos*. Nonetheless, this "tip of the iceberg" understanding of the *korbanos* should enable us to appreciate the numerous complex layers of significance associated with the *korbanos*. Unfortunately, in modern times, where the world is spiritually impoverished and where reasonable questions can be raised regarding morality, we have a difficult time relating to the concept of *korbanos*. Nevertheless, one can imagine the impact the sacrificial system would have had on individuals who were more spiritually attuned and sensitive to the condition and improvement of their souls.

Operating under the premise that the soul yearns for God, or rather closeness to God, *korbanos* would have been "food for the soul," so to speak. They would have had "curative properties" by providing "nutrients" to the soul by means of enabling one to draw closer to Hashem. The *Ramban* captured this concept eloquently when he wrote: "Anyone who possesses the power of sight and perceives what is written in Scripture will indeed admit that the subject of the offerings is of a very wondrous nature [and is analogous to] any curative substance whose essence is unknown. [Despite its indefinable nature,] its power and importance are [nevertheless] indicated by its healing effect."[48]

II: WOMEN'S ISSUES

As I mentioned in the introduction, people cite a plethora of verses they find distasteful in the Bible, even if the Bible does not actually condone what was done. Context is frequently ignored, and people often have an agenda of portraying the Scriptures as evil without bothering to probe deeper to develop a more thorough understanding. In this book, we are assessing the verses within the value system of the Torah, not twenty-first century Western society. The Bible is not a book of political correctness meant to cater to our oversensitive egos. The Bible says what we need to hear, which is sometimes critical and/or a rebuke, and its purpose is to enable humanity to have a meaningful relationship with God. Finally, and most importantly, the Bible teaches what should be obvious: that men and women are different—different but equal. Men have strengths and attributes that women typically do not, and women, likewise, have certain advantages and characteristics that men normally do not. This is not something undesirable. Within a proper framework, these differences complement each other and enable men and women to optimize their contribution to their relationships and families.

Equality in Judaism is not viewed in terms of sameness; people are not viewed as the same. Rabbi Dovid Gottlieb said it well in a lecture: "The fact that the roles are different doesn't necessarily mean there is a difference in value."[49] Equality in Judaism means that through different roles, people have an equal opportunity to serve God in a unique way while having access to equal reward for their Divine service.

In one of his lectures, Rabbi Yisroel Reisman makes a salient point giving evidence for the conviction of the Torah maintaining that neither man nor woman is superior to the other in the eyes of God. Rabbi Reisman quotes the comment of the most well-known commentator on

---

48   *Writings of the Ramban*, vol. 1, p. 248.
49   Rabbi Dr. Dovid Gottlieb, "Dealing with Issues—Feminism," lecture.

the Torah of all time, *Rashi*, regarding a verse in Genesis: "Hashem, God, said, 'It is not good for the man to be alone. I will make a helper opposite him.'"[50] *Rashi* explains why it is not good: "So that they [the heretics] do not claim that there are two dominions. God, above, is alone without a mate, and this one [man], below, [is] without a mate." Rabbi Reisman makes the observation that the heretic's claim of dominion of earth is only alleviated if the woman (helper) is equal to the man.

In the 1850s, Alexis de Tocqueville, a French philosopher, observed upon his visit to the United States: "The American's passion for equality will demand that everyone will be treated identically because that is the easiest way for simple minded people to enforce equality." This being said, we should deepen our understanding of equality by acknowledging that being treated identically is not bringing justice to women but rather the opposite: It brings a great injustice upon the woman that she is only valued in society if she takes on the role of a man. At its core, this is a form of sexism, one that is very demeaning and destructive to womanhood. Keeping these fundamental points in mind will aid the reader's understanding of the upcoming Biblical verses.

Genesis 3:16

"To the woman, He said: 'I will greatly increase your suffering and your childbearing; in pain shall you bear children. Yet your craving will be for your husband, but he shall rule over you.'"

The *Ramban* commented on this verse: "The soundest interpretation in my view is that He [God] punished her in that she would long very much for intimacy with her husband, and would not be concerned about the ensuing pain of pregnancy and childbirth (that are the direct outcomes of intimacy)." Rabbi Dovid Orlofsky explains the part of "ruling over her" to refer to the man traditionally initiating and directing intimacy.[51] This means it is the desire of the woman to please the man in this matter.[52]

---

50 Genesis 2:18.

51 See *Rashi* on the verse, and *Eruvin* 100b.

52 While exceptions to this exist, this trend remains generally true today.

Unfortunately, historically, this verse has been used out of context with an incomplete understanding by men who have misconstrued its intention to subdue women. However, in Judaism the man has a halachic obligation (according to Jewish law) to satisfy his wife's need for intimacy. Thus, the concept of "ruling over her," i.e., the initiation and direction of intimacy, does not connote male dominance or superiority but rather ensures that the man satisfies his wife's "craving for [her] husband." With this understanding, one should be hard pressed to make claims of chauvinism or sexism.

Genesis 19:4–8

Lot offers his daughters to strangers so that they will not rape his guests.

Lot's behavior was condemned by the Torah. In the commentary of the *ArtScroll Tanach Series*, we see this clearly explained: "The narrative up to this point explained Lot's hospitality; now it relates his wickedness. He made every effort to protect his guests because they had come into his home, but he shows himself ready to appease the Sodomites by offering his daughters for immorality, which apparently was not repugnant to him, nor did he feel he was doing a great injustice to his daughters…It is for this reason that the Sages have said [*Tanchuma, Vayeira* 12]: Usually a man will fight to the death for the honor of his wife and daughters, to slay or be slain, yet this man offers his daughters to be dishonored!"[53]

Genesis 38:16–24

The incident with Judah and Tamar.

The story of Judah and Tamar is a favorite among those who, based on a superficial reading of the text, adopt an agenda to portray the Bible as pure barbarism. This results in the abuse and exploitation of one of the Bible's most mysterious passages as an example of male chauvinism and injustice toward women. Read only at face value, it is understandable how one could conclude that Scripture has an unbalanced view of men and women.

---

53   Genesis, vol. 1, p. 638, based on the *Ramban*'s words on the episode.

In this story, Tamar resorted to deception to become impregnated by Judah in order to be the bearer of the royal line. She achieved this by acting as a harlot in order to get Judah to come to her. When Judah finds out that his daughter-in-law has committed harlotry, he says she should be taken to be burned. Judah, the one who committed the act of being with a harlot, seemingly had no problem with commanding that his daughter-in-law be killed for the act of harlotry. It is not difficult to see how one who is unfamiliar with the context of the situation (using the written and oral law) would find this passage difficult. At the end of the story, "Judah recognized, and he said, 'she is more righteous than I, inasmuch as I did not give her my son,' and he was not intimate with her anymore."[54]

In order to gain a better understanding of the incident, one needs to know some background information: Tamar was originally married to Judah's son Er, but Er died because of his evil ways. Then she married Er's brother, Onan. Onan also fell due to his evil ways, and Tamar was twice-over a widow. Judah did not like that the deaths of his two sons suggested a pattern, and so to spare his third son from what appeared to be likely death, he withheld Shelah.[55] Yet, at the end of the passage, Judah recognized the gravity of withholding his son from Tamar. What was the big deal about Judah withholding his son from Tamar?

In Deuteronomy, there is a commandment that if a man dies before having children, one of his brothers is obligated to carry on his legacy by marrying the widow and having children.[56] *Sefer Hachinuch* explains the importance and meaning of this commandment:

> At the root of this precept lies the reason that after she is wed to a man, a woman is as one of his organs or limbs. For so is it inevitable in nature, because of the incident with the first father [Adam], since one of his ribs was [sic] taken, and from it, God fashioned a wife for him. Now that this man

---

54   Genesis 38:26.
55   See *Yevamos* 64b.
56   Deuteronomy 25:5.

has died without children, who would have been a part of
him remaining as a memorial for him and a replacement in
the world for the service of the Creator; and moreover, there
is not a vestige of him [now] in the physical world except this
woman who is a 'bone of his bones, and flesh of his flesh'—it
was God's kindness toward him to raise up progeny from her
by means of his brother, who is also like half his flesh. In order
that his progeny will take his place, serving his Creator in his
stead, and he will gain virtue through them in the spiritual
world where he is—as it is known, that a son gives his father
merit. For the Sages of blessed memory said, "a son brings
a father merit; a father does not bestow merit on his son." And
so too, in truth, to the living brother who begets the children
with the yevamah [his brother's widow], a share in them
is likewise credited, and he too gains some of the merit for
them…This is why the Sages of blessed memory say [Yevamos
22a–b] that as long as his brother has any remembrance at all
in this world—a son, daughter, or grandsons from another
wife, even a male or female bastard—they free his wife from
the obligation of levirate [a brother marrying the wife of his
deceased brother] marriage. It is thus apparent that the aim is
nothing but to memorialize his name and give him a share and
merit in this material world.[57]

Therefore, by withholding Tamar from Shelah, Judah was forgoing this incredible merit of carrying on his other sons' legacies through levirate marriage. Tamar's trickery to accomplish this shows how her womanly intuition to do the right thing was ultimately approved by God, who intervened and led Judah to her, even against his better judgment, so that he would instead perform the levirate marriage himself.

On top of this, the wife or the perspective brother-in-law can be released from this obligation by a mechanism known as *chalitzah*, found in Deuteronomy 25:9. This is a prime example of how the Torah

---

57   *Sefer Hachinuch* #598.

is sensitive to the woman's needs/desires. In other words, if she doesn't want to marry her brother-in-law, she has an "out."[58] The Torah isn't forcing her to marry to fulfill some "chauvinistic" commandment.

Returning to the story of Judah and Tamar, it is difficult to imagine that Judah, one of the sons of the holy Jacob, would have intentionally approached a harlot to acquire her services. In truth, what transpired was the result of supernatural intervention. In fact, the Midrash says that "Judah wanted to pass her by, but Hashem readied His angel who is designated over lust to intervene."[59] Furthermore, *Rashi* comments on the words "it is from me that she is pregnant"[60] by quoting the Talmudic Sages who said, "The Divine voice went out and said, 'It is from Me, My doing that these events emerged.'"[61]

One can even see the "Master Plan" being laid out by inference from Tamar's words. As Rabbi Moshe Weissman put it: "All of Tamar's words contained glimmers of prophecy. With the words 'your signet ring,' she prophesied that kings and nobles would come from her. 'Your cloak' contained an allusion to the Sanhedrin, who wear *taleisim* and tefillin all the time and would also be her descendants. 'Your staff' referred to Mashiach [the Messiah] to be born from the tribe of Yehudah [Judah], of whom it is said (Isaiah 11:1), 'And a staff shall come forth from the stump of Yishai [Jesse].'"[62] A deeper understanding of this story clearly illustrates that this episode was not merely some chauvinistic story about a man satisfying his base animalistic desires at the expense of some poor woman. Judah's desire to "pass her by" and Tamar's prophetic words and intentions combine to portray the truly profound and complex nature of this event, something that is lost with only a cursory reading of the story.

The question is: Why did Hashem cause His angel who is designated over lust to intervene and increase Judah's desire for Tamar? Commenting on this incident, *Rashi* uncharacteristically uses the

---

58   *Yevamos* 4a; *Shulchan Aruch, Even Ha'ezer* 165:1.
59   *Bereishis Rabbah* 85:8.
60   *Rashi*, Genesis 38:26.
61   *Sotah* 10b.
62   *The Midrash Says, Bereishis*, p. 365; see also *Bereishis Rabbah* 85.

term, *taavah*, meaning lust. The *Maharal* notes that *Rashi* also used this same word, *taavah*, when discussing how Adam HaRishon [the first man] reunited with Chavah [Eve] after 130 years of separation following Cain's murder of Hevel. That "reunion" resulted in another son, Sheis [Seth]. Rabbi Baruch Adler comments that *Rashi's* use of the word *taavah* in both cases conveys a critical tenet that during certain pivotal moments in world history, when Hashem needs a certain individual to be born, Hashem resorts to increasing certain people's desire beyond the level of their normal desire, so that they will effectively bring into being the particular individual that Hashem needs on the world scene.[63]

Judah's condemnation of Tamar, before he realized that he was the one responsible for impregnating her, is also perplexing. The *Rambam* says that sexual relations with an unmarried woman were permissible before the giving of the Torah.[64] If this were the case, why did Judah sentence Tamar to death for something that was permissible at that time? The answer is that the crime of which Tamar was accused was: "The wife of the dead man shall not be (wed) outside to a stranger,"[65] applied in a manner consistent with law before the Torah.[66]

As we have shown, delving deeper into this episode reveals prophetic insights, multifaceted laws, uncharacteristic word choices, and other complexities that illustrate numerous intricacies within the Torah. This episode, in particular, serves as the foundation for Mashiach, the ultimate redeemer—something that is not apparent from a superficial reading of the text.

Exodus 21:4

Women and children are the property of a master.

This is a very specific case where an *eved Ivri*, Jewish indentured servant,[67] is given a gentile maidservant as a "wife" during his tenure as

---

63   *Foundations*, pp. 116–17.
64   *Rambam, Mishneh Torah, Ishus* 1:4.
65   Deuteronomy 25:5.
66   Rabbi Avigdor Miller, *The Beginning*, p. 567.
67   Who is already married to a Jewish woman.

a servant by his Jewish master. When he has completed his service, he leaves his servitude with his Jewish wife and their children, while the gentile maidservant and any children born from him remain with the master. The *Me'am Loez* comments:

> *One may wonder why the Torah permits such a thing at all. Since this slave is Jewish, why may his master pair him off with a gentile slave woman? Furthermore, this rule seems to oppose logic. Logic indicates that if he does not have a Jewish wife, it would not be so bad to mate him with a gentile slave. But if he already has a Jewish wife, why permit him a second mate? But the Torah mandates that the master should support the wife and children of the slave. The Torah therefore permits the master to pair him off with a gentile slave woman. Since the master stands to gain more slaves through this union, he will agree to buy a married slave, even though he has to support his family. Without this provision, no one would want to buy a married man as a slave. If the courts were not able to sell him, the theft would never be repaid.[68] If the master gave a Jewish woman as a wife, the master would have no benefit from it. Any children born from such a marriage would not be slaves but free men, just like any other Jew. However, if the slave is paired with a gentile slave woman, then the children are slaves just like their mother...However, if a man is still single, there will be many people who want to buy him as a slave. Therefore, the incentive to marry him off to a gentile slave woman is not necessary.[69]*

This certainly is not a romantic arrangement, but it is very pragmatic for all parties involved. For the Jewish slave with a family, this arrangement will give him more market value[70] and enable him to see

---

68   A Jewish person becomes a servant when they steal and are unable to repay what they stole.
69   *Me'am Loez*, Exodus 21:4.
70   See below. He only goes into slavery if he sells himself for monetary reasons or if he stole and is not able to repay what he took.

that his family is provided for. The gentile maidservant has already agreed to be a slave,[71] and she is fulfilling part of her agreement with the master. Regarding the children born into slavery, it is true that they do not have a choice regarding circumstances in which they are raised, but which children do? For people in their situation, the question for them normally was not if they were going to be a slave, but rather whom they were going to serve. As I will demonstrate below, to be a gentile slave under Jewish ownership was positive compared to the alternatives.

Exodus 21:7–11

"If a man will sell his daughter as a bondswoman, she shall not leave like the leave-taking of slaves. If she is displeasing in the eyes of her master, who should have designated her for himself, he shall assist in her redemption; he shall not have the power to sell her to a strange man, for he had betrayed her. If he had designated her for his son, he shall deal with her according to the rights of young women. If he shall take another in addition to her, he shall not diminish her food, her clothing, or her marital relationship. If he does not perform these three for her, she shall leave free of charge, without payment."

This passage of the Bible is often quoted as an example of the archaic nature of Scripture. Critics of the Bible love to quote the above verses, painting the perverse picture that it was a normal and accepted practice to sell your daughter for monetary gain. These claims, however, are short-sighted, misinformed, and result from assumptions stemming from a cursory reading of the text.

Rabbi Samson R. Hirsch explains the aforementioned verses by indicating that they refer to a specific kind of marriage that is directly connected with the sale of the daughter. In other words, this is basically if the "buyer" has the intention of eventually marrying the girl, in which case, the money given to the father is considered as a betrothal gift. This sale can only be made during the ages where the earnings of the child legally belong to the father and where the father has legal authority to

---

71   See below, p. 132, "Slavery."

contract his child into a legally binding marriage and receive a betrothal gift in her stead. This refers to the period where she is still a minor according to halachah.

In short, the intended eventuality of marriage is the predominant idea and ultimate goal of the "sale." The girl only remains in servitude while she is not yet of marriageable age. As soon as she becomes marriageable, however, the master must either marry her or let her go "free of charge, without payment." However, it is critical for one to note that this "sale" could only happen under the most extreme, bitter, and dire circumstances, because according to halachah, the father must first have sold his house, land, livestock, and possessions, including his last shirt, before he is forced, as an absolute last resort, to take this undesirable step and sell his daughter.

Furthermore, Rabbi Samson R. Hirsch elaborates that, in general, a father should not use his legal authority to give his little daughter into marriage during her minority. Moreover, under normal circumstances, it is actually considered forbidden. The halachah clearly states that it is forbidden for a man to give his daughter into marriage while she is a child, until she has grown up and declares: "That is the man I want to marry." Importantly, this not only renders any forced marriage sinful and forbidden, but the same also extends to the, unfortunately, all-too-common practice of persuading a daughter into a marriage. The Torah gives the father the legal power to do so only in cases of extreme urgency when such an arrangement regarding the child's future serves as the means of her salvation and well-being. The Torah calls the father's behavior, from the child's standpoint, a betrayal, "for he had betrayed her." This is contrary to what a child can usually expect from her father and is regarded as an exception.[72]

The various intricacies and the specific set of circumstances governing the permissibility of this situation are absent from a superficial reading of the Biblical verses. Hopefully, the foray into the deeper complexities of this situation illustrates that, counter to what Biblical critics allege,

---

72   Rav Hirsch, Exodus, pp. 297–98.

fathers did not have "free license" to sell their daughters purely for monetary gain, and these sales were clearly not common practice but rather only happened under extreme and rare circumstances. Furthermore, these verses are not indicative of a discriminatory, sexist, or chauvinistic society, but instead indicate Judaism's sensitivities and concerns for the future and well-being of a young Jewish girl whose family is in a desperate financial situation.

Leviticus 12:2–5

A woman is "contaminated" twice as long if she gives birth to a girl rather than a boy.

None of the various understandings of this verse indicate that women are contaminated twice as long due to some inherently unclean element related to the baby being female; something like that would be a ridiculous assertion. Rabbi Zalman Sorotzkin provides a very interesting and esoteric explanation of this concept. He states that in addition to the period of contamination being twice as long for birthing a female compared to a male, the "blood of purity" also continues twice as long. Why? He answers:

> The duration of contaminated blood and "blood of purity" depends upon the amount of blood involved in the birth. Man was created from the earth, a substance that does not contain blood. This earth was molded into human form after being mixed with water. Then God infused it with the breath of life, "and man became a living soul" (Genesis 2:7). Only afterward did the water become blood ("for the blood is the soul," Deuteronomy 12:23), and the earth became flesh. As a remembrance of the original creation, when man's blood stemmed from his spiritual source (God Himself breathed a soul into him), but not from his material source (earth and water), the birth of a male involves relatively little blood. Woman, on the other hand, was created from man's flesh. Her creation involved a double portion of blood—both from her spiritual source and her material source. Therefore, the duration of

*blood—both contaminated blood and "blood of purity"—with
a female's birth is twice that of a male.*[73]

Rather than discriminating against females simply for being female, Rabbi Zalman Sorotzkin's beautiful explanation of these verses clearly highlights the fact that the concept of contamination, in these verses, is rooted in the primordial differences between the creation of the original man and woman. Framed in this way, one can better appreciate the difference as not some arbitrary or petty sexist or societal injunction, but rather as being related to something that results from an intrinsic difference between males and females.

Leviticus 15:19

"When a woman has a discharge," *Niddah* laws.

Rabbi Nechemia Coopersmith explains the concept of "the impurity of menstruation" quite nicely in his book, *Eye of the Needle*. Purity and impurity are poor translations of *taharah* and *tumah*, respectively. Instead, the open presence of God is what we call "*taharah*," while a state of God's hiddenness is what we call "*tumah*." In other words, "*tumah*" is really a "*taharah*-vacuum." The state of *tumah* can develop upon men, women, and animals. When the open presence of God—the *neshamah*, or life—leaves (i.e., as a result of death) a man, woman, or an animal, that body becomes *tamei*. The highest "*taharah*-vacuum" is a dead body.

Let's go back for a moment to the English concept of "*tumah*" as "spiritually undesirable" or "dirty." Which do you think is more spiritually unclean: a dead dog or a dead human being? Most people would think of a dead dog as being more "spiritually unclean" because it is a lower form of existence than a human being. But, in actuality, the dead body of a human being contains a much greater degree of *tumah*. Why? Because the human body, when it is alive and filled with a *neshamah*—the open manifestation of God's presence—has a much greater condition of *taharah*. The manifestation of Godliness within a human being is far greater than that within an animal. Therefore, when the *neshamah*

---

73 Rabbi Zalman Sorotzkin, *Insights in the Torah*, pp. 165–66.

departs, it leaves behind a much greater vacuum of *taharah*, a much stronger *tumah* than that of an animal."[74]

Rebbetzin Rivkah Slonim explains:

> When stripped to its essence, a woman's menses signals the death of potential life. Each month a woman's body prepares for the possibility of conception. The uterine lining is built up—rich and replete, ready to serve as a cradle for life—in anticipation of a fertilized ovum. Menstruation is the shedding of the lining, the end of the possibility. The presence of potential life within fills a woman's body with holiness and purity. With the departure of the potential, impurity sets in, conferring upon the woman a state of impurity or, more specifically, niddut. Impurity is neither evil nor dangerous, and it is not something tangible. Impurity is a spiritual state of being; the absence of purity, much like darkness is the absence of life.[75]

Why seven days? There are various explanations for this, but I would like to share, in my opinion, what is the most practical from Rabbi Meir in the Talmud: "For, since the husband is accustomed to his wife, he may begin to find her unpleasing. Therefore, the Torah said to let her be forbidden for seven days so that she will be as dear to him as the day of his marriage."[76]

Rabbi Moshe Meiselman explains how this principle is applied to marriage through the laws of *niddah*:

> The laws of niddah enrich the relationship between husband and wife. They were not meant to make women feel taboo or unclean. The Halakah (Jewish law) casts no aspersions on the physical state of menstruation, and surely a very bankrupt set of values is indicated if a woman feels she has lost her self-esteem when she cannot have marital relations for a week

---

74   Rabbi Nechemia Coopersmith, *Eye of the Needle*, p. 107.
75   *Jewish Women Speak about Jewish Matters*, p. 77.
76   *Niddah* 31b.

*and a half. If anything, the laws of niddah make it possible for
a woman to be valued as a person rather than as a mere sex
object. No knowledgeable Jew, for whom these laws are part of
everyday life, has ever viewed them as a means for ostracizing
women, condemning them, or destroying their self-esteem.
On the contrary, every generation of Jews, each individual in
his own way, has found that the laws on niddah inject[s] the
Divine Presence into a sphere where it can all too easily be
forgotten, serving as a reminder that there is no area of life in
which God is absent.*[77]

Leviticus 27:3–7

God places lesser value on women than men (of similar age).

The valuation mentioned here is of a very specific type. The type of
valuation that this chapter is dealing with is what is called in Hebrew
"*Arachin*." This particular valuation method was employed when someone used a certain vow (*erech*) to pledge his "worth" (or the "worth" of
another individual) towards the maintaining of the Tabernacle (later to
be the Temple). Rabbi Samson Raphael Hirsch explains its nature: "This
value is given as a fixed one; it has absolutely nothing to do with physical, spiritual, intellectual, moral or social qualities, and rises and falls
purely according to sex and age."[78] Rabbi Elie Munk echoes Rabbi Hirsch
in his commentary on Leviticus: "The laws of valuations are not related
to market prices or some other scale that we can understand. A person
may be the wisest of all men or a fool, but his assessment remains fixed
at fifty shekels as long as he is between the ages of twenty to sixty.
Thus, according to the opinion of the *Ibn Ezra* and many others, these
laws are classified as *chukim*, arbitrary decrees,...and are not subject to
logical analysis. Diverse solutions are put forward by the *Abarbanel*, R'
Chaim ben Attar, R' Yitzchak Arama, and others, but questions can be
raised in every case."[79]

---

77   *Jewish Women in Jewish Law*, p. 127.
78   Hirsch, Leviticus, vol. 4, p. 812.
79   *The Call of the Torah*, vol. 3, p. 331.

Numbers 5:11–31

Fidelity test required for women who were suspected of cheating, but not men.

The reason for this is because a woman who has been unfaithful cannot remain married to her husband, whereas an unfaithful husband can remain married to his wife (if the wife so desires; ultimately, the decision is hers, thus empowering the woman, not discriminating against her). It is important to point out, however, that the fidelity test only worked if the husband was not involved in immoral practices.[80] If the woman was guilty, then not only did she miraculously die, but so too did the man with whom she had been unfaithful.[81]

I once heard an explanation from one of my rabbis, Rabbi Dovid Stefansky, explaining why a woman cheating on a man is viewed more harshly. It was a psychological observation that, generally, when a man cheats, it is because he falls prey to his base desires (succumbing to the vice of lust) and not due to anything intrinsic to his relationship, whereas, generally, if a woman cheats, it is a testament to how she values the relationship (e.g., "I'll show him!" Or, "he doesn't love me!"). Because the woman typically values the relationship more than a man, it is considered more treacherous when she is disloyal. Furthermore, in cases where a woman was innocent and remained faithful, the fidelity test served as a means of "clearing her name." Only in these cases would Hashem allow His holy Name to be erased, something that is forbidden in the Torah, in order to assure the couple, in their minds and hearts, of the faithfulness of their relationship. If a woman survived the ordeal, it served as irrefutable proof that she was innocent and would thus assuage any potential lingering doubts the man might have had. Moreover, as a reward for proving her innocence, she would be blessed with a child, one who would always serve as a symbol of the faithfulness and integrity of her marriage. Ultimately, one should be able to see how this fidelity test actually aided women rather than discriminated against them.

---

80   *Rambam, Mishneh Torah, Sotah* 2:8.
81   See *Sotah* 28a. I am indebted to Rabbi Elie Ginsparg for this explanation.

Numbers 30:4–16

Fathers can annul daughter's vow, and husband can annul wife's vows.

A father can only annul his daughter's vows if she is (1) under his jurisdiction, and (2) between puberty and "mature puberty," i.e., between eleven and twelve-and-a-half years old.[82] The truth is that basically most vows of minors are non-binding.[83] Hence, the Torah does not discriminate between a son and a daughter when it comes to annulling a child's vow, except for the six-month window leading up to "complete adulthood" for the daughter. Rabbi Avigdor Miller asks: "Why is the daughter under the father's jurisdiction during the short period (*naarus*), but not the son? In this brief period of physical change-over from childhood to young adulthood to young maidenhood, the emotional imbalances might motivate a vow that would be an obstacle to marriage."[84]

Regarding a husband being able to annual the vows of his wife, he may only do so in two instances: (1) if she makes a vow of personal affliction; and (2) if the vow negatively affects the husband.[85] It must be noted that the husband is not capable of annulling his own vows, but must seek out a Rabbinical court to accomplish such a feat. It was with the specific exception of a woman's vow that negatively affects the marriage[86] that the Torah granted a husband the opportunity to annul the vow without having to take it to a Rabbinical court.

This clearly does not give free license to fathers and husbands to annul anything they wish to annul. Rather, a father can only annul vows under specific circumstances where, due to the immaturity and limited perspective of his daughter, she is unable to foresee the full impact of her vow in the future. Similarly, a husband may only annul his wife's vows if they would be detrimental to her or him and to the sanctity and integrity of their marriage. Moreover, this affords the husband the

---

82   See *Nedarim* 70a.

83   *Niddah* 45b.

84   *Journey to Greatness*, p. 414.

85   See *Nedarim* 79a–b.

86   The *Ha'Kesav V'Ha'Kabbalah* writes that even the vows of "personal affliction" affect the husband.

opportunity to annul certain, potentially intimate vows that may be embarrassing for her to have to admit in front of a Rabbinical court.

The follow-up issue would be why do girls need protection more than men in this area. In order to understand this, a little background is in order. The cognition of men is different from that of women. It is true that there is overlap, and both men and women have the qualities of the other, but that does not change the fact that different qualities are generally more pronounced in one sex than the other. Women, the Torah teaches, have a *"binah yeseirah,"* enhanced understanding of things and people.[87] In other words, women often have more perception, intuition, and foresight than men.

On the other hand, men have a more pronounced quality of *"daas,"* which is loosely translated as knowledge. A better way to understand what kind of knowledge this is is articulated by Marina Goodman: "Men have a greater measure of *daas. Daas* is when one understands something by first separating one's ego from the subject. In psychology, this is called 'separate knowing,' which has been recognized as dominant in men."[88]

The Talmud says that women have *"daas kalah,"* light *daas.*[89] This does not mean that women are light in intelligence. The famous commenter on the Talmud, *Rashi,* explains the term *"daas kalah"* as a description which means that women are more easily enticed in a relationship. One way to understand this is that women are more easily moved to emotion or take action based on impulse or temptation of the moment in relationships. One could say a reason the husband is given permission to annul his wife's vow with regard to what affects their relationship (and not the other way around) is that he is more calculated and objective regarding the relationship and thus was given special permission in this limited circumstance. Finally, it is worth mentioning that the vows that the husband was given special permission to annul are vows that his wife **wants** annulled. The Talmud even says that if a husband

---

87 *Niddah* 46b.

88 *Why Should I Stand Behind the Mechitzah When I Could be a Prayer Leader?*, p. 47.

89 *Kiddushin* 80b.

does not annul the vows of his wife that she wants annulled (that he had the power to annul), it is grounds for divorce.[90] In other words, this is meant as an advantage for a woman that her husband in certain circumstances can annul her vows, not a disadvantage.

Deuteronomy 21:10–11

"When you will go out to war…and you will see among its captivity a woman of beautiful form, and you will desire her, you may take her to yourself as a wife." The *Eishes Yefas To'ar* (woman of beautiful form).

It might come as a surprise to many people, but this section of the Torah is one of the most enigmatic sections that exist. For an ancient text to condone the taking of women in the heat of battle is quite standard, but we would expect something different from the Bible. Even for the person familiar with the Oral tradition, this case is very perplexing indeed!

The reasons for this perplexity are multifaceted. First, soldiers were expected to follow the law by acting righteously as one of God's holy people. So, the question arises as to why these holy individuals were allowed by the Torah to commit what is normally considered a grave sin, despite being in the heat of battle? Second, the Torah does not ordinarily concede to people's desires, so why is this case seemingly different?

Rabbi Uziel Milevsky brings up a number of salient points by questioning why the Torah uses certain phrases that seem to be redundant. First, he asks why Scripture says: "When you wage war against your enemies, and God delivers them into your hands, and you will take the captives."[91] He points out that we believe all victories in war are delivered from God. It seems redundant to mention His intervention. Moreover, he asks, "Why, in stating that 'you will take captives' in the war, does the Torah use the double terminology of *'ve'shavisa shivyo,'* which means literally, 'and you shall imprison its prisoner'?" After providing evidence that these were not average soldiers but rather an army

---

90 *Kesubos* 70a.
91 Deuteronomy 21:10.

composed of righteous men who would immediately recognize Divine intervention, Rabbi Milevsky asks: "How could an army of completely righteous men even contemplate abducting the woman, and even if they did, how could they fail to control their impulses?" He answers:

> *The Ohr Hachaim tells us that it is indeed extraordinary that such a thought should occur to one of these righteous soldiers. But, if it does, it is due to a very specific cause and relates to the origin of the souls of the individuals involved. The Kabbalists explain that, contrary to what we might think, a soul is a separate entity from the person in which it resides. God gave us a soul, but the soul is not us. Thus, more than one person can share the same soul, in a repetition of the soul-giving process. We are told that Rabbi Akiva shared his soul with Moshe Rabbeinu [Moses our teacher]; thus, the two of them shared certain spiritual characteristics. In some cases, if a soul has been flawed in some way, it will come back to this world and enter someone's body in order for that person to rectify what is lacking in the soul. In this way, a Jewish soul can enter a non-Jewish body. When that happens, the non-Jew feels a natural drive to rectify the soul he was given by converting to Judaism. The Arizal writes that every gentile who has converted wholeheartedly to Judaism possesses a Jewish soul that entered a gentile body. If a non-Jew can possess a Jewish soul, then we can be sure that this Jewish soul has a zivug, a pre-destined mate. The Talmud explains the concept of zivug in terms of coalescence of two halves of a complete soul. The person who goes to war, as described in the Torah, is a tremendous tzaddik, righteous person, someone who feels he has nothing to rectify in his relationship with God. When this person experiences a very intense attraction to a gentile woman captured in war, it is likely that this attraction has a deep spiritual meaning. We can conclude in this case that his zivug, his second half, is imprisoned in the gentile body and wants to be released. This is what is implied in the Torah's phrasing, 'and you shall imprison*

its prisoner.' Someone who is destined to convert to Judaism is
an imprisoned person, one who has been imprisoned within his
or her own body. This passage, then, refers to the extraordinary
experience of two half-souls meeting each other and realizing
that they belong together.[92]

This beautiful explanation answers the first two of Rabbi Milevsky's questions. The seemingly redundant mentioning of God's intervention (Rabbi Milevsky's first question) is really illustrating one of the many means by which God guides two halves of one soul toward each other. In this context, mention of God's intervention comes to add onto the fact that all war victories emanate from God and is thus not a repetition. Rabbi Milevsky's second question about the double terminology (i.e., "imprisoning its prisoner") was answered by the *Ohr Hachaim* as referring to a "captive" soul that is destined to convert to Judaism. Rabbi Milevsky's third question about the righteous men controlling their impulses requires further investigation.

In order to ensure that these soldiers had proper intentions (of ultimately uniting with the other half of their soul) and not merely succumbing to their base impulses, the Torah adds some precautionary measures for the soldier to know whether the woman he desires is the one he is destined to marry. She must shave her head, let her nails grow, and is prohibited from adorning herself.[93] Rabbi Milevsky observes: "By removing all of the physical circumstances that may create the appearance of a spiritual experience, by seeing the *eishes yefas to'ar*, the woman of beautiful form, for a period of thirty days without the accessories that add to her physical beauty, he can make sure that his attraction to her was not merely physical. If, after thirty days, he still feels that he wants to build a home together with her, then he should marry her, for he has found his mate."

Rabbi Milevsky then goes on to make his final point: "The first time the Torah mentions the Jewish man's desire for the *eishes yefas to'ar*, it

---

92   *Ner Uziel*, vol. 2, pp. 278–82, s.v. "Souls that belong together."
93   Deuteronomy 21:12.

uses the word *'chashakta,'*[94] from the root *cheishek*. When it describes his desire after thirty days have passed, the Torah uses the word *'chafatzta,'*[95] from the root *cheifetz*. The word *cheishek* refers to a physical (base) desire for something. On the other hand, the word *cheifetz* refers to a rational (cognitive) desire that is a product of a rational decision pertaining to what is good for the person (as in *'Mi ha'ish he'chafetz chaim*—Who is the man who desires life?'). The Torah uses the words as it does here to describe the sequence of events when a Jewish man takes an *eishes yefas to'ar*: In the beginning, he must always suspect that his desire is a *cheishek*, a physical desire, even if he is a complete *tzaddik*. He must put his feelings to the test; the more one is a *tzaddik*, the bigger is his *yetzer hara*, evil inclination. However, after the thirty-day period, if he still has the same strong desire to be with the *eishes yefas to'ar*, then he can be assured that his desire stems from a *cheifetz*, a rational decision, and not a *cheishek*. In that circumstance, he has met his *zivug*, and the decision to marry her and build a home with her stems from that deeper spiritual connection."

Finally, the Talmud says: "The Torah speaks only in deference to the *yetzer hara*, evil inclination, regarding the case of the '[*eishes*] *yefas to'ar*. It seems here that the Torah is permitting what is normally forbidden."[96] Rabbi Zalman Sorotzkin sheds some light on this very confusing exception that the Torah makes:

> *"'You may take her for a wife.' The Torah only spoke in consideration of the evil inclination, for if God did not permit this woman, the man would marry her even though she was forbidden." This is difficult to understand. The danger of the evil inclination overpowering man and causing him to sin is present whenever something is forbidden, particularly in sexual matters. Yet, God did not issue a blanket exemption for all prohibitions just to pacify the evil inclination! Why is the*

---

94   Ibid., v. 10.
95   Ibid., v. 14.
96   *Kiddushin* 21b.

case of the eishes yefas to'ar different? We can suggest that
this halachah is not intended as an appeasement for the evil
inclination but rather as a medicine against it.[97] For instance,
the gentile harlots used to adorn themselves to attract enemy
soldiers at a time when these soldiers were separated from
their wives. Because the evil inclination for sexual desires is so
strong, the "permissibility" of the eishes yefas to'ar served as
a medicine (in the sense that the process helped the soldier to
figure out the true motive for his desire) to combat the lustful
"symptoms" of the soldiers.

In short, Rabbi Sorotzkin explains that the system of the *eishes yefas to'ar* was a deterrent for the solider to prevent him from falling into the trap of sexual desire. It was a system that channeled his desires in a way to force him to cool off and make sure he was not acting out of sexual desire.

It should be noted that it is not as if the *eishes yefas to'ar* was collected from a village and the soldier pillaged a town and came back with the women as loot; the women were active participants in the battle.[98] She is not forced to marry him against her will,[99] and Rabbeinu Bachya comments explaining the parameters of what was allowed: "Our Sages teach, based on this verse, that the soldier must not rape the prisoner as an act of war, but must conduct relations with her on a basis of mutual consent in a private location."

At this point, critics may say: "Very nice, but the picture painted here was contrived to mitigate the severity of wrongdoing on the part of the Bible." Although I certainly can see the thinking in making such a criticism, I believe it fails on two accounts. First, who says that this was not the intended message of the Bible as laid out by its interpreters? Are there any traditional Jewish explanations that contradict the overall

---

97   Sorotzkin, *Insights*, pp. 252–53.
98   She was not an innocent person; see *Rashi*, Deuteronomy 21:13, who says that she was on the "playing field" being used to ensnare our troops.
99   *Rambam, Mishneh Torah, Melachim* 8:5.

understanding of this section of Scripture?[100] And, if not, what positive evidence does the critic have to support his or her understanding of the text to be more authentic? Second, the commentaries of the Sages of the Talmud and the Middle Ages not only fit into the text nicely, but they also precede "woman's lib" by hundreds of years. What possible incentive would they have to fabricate an understanding of the text to the people of their time? In other words, it was the norm when these commentaries (all the more so, the Bible) were written that women were considered legitimate spoils of war to defy them as one pleased (other nations bragged as such!). Therefore, if the Jewish interpretation rejects this idea (that women are spoils of war to be defiled) and ascribing motivations to something else, we have no reason to think the interpretation was influenced by anything outside of the principal of giving over the true meaning of the verse.

Deuteronomy 22:13–19

Defamation of a married woman.

The wronged woman that Scripture refers to here is not required to stay married to the man who slandered her. He is the one who is no longer allowed to end the relationship; it is he who cannot divorce her. If she wanted to, she could divorce her husband.[101] This clause in the Bible was put here for the benefit of the wife, not the husband. Even though it may not romantically make sense, it does have pragmatic value. In truth, even though she was exonerated, her likelihood of finding someone willing to commit to a woman with this sort of history is

---

100   Some might infer from *Rashi's* connecting this episode with the "rebellious son" episode as an example of a traditional commentary who disagrees with the interpretation just mentioned. However, Rabbi Boruch Adler (*Torah Secrets*, p. 490) quotes a *Chasam Sofer*: "This Torah forbearance is only intended for the individual who could not exercise self-control. However, an individual who is poised and can practice self-control is not included in this Torah leniency. Should a person take opportunistic advantage of this special legal loophole, which was never intended for him, then the Torah warns of possible dire consequences." In other words, *Rashi* only connects the rebellious son passage to a person who would be dishonest about his true motivations.

101   Rav Hirsch, Deuteronomy 22:19.

minuscule.[102] Therefore, the Bible provided her the option to remain married and have the benefits that come along with marriage if she would choose that arrangement (as unlikely as it is that she would!).

It is important for one to realize that the Torah is not "forcing" the woman to stay married to this man who falsely accused her; she has the option to remain married if she chooses. This portion is not discriminating against women, as critics claim. On the contrary, the inclusion of these verses in the Bible clearly indicates the concern for women's rights. After falsely accusing his wife, the husband's right to divorce her is stripped away. The "power" is now entirely the wife's jurisdiction. She becomes completely in charge of her marital future. Furthermore, the husband who makes such a claim against his new bride is only doing so to spare him from forbidden relations (for if she did have relations during the betrothal period, she would be forbidden to him), for the Talmud declares that "a person doesn't make a meal [i.e., go through with the wedding] for naught," and thus he would only claim against her virginity if he has a good reason to do so.

Deuteronomy 22:28–29

"If a man will find a virgin maiden who was not betrothed, and takes a hold of her, and lies with her, and they are discovered, then the man who lay with her shall give the father of the girl fifty silver [shekels], and she shall become his wife, because he had afflicted her; he cannot divorce her all his life."

The woman who is raped is not obligated to perpetually stay with the person who raped her.[103] This injunction has two functions. First, it is used as a deterrent to keep a man from engaging in this act of wickedness, as the *Sefer Hachinuch* writes: "At the root of this precept lies the purpose to chastise and restrain scoundrels from this evil deed."[104] Second, if the girl for whatever reason would desire that he take care of her as his wife, then the option is available to her to have him take care

---

102 Due to her public humiliation and her having lost her virginity (a bigger issue in Biblical times).

103 *Kesubos* 39a–40a.

104 *Sefer Hachinuch* #557.

of her as a permanent form of payment for his actions, i.e., a sentence without parole.

Ecclesiastes 7:26

"More bitter than death, the woman…"

Rashi understands this as a metaphor referring to heretical ideas. Similarly, the *Ibn Ezra* understands it to be metaphorically referring to sexual desire.[105] Moreover, Rabbi Meir Zlotowitz, of the *ArtScroll Tanach Series*, explains the verse in unambiguous terms: "It is abundantly clear that Solomon refers only to evil, licentious women, who erotically trap men into evil ways. This is not a wholesale condemnation of all women."[106] The Biblical critics' claim that this is an example of the Bible's outright chauvinistic and sexist view of women once again stems from a superficial and cursory reading of the text. By delving deeper into the various commentaries, it becomes evident that this is not denouncing women as a whole, but rather is aimed at a very specific "type" of woman who behaves in a manner that causes others to sin.

Polygamy

Polygamy in the Torah is taken for granted by people whose first inclination is to group the practices of the Torah with the surrounding cultures at the time. Most relationships in married Jewish life, however, were monogamous. Rabbi Tzvi Freedman zeros in on the heart of the matter in a response he gave to the question of why the Torah allows polygamy. He writes:

> *Just to magnify [the] question somewhat, you'll note the Torah presents the original paradigm of marriage—that of Adam and Eve—as monogamous. Furthermore, virtually every instance of polygamy recounted in the Torah is directly related by the narrative to some sort of calamity—whether strife between competing wives, as was the case with Hannah and Peninah (I Samuel, chap. 1), or between rivaling half-siblings,*

---

105   See *Rashi* and *Ibn Ezra* on the verse cited.
106   On Ecclesiastes, p. 144.

e.g., Jacob's (Genesis, chap. 37) and King David's sons (I Kings, chap. 1). Even the very verse (Deuteronomy 21:15) in which the Torah provides a green light for polygamy frames it within an undesirable circumstance: "If a man will have two wives, one beloved and the other hated..." Why then make room for trouble? If the ideal union of a man and a woman is an exclusive one, why should a "nation of priests" and a "holy people" compromise? The simple answer is that Torah deals with life on earth, and the gamut of social life and human experience over all history and world geography is too diverse to be restricted to one moral ideal.[107]

As it will be explained below, the taking on of multiple wives was always a response to a unique situation and was never the standard family model. These were not, God forbid, Hugh Hefner–style relationships; they were weighed with caution and care. It is also worth mentioning that every wife in the family unit was entitled to "food, clothing, and conjugal rights commensurate to her needs, his capacity."[108]

The cases of polygamy found in the Torah were all motivated by reasons other than the mere desire of the male involved. Of the famous Biblical figures who practiced it, we find the first is Sarah, Abraham's wife who was barren. At Sarah's recommendation,[109] Abraham married Hagar with the hope that, through her, children would come into the family.[110] Jacob also was not looking for multiple marriages; he was tricked into marrying Leah before he got to marry Rachel.[111] Hannah, due to being barren, encouraged her husband to take another wife (Peninah).[112] As for King David, Solomon, and others in the monarchy, their arrangements were for political reasons. In the Jerusalem

---

107   "Why Does Torah Allow Polygamy?" Chabad.org.

108   See Exodus 21:10, and *Rambam, Mishneh Torah, Ishus* 14:3.

109   See Genesis 16:2.

110   Furthermore, in the merit of Sarah giving her husband another wife, her maidservant, she would merit having children of her own.

111   See Genesis, chap. 29.

112   I Samuel 1, with the explanation of the *Yalkut Shimoni* and *Malbim*.

Talmud,[113] we find a case of a sage with more than one wife—perhaps the only case of a sage of the Babylonian and Jerusalem Talmuds combined having multiple wives—named Rabbi Tarfon. The Talmud records that during a famine in the land, Rabbi Tarfon took in three hundred wives; he did this because he was a Kohen and thus received priestly tithes, which would enable them to eat the tithes and spare them from starvation. Hence, even in this case, the marriages were driven by motives concerned with the welfare of others.

About one thousand years ago, a great rabbi and widely revered authority in Jewish law known as "Rabbeinu Gershom *me'or ha'golah*—Our Rabbi Gershom, light of the exile" felt that it was necessary to put a *cherem*, ban, on people who engaged in polygamy. The reasons he felt the necessity for the ban were multifaceted. Rabbi Naftali Silberberg summed up the reasons succinctly:[114]

- To prevent people from taking advantage of their wives[115]
- To avoid potential infighting between rival wives[116]
- To avoid, as Rabbi Gershom was concerned, the husband not being able to provide for multiple women[117]
- To minimize the chance that a man whose two wives in different locations will have offspring that will come to marry, which the Torah forbids[118]

The ban was accepted by the total spectrum of Ashkenazic Jewry[119] and some Sephardim.[120] However, some Sephardic communities, especially those in Yemen, never accepted the ban. In our current times, with the combination of the ban of Rabbi Gershom and the fact that most countries prohibit polygamy by law,[121] it is very rare to find polygamy

---

113 *Yevamos* 4:12.
114 Rabbi Naftali Silberberg, "Does Jewish Law Forbid Polygamy?" Chabad.org.
115 *Maharik*, in the name of the *Rashba*, cited in *Darkei Moshe, Even Ha'ezer* 1, note 10.
116 *Mordechai, Kesubos* #291, cited in *Darkei Moshe* ibid., note 12.
117 *Maharam MiPadua* #14; *Mishkenos Yaakov* #1.
118 *Mishkenos Yaakov* ibid.
119 Jews of European descent.
120 Jews from Spain, North Africa, and the Middle East.
121 Including Israel, though it should be mentioned that the refugees who came to Israel in

in the Jewish community. The exception would be the Arab countries where the Jewish community didn't accept the ban and where the law of the land allows such relationships. Even in this case, it is not the norm for people in these Jewish communities to engage in polygamy, and in their wedding contracts (*kesubah*), they stipulate that marrying subsequent wives requires permission of the first.

In a more direct answer to the question, why weren't women allowed to have multiple husbands? There are two main reasons for this. First, the commandment to have children[122] is upon the man, not the woman, and therefore, there is no reason why a woman would need another husband to fulfill an obligation that she does not have. Second, before the era of DNA testing, it would have been impossible to know which father the child belonged to. For a multitude of reasons, it was imperative to be able to trace one's lineage, including some of them being in the best interest of the wife. For example, if a woman has multiple relationships going on at the same time, and if one (or more) of the husbands want out of the relationship—and if children are involved—how would one prove (in a pre-DNA testing era) who is the father obligated to be responsible for the children? In addition to this, if a Sephardic man can only marry an additional wife with the permission of the current one,[123] and Ashkenazim are not allowed at all due to the ban of Rabbeinu Gershom, why would women be allowed?

Final Thoughts

Although Biblical critics would have one believe that the Bible is chauvinistic, sexist, and discriminatory toward women, this is a false accusation brought about, in part, by a limited, cursory reading of the text and in some cases a particular "agenda" of the individual. A deeper more comprehensive understanding paints a very different

---

the founding of the state from Yemen were permitted to maintain their polygamous relationships.

122 *Shulchan Aruch, Even Ha'ezer* 1:13; *Rambam, Mishneh Torah, Issurei Biah* 21:26; ibid., *Ishus* 15:2. Since childbirth can be life-threatening, the Torah did not obligate women in it; *Meshech Chochmah*, Genesis 9:7.

123 This is how some marriage contracts are written; see above.

picture—one that is not only supportive and respectful of women but one that is, in many cases, favoring women's needs. Everyone has a different "job" to do and a different role to fill, which doesn't make anyone better or worse than anyone else but different—different but equal. Operating off of a superficial reading of the Bible, it is easy to see how one could arrive at some of the accusatory conclusions that critics often concoct. However, a more profound understanding reveals the beauty and equality that is inherent in the Torah and Judaism.

III: SLAVERY

The institution of slavery in the Bible is one of the most often-invoked passages used to support the supposed condoning and encouragement of barbaric practices in Scripture. The truth is, however, that in contrast to the institution of slavery in other cultures, which was used as a way to take advantage of others for personal gain, the institution of slavery in the Bible was enacted as an intended benefit not only for the slave owners but also the person who was in servitude. Whether the case was a Hebrew servant (*eved Ivri*) or a gentile servant (*eved Canaani*), the person was placed in his predicament not to be taken advantage of but rather for him (and his master) to achieve greater spiritual heights. Additionally, although "*eved*" is often translated as "slave," a more appropriate translation is "servant." The reason for this is that the word "slave" has become a loaded term[124] that could impede one from achieving an unbiased assessment of the condition of the *eved* according to Biblical law.

Eved Ivri: The Jewish Servant

There are two different cases where a Jew could become a servant. The first case is where he sold himself as an escape from extreme poverty.[125] The second case is if he stole something and was unable to return the stolen item or pay back the monetary value of what he stole, including

---

124   This is especially true in America, where the word evokes the slavery of the South.
125   Leviticus 25:39.

penalties, then the court was permitted to sell him[126] as restitution to his victims.[127]

While the servant is expected to work off his debt, there is a special commandment making sure that the "indentured servant" is treated with dignity.[128] In fact, if the servant is married, the master must support him and his wife (and children). The servant receives the same quality of food and sleeping arrangements as the master, to the extent that the Talmud teaches: "One who acquired a servant is as if he has acquired a master."[129] The servitude could be so benign that there was a concern that when it came time for the man to go free he would elect to stay with his master![130]

It's standard today for thieves to be punished with prison. The Torah's view is rather novel—offering the person a chance to repay his debt, while being placed in excellent living conditions, placing a limitation on how long he's meant to be in such circumstances. Moreover, he's not placed with other criminals from whom he can increase his knowledge of his trade and likely continue to commit such crimes when he has "paid his time," but instead he's housed with a decent family who must treat him respectfully.

What is the spiritual benefit that servitude brings a person? Rabbi Yisroel Belsky provides a penetrating insight:

> *Indeed, not every poor person elects to sell himself into servitude, and not every thief is sold. The experience of avdus, servitude, is meant to teach him a lesson and to help him overcome the source of his troubles. The main lesson of avdus is to teach a man that he is, in essence, a free and independent person. True independence, therefore, is not measured by one's outward freedom to act but by the level of control he exerts over*

---

126 Him and not her. The Sages interpret from the wording, "his theft," that a woman may not be sold; *Sotah* 23b.

127 Exodus 22:2.

128 See Leviticus 25:43.

129 *Kiddushin* 22a.

130 Exodus 21:5–6.

his urges and desires. In the above Gemaras, Chazal [Rabbis of the Talmud] are telling us that a person who becomes an eved Ivri must have possessed some character flaw, some element of avdus through which he was completely enslaved to certain desires and temptations, to his yetzer hara, animal-like inclination. This type of slavery is often hidden from a person. The avdus to his yetzer [hara] is an intangible process that is difficult for him to recognize unaided. Indeed, he may even make elaborate justifications for his failings, transforming them into positive attributes. When a person becomes completely enslaved to his greed and pleasure-seeking that he begins to conduct his life in an unlawful manner, the Ribbono Shel Olam, Master of the Universe, helps this person to free himself from this inner ailment. His punishment takes the form of a tangible, recognizable form of avdus, and is designed to serve as both a lesson and a cure.[131]

Ultimately, one should note that *avdus*, servitude, serves a much loftier purpose than simply being a mere punishment. Doing whatever one wants, contrary to what many modern people espouse, is not true freedom. These modern thinkers are most likely slaves themselves—slaves to their own passions, desires, and *yetzer hara*. When one has become so enslaved to his base desires and his *yetzer hara*, the only remedy is *avdus*. Through becoming subservient to someone else, a person will hopefully come to recognize his own shortcomings and will hopefully return to the proper path of worshipping and serving God, not his own greed and desires.

Earlier, we mentioned a concern that the servitude could be so benign that the servant might elect to stay a servant to his master instead of going free. Now we can understand why this was a concern. This servant is clearly still only focused on the physical, animalistic side of life. Opting to remain in servitude would be a clear indication that he didn't "hear the message"; he missed the big picture. This is why, if a servant

---

131   Rabbi Yisroel Belsky, *Einei Yisrael*, pp. 211—12.

elects to stay with his Master, we pierce his ear; it indicates that he clearly didn't hear the message he was supposed to.[132]

Eved Canaani: The Gentile Servant

Someone who is a little more Biblically astute may argue: "That is all well and good for the Jewish guy, but what about the poor gentile fellow who was not afforded the extra protection given to the Jew?" After all, the gentile slave was not a thief or someone who sold himself due to his financial standing; he just became owned.[133] I use the word "owned" because the Torah calls him "property"[134] and allows his master to beat him as long as he doesn't die immediately. On top of that, he is never allowed to be freed (aside from specific cases that will be discussed later).[135] However, although the gentile servant is treated differently from the Hebrew one, the condition of the non-Jewish servant is not as undesirable as a peripheral reading of the Bible would *seem* to indicate.

(A) How Does One Become an Eved Canaani?

Rabbi Samson Raphael Hirsch explains the process eloquently:

> *The consideration of certain circumstances is necessary to correctly understand the fact that the Torah presupposes and allows for the possession and purchase of slaves from abroad to a nation itself just released from slavery. No Jew could make any other human being into a slave. He could only acquire by purchase, people who, by the then universally accepted international law, were already slaves. But this transference into the property of the Jew was the one and only salvation for anybody who, according to the prevailing laws of the nations, was stamped as a slave. The terribly sad experiences of even the last century [Union, Jamaica 1865] teach us how completely unprotected and liable to the most inhumane treatment was*

---

132 Exodus 21:6.
133 Leviticus 25:44.
134 Exodus 21:21.
135 Leviticus 25:45–46.

the slave who in accordance with the national law was not emancipated, and even when emancipated, wherever he was, was looked upon as still belonging to a slave class or at best as a freed-slave. The home of a Jew was to them a freedom. There, he was protected by law against mishandling; the law courts were accessible to him.[136]

We see from here that the slaves were not taken in battle as spoils of war, but rather from a non-Jewish slave market already in operation.[137] The gentile servant, upon agreement, starts his tenure as a servant for the Jewish family who bought him from the market. I mention "upon agreement" because according to Jewish law, even if he was bought on a slave market, he still had to agree with the arrangement in order for him to become a slave to a Jew.[138]

(B) Was an Eved Canaani Really Considered Property?

Designating the servant as "property" was not done to take advantage of or demean the servant. Rather, this very specific status is used so that the master will appreciate the ramifications of having a servant. Rabbi Abraham Isaac Kook explains this concept well:

Slavery, Rav Kook explained, is like any other natural phenomenon. It can be used properly and responsibly, or it can be abused. As long as some people are wealthy and powerful, while others are poor and weak, the wealthy will hire out the poor to do their labor and control them. This is the basis of natural servitude, which exists even if slavery as a formal institution is outlawed. For example, coal miners are de facto slaves to their employer and, in some ways, worse off than legal slaves. The mine owner often cares more about his profits than his workers. He allows his miners to work without proper light and ventilation in poorly built mines. The owner is not

---

136   Rav Hirsch, Commentary on the Torah, vol. 2, p. 156.
137   Leviticus 25:44.
138   *Yevamos* 48b; *Rambam, Mishneh Torah, Avadim* 8:12.

perturbed that his workers' lives are shortened due to their abysmal working conditions. He is not overly troubled that the mine may collapse, burying alive thousands of miners—he can always buy more. Yet, if these miners were his legal slaves for whom he paid good money, then the owner would look out for their lives and welfare just as he watches over his machines, animals, and the rest of his property that he has made an investment into. For this reason the Torah emphasizes that a slave is his master's property. When it is in the master's self-interest to look after his slave's welfare, the servant can expect a better, more secure future.[139]

In today's world, people go to great lengths to protect their property. We install security systems, we have locks on our doors, we have pass codes on our electronic devices, etc. We guard and protect our property diligently so that it doesn't get stolen and so that we can maximize its utility. Just like one would be foolish to treat one's car as if it were expendable and easily replaceable, one ought to views one's slave in a similar fashion. In doing so, one will come to treat one's slave properly.

Rabbi Dovid Orlofsky explains a different facet of the motivation for the Torah to call the servant his "property."[140] He points out that the role of the servant was primarily to do mundane tasks so that the Jew would be better able to focus on serving God.[141] Hence, the function of the servant was to enable the Jew to serve God. The Talmud says, "To a righteous person, his money is worth more than his body."[142] The reason for this is that a righteous person uses his money to achieve service of God, which is the focus of his life. In a census recounted in the book of Exodus,[143] the Jewish People are told to give God an atonement for their souls. The counting and atonement were accomplished by giving

---

139 Rabbi Chanan Morrison, *Gold from the Land of Israel*, pp. 139–40, adapted from *Igrot Ha'reiyah*, vol. 1, p. 89.

140 Rabbi Dovid Orlofsky, audio tape, *Parashas Mishpatim* 5759, PA 32—"A Jewish Guide to Slave Owning."

141 See *Sefer Hachinuch* #347.

142 *Chullin* 91a.

143 Exodus 30:12–13.

a half-*shekel* (coin). This teaches us that our life and our money are the same thing; you can count a person by the effect he is having on the world. The concept that a servant is one's property means that just as money helps one serve God, so too does one's servants help a person serve God.

(C) Did the Torah Condone Beating an Eved Canaani?

The short answer is no; the Torah does not condone beating one's slave. This unfortunately common misconception that the Torah condones this heinous act is derived from a couple of verses in Exodus: "If a person should strike his (non-Jewish) servant or maidservant with a staff, and he dies by his hand, he shall be avenged. But if the [servant] survives for a day or two, then he shall not be avenged, for he is his (master's) property."[144] These verses seem to support the idea that as long as the poor guy does not die immediately, you can do whatever you want to him without fearing judicial recourse, which is the meaning of "avenged" in the verses. However, this is clearly not the case.

In fact, the gentile slave actually had quite a bit of protection from being physically assaulted. A couple of verses in Exodus teach us that if the slave were struck by the master and as a result became blind (even partially) or lost a tooth, then the slave was to be set free.[145] The only tools allowed to be used to hit the slave were a staff or an object used for discipline; any other tool that was specifically designed to inflict damage was not subject to the "if he lingers for a day or two" rule.[146] Given all of the responsibilities that a master has to his servant, all of the "benefits" a servant provides to his master (e.g., freedom from labor in order to better serve God), and the monetary investment the master has in his servant, it would not be in the master's best interest to kill his servant. The master would not want to have the expense of procuring another servant, and neither would he want to perform all of the work that the servant had been doing. More importantly, he would not want

---

144   Ibid., 21:20–21.
145   Ibid., v. 26–27.
146   *Rambam, Mishneh Torah, Rotzei'ach* 2:14.

to have to deal with the legal headache and/or punishment for killing his servant. Therefore, because it is not in the master's best interest to kill his servant, one could logically deduce that, in this case, where the servant later dies, the death was accidental. However, if the servant were killed as a direct result of a beating (and not because of discipline), even if one used a staff or an object normally used for discipline, then the master would be culpable for the crime and would receive the death penalty—the same punishment as any other murder.

In summary, although the Torah does not condone beating one's servant, it does allow for one to discipline his servant. The Torah recognizes the fallibility of humans, and therefore it sets forth laws to guide us in such cases. In the case of outright misconduct,[147] where the master beats his slave, the Torah is clear in teaching us that the master is culpable. However, in the second case,[148] the Torah is teaching us that the (delayed) death was accidental, and as such, the master is not accountable as he was in the previous case.

(D) Did an Eved Canaani Really Have No Out?

As we mentioned above, if a servant was not being treated properly, he was to be set free.[149] Given that there are situations where an *eved Canaani* could be freed; one may wonder why there is a prohibition against freeing a servant without just cause? Rabbi Avigdor Miller explains: "There is an especial benefit to those in the status of slaves among the holy people, for they gain happiness both in this life and also in the eternal afterlife. By setting free the slave, the master deprives a free man of the influence of the holy ways of the Jewish family in which the slaves live more temperately and more safely, and from which they derive the merit of good character and good deeds which bestow eternal reward."[150] As we see from the words of Rabbi Miller, the prohibition of freeing a servant without just cause prevents the master from depriving the servant and the family of spiritual and physical benefit

---

147   Exodus 21:20.
148   Ibid., v. 21.
149   Ibid., v. 26–27.
150   Rabbi Avigdor Miller, *Kingdom of Cohanim*, p. 315.

of the relationship. Nevertheless, the *eved Canaani* wasn't "trapped"; he had options and "outs."

Final Thoughts

If the servant, Jew or gentile, and the master truly embraced the intended design of this system, it was a privilege. How could fetching your master a glass of water be a privilege? When the person you are serving is someone you look up to and desire to emulate, then serving him is an honor and not an embarrassment. Examine, for example, the relationship between a Chassidic Rebbe[151] and his students. His students consider it an honor to serve their Rebbe—to the extent that they almost "fight" over who gets the privilege. This concept is not relegated to the religiously devout either. Take for example a person who is a gigantic baseball fan who one day gets offered to be a bat boy for his favorite team. Would he say, "No thanks, let them get their own bats!"? Not likely. He would more than likely be elated to be honored with the opportunity to serve the people he admires and looks up to. It is all a matter of perspective. In truth, the institution of Biblical slavery would not work for us today, though not because we have evolved into a morally superior society, but rather because we are not worthy of it and would not utilize it in a proper way.

IV: THE CHOSEN PEOPLE

(1) What Does It Mean to Be Chosen?

For the student of the Bible, the unambiguous notion of the Jewish People being chosen by God is attested to ample times in Scripture.[152] The question is: What does it mean to be chosen?

First, I will explain what it does not mean. It does not mean only Jewish People can go to the afterlife; the Talmud teaches explicitly that the righteous members of the nations have a place in the World to Come.[153] It does not mean that the Jewish People will rule over

---

151   Grand rabbi of a Chassidic dynasty.
152   Exodus 6:7, 19:5–6; Leviticus 20:26; Deuteronomy 7:7–8, 10:15; Isaiah 43:10, 51:16.
153   *Sanhedrin* 105a; *Rambam, Mishneh Torah, Melachim* 8:11.

the earth. In fact, it means the opposite: that God will rule over the Jewish People with special providence in order to reveal His Presence in the world.[154]

The role of being chosen is more of a responsibility than a mere privilege, primarily because the Jewish People have the incessant mission of proclaiming God's teachings to the world.[155] This is evidenced by, "I, Hashem, have called you in righteousness...and have set you as a covenant of the people, for a light to the nations."[156] The Jewish People's mission is to bear witness to God, as the prophet Isaiah says: "You are my witnesses says Hashem, and my servant whom I have chosen."[157] The concept of being a witness to God is that good things happen to the Jewish People when they do what they are supposed to do,[158] and bad things happen to them when they do not live up to God's expectations.[159] This is the meaning behind the joke where Goldberg tells God: "Lord, we have been the chosen people for so long; could you please choose someone else?"

Rabbi Samson Raphael Hirsch articulates the concept of being chosen succinctly: "The selection of the Jewish People was not meant as a rejection of the other nations, but, on the contrary, as a crucial service to them. The 'Chosen People' were meant to preserve and demonstrate to the world the verities that ultimately were to be upheld by all of humanity. If the rise and fall of empires were to reveal the hand of God in history, it was the role of the Jewish People in particular to drive home the lesson that God is the Master of history."[160] In summary, being cho-

---

154 The sovereignty that will be granted to the Jewish People in the end of days (due to their fulfillment of their chosen role) will be accepted and desired by the nations of the world due to their acknowledgment of God's Kingdom.

155 *Vayikra Rabbah* 6:5.

156 Isaiah 42:6.

157 Isaiah 43:10.

158 See the blessings in the Torah that God offers as a reward for observing His commandments: Deuteronomy 28:1–14; Leviticus 26:3–13.

159 For example, "You will be a source of astonishment, a parable, and a byword, among all the peoples where Hashem will lead you;" Deuteronomy 28:37.

160 Rabbi Joseph Elias' commentary on Rabbi Samson Raphael Hirsch, *The Nineteen Letters*, p. 108.

sen doesn't mean that the Jewish People have a lush life of privilege, but rather that they have a life full of responsibility. Although, one could say that it is a true privilege to have this responsibility.

(2) Why Were the Jewish People Chosen?

Abraham was the founding father of the Jewish People. Unlike other alleged Divine revelations, where God revealed Himself to a passive individual, Abraham actively sought out God and the truth of the Universe. Our rabbis teach us that Abraham had no teachers of monotheism. His belief in a singular, unified Creator was not the product of his education or something that he inherited. Rather, his beliefs were attained by pure logic and a desire to know the truth. Then and only then did God communicate with Abraham.[161]

Rabbi Zev Leff mentions how, in Telshe Yeshiva, they had an expression: "*Yichus*, pedigree, is like a bunch of zeros. If you make something of yourself and put a digit before the zeros, the number will be astronomical. If not, you are only left with a bunch of zeros." There is a concept that just like in physical reality (genetics), in which certain attributes can be passed down to give the descendants who utilize them an advantage, so too, in spiritual reality, people can inherit a potential that gives them a certain advantage once cultivated.[162]

It is important to note that both physical and spiritual potentials are only predispositions, not guarantees. Having a genetic predisposition for strength doesn't guarantee that one will be strong. Compared to others, one may have an easier time building muscle, but one will only gain that strength advantage if one cultivates it (e.g., exercises, lifts weights, etc.). If one passively squanders this trait by being a couch potato, then that genetic expression for strength will not manifest itself. Likewise, a spiritual predisposition to spiritual leadership or wisdom needs to be cultivated in order for those advantages to come to fruition. Abraham, as the founding father of the Jewish People, imbued the entire Jewish

---

161 See *Bamidbar Rabbah* 14:2, and *Zohar* 186a.
162 See *Megillah* 13b.

line with his spiritual "gene" of leadership by actively pursuing truth and seeking God.

If used wisely, the Jewish "gene" for spiritual leadership is certainly a blessing that the Jewish People are privileged to inherit (but a curse if wasted). The Jewish People were given these special abilities to be used as an instrument for leading the world to spiritual perfection. In Hebrew, Abraham is an abbreviation of "father of nations." Hence the verse: "Abraham shall surely become a great and mighty nation, and all the nations of the earth shall be blessed through him. For I have known him, and I know he will instruct his children and his household after him, that they will keep God's way, and maintain righteousness and justice, so that God will be able to grant him everything He promised him."[163] Just as Abraham was chosen to lead the masses for a Divine purpose, so too have his descendants been charged with the responsibility of being a "light to the nations" in order to demonstrate the best way to live up to our Divinely endowed potential.

(3) Why the Separation?

(A) Not Racism...

The fact that the Jews are referred to as God's chosen people has often been labeled as a form of racism or blood purity. This ludicrous accusation is put forward by secular Bible scholars such as Hector Avalos. He writes:

> *The idea of blood purity was, in turn, dependent on even older notions that one's genealogy was located in the blood. This idea may be found in Judaism, as evident in comments found in Jewish literature concerning the story of the murder of Abel by his brother Cain. According to Genesis 4:10, [God] tells Cain that he knows of Abel's murder because 'the bloods of your brother [Abel]' are crying from the ground. The Hebrew text latterly has the plural, 'bloods of your brother' [d'mei achicha], an odd fact commented upon in the Talmud (Sanhedrin 37b) as*

---

163   Genesis 18:18–19.

> *well as in the commentary of the great medieval Jewish scholar,*
> *Rashi, on Genesis 4:10. One of the explanations recorded in*
> *those sources is that 'bloods' refers to the descendants of Abel.*[164]

Many may nod their heads in silent agreement, reflecting inwardly: "another example of primitive tribalism." However, a person with a solid third-grade Jewish education understands that "the bloods are crying from the ground" because Abel had the potential to have many children. Cain's act of murder obliviously prevented Abel from procreating and leaving over future generations.[165]

In truth, Judaism is different from racism in at least two major ways. First, adherents to Judaism, while being primarily white (from European, North African, and Middle Eastern lineage), are found in practically every race: African, Asian, Hispanic/Latino, and the list goes on. Clearly, no racial group is excluded from Judaism. Secondly, a person can convert to become a Jew! When it comes down to what the Jewish texts teach, exclusiveness is limited to spiritual matters, but the club is literally open to everyone.

(B) In Order to Fulfill a Mission...

God desires that the Jewish People should be a nation set apart.[166] The reason for this is that assimilation with other nations is a sure-fire recipe for disaster when it comes to keeping the Jewish People focused on their sacred mission for the world. The combination of assimilation and intermarriage, which often go hand in hand, that constantly hammer away at Jewish demographics is clear evidence of how failing to remain separate inevitability leads to a loss of one's Jewish identity

---

164   Avalos, *Fighting Words*, p. 315.
165   This is merely one example of Avalos' unprofessional scholarship; this feeling is not relegated to Orthodox Jews such as myself, however. In his book, *The Peace and Violence of Judaism*, Professor Robert Eisen says of Hector Avalos: "I must also note here that Avalos's interpretations are marred by a poor reading of the sources, a one-sided selection of biblical passages, erroneous statements about Judaism in general, and unfair criticism of fellow scholars..." (22) Eisen goes on (pp. 22–23) to list numerous blunders and flaws in Avalos's scholarship and approach in general.
166   Leviticus 20:26.

and unique, sacred mission. In looking at the intermarried/interfaith family, we may see that the Jewish parent has a desire to "raise his children Jewish" or at least expose them to their heritage; however, those children see their parent not truly committed to Judaism and not living a Jewish life. These same children may light Chanukah candles one day and go to Christmas Mass the next. More often than not, these children won't feel a strong connection to Judaism because of the mixed messages they receive from their parents, after whom they model their behavior. Unfortunately, more often than not, the grandchildren (or great-grandchildren) aren't even raised with any exposure to Judaism whatsoever. Thus, that "Jewish line" becomes severed and the sacred mission abandoned.

The point of being separate is intended to better enable the Jew to focus on his sacred mission. Academics associate with other academics, scientists with scientists, doctors with doctors, etc., all in order to better concentrate on their "missions" within their respective fields. since Judaism is a mission that encompasses all of their lives, they need to separate from those who aren't similarly charged during all relevant times, i.e., all the time.

The Jewish People are charged with the obligation of being a nation of priests to the world.[167] For observant Jews, the day is filled with work, prayer, Torah study, and acts of charity. Their social life centers around the various functions of religious institutions that support the Jewish community. An observant Jewish lifestyle is very time-consuming. Aside from building professional (i.e., work) relationships, observant Jews do not have a plethora of "free" time that they can devote to things other than their sacred mission.[168]

---

167   Exodus 19:6.

168   It is noteworthy to mention that if observant Jews have family relationship(s) with non-Jews due to circumstances of their life previous to their observance, they are still required to respect their family members as family members (*Shulchan Aruch, Yoreh Deah* 269). However, clearly the relationship(s) have to change with regards to maintaining standards of Jewish law (i.e., kosher food, laws of modesty, keeping away from influences that would challenge observance, etc.).

In his book, *To Heal the World*, Jonathan Neuman writes:

> *Actually, this [separation] isn't unique to Jews. Some sort of distinction is a critical characteristic of any religion or ethnicity—at least to some degree. For one thing, every religion considers itself necessary—otherwise why should its adherents make the sacrifices their religion demands? And if religion is necessary, it will usually need to endure. In order to do that, it needs to keep itself somehow distinct from the rest of society. That's what traditional Judaism tries to do...To reiterate, if Jews and gentiles come from the same place, have exactly the same rights and obligations, owe those obligations equally to everyone else, and share the same destiny as the rest of humanity, then there is nothing special, extraordinary, or necessary about the Jews.[169]*

He later quotes the essayist Hillel Hankin: "If ethics are what make the Jew like anyone else, they cannot also be what make him a Jew."[170]

As mentioned previously, being chosen and living a separate life devoted to serving God is not just a tremendous responsibility, but it is an extremely great privilege too.

(C) Is It Intolerant to Believe Others Are Wrong?

One of the great untruths that permeates Western society in general, and academia specifically, is the perfunctory reasoning that it is possible to accept two mutually exclusive truth claims as true. Moreover, if one rejects someone else's truth claim, it is parallel to rejecting the person. It is by no means an exaggeration to say that this insidious idea is dominating American culture; this notion has become sacrosanct.

While this idea certainly appeals to the emotions, such sophistry is exposed as the façade that it is when examined with an objective, intellectually honest mind. If we are authentically committed to our convictions, then, by definition, we cannot respect positions, traditions,

---

169   Jonathan Neuman, *To Heal the World*, pp. 47, 50.
170   Ibid., p. 203.

or beliefs that are contrary to our perception of truth. When it comes to theological matters (though clearly this is not limited to them), people's traditions and beliefs are often mutually exclusive. One can't say, "I believe in a God that revealed His will," and, "I don't even believe in a Creator," yet we are both right. However, that is exactly the mistake that is perpetrated daily by people who refuse to follow their positions to their logical conclusions.

The supposed "universalistic acceptance" of different values and positions only works if one has some sort of existentialist, "cash value" pragmatic approach to the issues involved. This understanding of people's understanding works only on a conceptual level at best, if at all. When it comes to issues that affect real people, in life however, even the staunchest relativist becomes an advocate for limiting the influence that is in opposition to their cherished ideals. While one might say, "Even though I am secular, I still believe religious fundamentalists are entitled to their convictions," it is another story when those convictions judge the lifestyle of another person who does not hold of those principles. I have seen the sweetest and seemingly compassionate people descend into the depths of bigotry and hate when confronted by people who strongly oppose ideas they cherish and hold dear.

Based on common media images and the general populace, it is easy to see how one could draw the conclusion that only people with "rigid religious and political" beliefs are intolerant. Conveniently, it rarely dawns on people that the most intolerant of all are those who bow down to the god of relativism, which demolishes and demonizes anyone who does not subscribe to a belief in relativism. Take, for example, how professor, psychologist, and editor of the book series, *The Destructive Power of Religion*, has no qualms with vilifying and stereotyping people who he perceives as intolerant based on nothing more than religious affiliation. Observe how J. Harold Ellen's sanctimoniously tolerant behavior becomes manifest when he judges those "intolerant religious fanatics" with a verbal assault that makes the comments of Jerry Falwell seem tame:

> *Fundamentalism is inherently heresy...Orthodoxy, which claims to be orthodox precisely because it dogmatically insists*

that it is the one and only formulation of truth, is always,
therefore, exactly the opposite of what it claims...All three
of the great Western religions that derive from the ancient
Israelite religion of the Hebrew Bible are plagued by the
presence of this sick psychology and its heretical products.[171]

Rabbi Shraga Silverstein provides the best response to Ellen: "Some take moderation to extremes."

Ellen also has the not-so-fine habit of associating people who share little if anything in common with his target of spite in an effort to include a diverse crowd to his fundamentalist bashing:

Fundamentalists have reared their ugly heads in every
field of human endeavor throughout history and have been
particularly noticeable in the fields of religion and ethics. One
might cite the history of the Spanish monks who mounted the
Inquisition of the late Middle Ages, some Gnostic forms of early
Christianity that thought to suppress others, the Hassidim in
the Israelite religion, and the framers of the doctrines shaping
al-Qaeda today.[172]

Let's see, people behind the Inquisitions, suppression, and al-Qaeda... what do the poor Hassidim share with this group of people, many of whom spilled blood in the name of their cause, other than a fashion (in clothing) that went out of style quite a long time ago? Was there some mass pogrom perpetuated by the Hassidim that was erased from the history books? This undignified libel is not worth the paper it is written on, and yet this bigoted propaganda is recommended reading at major academic institutions in America and around the world.

Ellen's attempt to spread the contempt is not limited to the religious; it also bleeds into the political sphere as we see from the following, "This would be interesting because it would provide for a rational understanding of the horrid phenomena with which the world is faced

---

171   *The Destructive Power of Religion*, vol. 4, p. 121.
172   Ibid.

in such persons as Joseph Stalin, Adolph Hitler, Osama bin Laden, Ariel Sharon, Yasir Arafat, and the like."[173]

So how does one tolerate people while not tolerating those people's convictions? Unfortunately, due to the challenge of making the distinction between people and their ideas, many have failed. This, however, is not an impossible hurdle to overcome. As the adage goes, one should, "Hate the sin, but love the sinner." It is imperative to have respect for people, and to have respect for their "right" to have their own opinions. As the saying goes, however, "Just because everyone has a right to an opinion, it does not make the opinion right."

It is indeed a topic I have had to struggle with very often. On the one hand, I come from a more pluralist background (which has some redeeming traits), and I am very reluctant to judge people. On the other hand, I have certain convictions that I cannot compromise for the sake of making people (including myself) happy or comfortable. This is a very delicate balance to maintain when I often find myself in conversation and seeking dialogue with people of radically different perspectives and traditions. What I try to do is judge the idea and its merits and not the person espousing them. The key is to respect the person, and his sincerity for having his convictions, but at the same time I am not obligated to respect another person's ideas if I find them to be at odds with my own convictions. This is a very challenging approach, but I believe it to be the best way to be a good person and stay consistent with my worldview. As Rabbi Shraga Silverstein said, "To tolerate everything is to respect nothing."[174]

(4) Zionism's Connection to the Concept of "Chosen People"

Many people like to use the modern State of Israel as an example of where the Biblical idea of being chosen is creating a conflict that would not otherwise exist. There are numerous flaws in this assessment:

---

173   Ibid., p. 124.
174   Rabbi Shraga Silverstein, "A Candle by Day."

1. This case succumbs to the fallacy of bifurcation (an argument that presumes that a distinction or classification is exclusive and exhaustive, although in fact other alternatives exist). A pristine example of this failure in logic is found in the writings of Hector Avalos:

   > *By most counts, tens of thousands of people have died violently since Israel became a nation. Figures published by Israel's Ministry of Foreign Affairs indicate that some 1,995 Israelis have died as a result of the horrific action between 1948 and 1999. Numbers for Palestinian deaths are more difficult to gauge, but most place them in the tens of thousands since 1948. Whatever one thinks of who owns what specific piece of land in Israel, it is fair to say that this conflict would not exist if it were not for the belief that God had given the land to Israel. The conflict would not exist if Jews did not see themselves as different from Muslims, and vice versa.[175]*

   I would venture to say all conflicts arise because people see themselves as different in some form or fashion. The differences between religions, ideologies, cultures, national interests, ownership of land, and resources are many, and they are often not mutually exclusive variables in fueling wars. To suggest that the only issue at stake in the Israeli-Arab conflict is religion is a demonstration of sublime ignorance of the political history of the region and the nature of war in general.

2. Except for certain isolated cases, Zionism is not to blame for violence in Israel. Even if this were the case, however, the concept of Zionism cannot be directly linked to the Biblical concept of being a chosen people. Most of the early Zionists were socialist atheists. The reason that there was such an attraction to Zionism in the early to mid-1900s was because it was perceived by many to be the answer to anti-Semitism.[176] How was a modern Jewish

---

175   Avalos, *Fighting Words*, pp. 136.

176   See the first chapter of Theodor Herzl's pamphlet, *The Jewish State*, in Arthur Hertzberg's book, *The Zionist Idea*, pp. 207–15.

state supposed to cure anti-Semitism? The leaders of the Zionist movement believed that if the Jewish People had a country like every other nation (notice how this was a move towards assimilation in the sense of making the Jewish People like everyone else, not towards creating barriers with others), then the Jewish People would finally be accepted among the nations.[177] In fact, Theodore Herzl, the Father of Modern Zionism,[178] suggested creating the Jewish state in Uganda instead of in Israel.[179] He was outvoted on the issue,[180] but this goes to show that the focus of Zionism was not on the sacredness of the Holy Land but rather on nationalism.

3. This point is illustrated well by Dr. Robert Eisen, professor of Judaic Studies at George Washington University, who says: "We also find instances in which secular Zionism entirely *rejects* Jewish ideas. Some secular Zionists were adamant about maintaining a strict separation between messianism and Zionism. Others openly rejected the notion of Jewish chosenness as a burden they did not want to carry. It was common for secular Zionists to speak about the desire for 'normalcy' for the Jewish People, to be a nation like all other nations. This, in fact, was Herzl's sentiment."[181]

4. What about the religious Zionists? Here are a group of people, clearly religious, quoting religious texts; surely, their ideology can be linked to the Biblical idea of the chosen people in their chosen land. It is true that religious Zionists are closer to the Biblical picture than the aforementioned group. It is important, however, to keep two things in mind. First, although religious Zionists have an impact on the government, it is a very minimal one. For example, religious Zionists do not have the political clout to effect changes in national military policy. Therefore,

---

177   Ibid.
178   At least the man who popularized the idea.
179   See Desmond Stewart, *Theodor Herzl*, pp. 202–3.
180   For cultural, not Biblical, convictions.
181   Robert Eisen, *The Peace and Violence of Judaism*, p. 198.

their vision of national politics is irrelevant in the grand scheme of things. Second, most of the aggressive actions perpetrated (rare and minimal though they may be) against the Arabs are not condoned by the religious Zionist establishment. It depends on where you draw the line, but some have suggested that much of religious Zionist thought is colored by a form of nationalism that permeates their ideology to the extent they will misrepresent sources to support their nationalism. "In their recent work on religious Zionism, both Dov Schwartz and Avi Sagi have argued that religious Zionism is largely the product of modernity. Chief among the modern forces shaping religious Zionism in early years was nationalism, which, we have already noted, was a basic element in all forms of modern Zionism. Religious Zionists also co-opted into their own thinking the modern notion that human initiative and activism shaped history."[182] In other words, the value of nationalism in religious Zionist circles is likely due more to the modern ideology of nationalism than the Biblical concept of a chosen people.

In closing, I would like to state for the record that I am anti-Zionist for theological reasons, not moral ones. In fact, it is my firm conviction that Israel should be praised for its treatment of Arabs considering the circumstances, and that the global condemnation of Israel is not justified whatsoever. When people such as J. Harold Ellens write: "It is surely the disposition and dynamics of the modern Palestinians and Israelis who seem forever ready to destroy their own world to save it,"[183] they distort the reality on the ground and blur basic morality, all in an effort to be "balanced." The sides are not morally balanced. One culture has glorified death and rewarded the use of children as suicide bombers,[184] while the other one has said, "We can forgive the Arabs for

---

182 Ibid., p. 183.

183 Ellens, *The Destructive Power of Religion*, vol. 2, p. 95.

184 "In Hamas-run kindergartens, signs read: 'The children of the kindergarten are the shahids (holy martyrs) of tomorrow'" (Jack Kelly, "Devotion, Desire Drive Youths to 'Martyrdom,'" *USA Today*, July 5, 2001).

killing our children; we cannot forgive them for forcing us to kill their children."[185] The good treatment of Arabs in Israel dwarfs the treatment of Arabs in their own homelands. No other country in the history of the world has withstood attacks on its people with such restraint, especially when Israel clearly has the ability to dish out a severe retaliation. Israel has not been flawless with the rights of the Arabs living in their land, but under the circumstances when 80% of a population wants to run Israel into the ocean, it is somewhat difficult not to put up inconvenient barriers for enhanced protection.

Final Thoughts

The concept of being a Chosen People is a call to global responsibility, not a club of blood purity. The need for separation is to ensure the longevity of the nation's ability to continue to follow the mission.

SUMMARY

In this chapter, we have covered animal sacrifices, seemingly anti-women verses, slavery, and the concept of chosenness. The animal sacrifices were shown to be a way to utilize animal life to help people improve themselves and thereby create a stronger connection to God. The verses seemingly being anti-women were put into context showing how they were often misunderstood and were often actually, at best, very favorable to women and, at worst, treated women indifferently, but not negatively. We discussed how the term "servant" is a more accurate translation than the term "slave." Finally, in our coverage of the Chosen People, we discussed how being "chosen" was synonymous with responsibility, and not some concept of ethnic purity.

---

185   Golda Meir, Statement to the National Press Club, Washington, D.C., 1957.

Chapter 4

THE SUPERIORITY OF A BIBLICALLY BASED MORALITY

U p until this point of the book, I have been primarily address-ing the moral indictments that critics have leveled against the Bible. This, the final chapter of the book, will build a case for the philosophical and pragmatic advantages that Biblical (i.e., what is commonly called Judeo-Christian in contemporary society) values have over secular humanism (and other atheistic value systems). When it comes to discussing morality and religion, there is a common mis-conception that when a person maintains that objective morality is impossible without God, he means to assert that atheists are viewed as evil people.[1] In truth, every time I have seen the issue of morality and religion debated or presented, the theist arguing that God is necessary for objective morality always adds the caveat that one does not have to be a believer to function as a moral member of society. It is obvious that just as theists can behave immorally, atheists can behave morally. In fact, knowledgeable theists would admit that when it comes to interpersonal morality, an atheist can be just as moral (sometimes even more moral) than a theist.

---

1   "Many theists maintain that if you do not believe in God—or have God as your prem-ise—then you cannot be good." Professor Paul Kurtz in "Is goodness without God good enough?" in Robert K. Garcia & Nathan L. King (eds.).

Another common misconception is that people think that just because God is infallible, His followers are supposed to be so as well. Every person, theist or atheist, faces the constant struggle to choose to be a moral individual. The point of this chapter is that God-based (Biblical) religion has a tendency to be more compelling, both philosophically and pragmatically, when it comes to leading a moral life.

I have primarily placed the philosophical arguments regarding this topic in Appendix B. This was done because much of the section may be intimidating for people without a background in philosophy, and because these arguments tend to interrupt the flow for those who are not interested in an in-depth treatment of such things. On the one hand, I didn't want to "overload" the reader not interested in in-depth philosophical coverage, but on the other hand, there are a number of well-known arguments (for example: the Euthyphro Dilemma) against traditional theological/philosophical arguments for "Divine Command Theory" (or variants thereof) that deserve more than just tangential coverage or argument. Therefore, the bulk (I could not avoid all) of the philosophical treatment of this important subject will be in Appendix B.

I: NATURAL LAW ACCORDING TO JUDAISM

In truth, Judaism has never had an official Natural Law Theory.[2] As Rabbi Dr. J. David Bleich wrote: "Nowhere in the vast corpus of rabbinic, legal, or philosophical literature is there to be found a fully-developed doctrine, nor, as Marvin Fox has pointed out, is the term natural law used by any Jewish philosopher or legal scholar prior to Joseph Albo in the fifteenth century."[3] Even Rabbi Albo's mention of Natural Law in his very notable philosophical work, *Sefer Ha'ikarim*, is somewhat short and cryptic.[4] Rabbi Bleich writes further:

---

2   Natural law theory is the idea that all of humanity shares common moral principles or notions that are intrinsic to human nature. This is relevant to the discussion of morality and how to assess it.

3   Rabbi Dr. J. David Bleich, "Judaism and Natural Law," *The Jewish Law Annual*, vol. 7, p. 6.

4   *Sefer Ha'ikarim* 1:7.

Nevertheless, it is remarkable that a philosophical doctrine which may be traced back as far as Cicero and which played a major role in the Latin tradition should not receive explicit reference, not to speak of detailed analysis, in Jewish philosophical or legal writings. Any argumentum ad silencium is weak at best, yet in the present instance, silence with regard to so significant a doctrine does constitute prima facie evidence that the notion of natural law was not taken seriously by Judaism. It was ignored because it played no significant role in the development of Jewish philosophy or legal theory.[5]

In fact, in an essay on Rabbi Albo and Natural Law, Ralph Learner gives us some insight into the importance that Rabbi Albo placed on Natural Law: "If Albo, unlike Sa'adya and Halevi and Maimonides, chose to speak of a natural law, it was not with any intention of vesting such prescriptions with added dignity and authority. If anything, it is Albo, more than any of these others, who came closest to maintaining outright that because the rationality of these *nomoi* or commandments is at least open to question and because they do not apply to all men as such, they ought most properly to be called 'quasi-natural' laws."[6] Nevertheless, there certainly is a plethora of sources in the classical Jewish corpus that lend to a conception of knowing what is moral based on using our rational faculties that is similar to the philosophical notion of Natural Law. Rabbi Bleich mentions this in the end of one of his essays: "There is, however, another sense in which Jewish thought may be said to reflect natural law theory...The simplest and oldest developed theory is found in the writings of the Stoics who observed that the entire universe is governed by laws which exhibit rationality...Reason, and hence natural law, requires the fulfillment of those ends and militates against any form of behavior which will serve to thwart such fulfillment. Common to all formulations of natural

---

5   Rabbi Dr. J. David Bleich, "Judaism and Natural Law," *The Jewish Law Annual*, vol. 7, pp. 6–7.

6   Ralph Lerner, *Natural Law in Albo's Book of Roots*, in Joseph Cropsey (ed.) *Ancients and Moderns*, p. 144.

law theory is the notion that man should seek to identify the rational principles inherent in the natural order and seek to guide himself by 'the light of reason.'"[7]

However, as one might expect, Jewish thought concerning Divine Command Theory and Natural Law Theory is not necessarily monolithic. Rabbi Dr. Michael J. Harris points this out in the introduction to *Divine Command Ethics, Jewish and Christian Perspectives*: "Contemporary Jewish scholars who address the issue of the attitude of Jewish tradition to Divine command ethics tend to take a rather monochromatic view, though in opposite directions. Some scholars—for example, Immanuel Jakobovits, Isadore Twersky, and Marvin Fox—think it clear that Jewish tradition supports Divine Command Theory, the notion that morality depends upon God's command. Others—e.g., Aharon Lichtenstein, Shubert Spero, Louis Jacobs, and Avi Sagi—think it equally clear that the tradition denies this view. This book argues that if a sufficiently sensitive analytical framework within which to examine the classic texts of Jewish tradition is developed, the picture that emerges from those texts yields a significantly more complex and nuanced stance concerning Divine command ethics than most of the contemporary literature is prepared to concede."[8]

While Rabbi Harris lists the different positions into fifteen categories,[9] there is a lot of overlap, and I don't think Harris meant to insinuate that there are actually fifteen individual philosophies. Rather, there are two main points of view: DCT (Divine Command Theory), and SMU (The Shared Moral Universe of God and humanity, i.e., the Jewish position that closely mirrors Natural Law). The rest are divided between the two with slight variations, depending on the scholar espousing it and the sources that he is using. I concur with Rabbi Harris that the gap between the two (DCT/SMU) theories is not as dramatic as it has been made out to be. The normative position is somewhere between the two extremes. In other words, regarding DCT,

---

7   Rabbi Dr. J. David Bleich, "Judaism and Natural Law," *The Jewish Law Annual*, vol. 7, p. 26.
8   Rabbi Dr. Michael J. Harris, *Divine Command Ethics, Jewish and Christian Perspectives*, pp. 1–2.
9   Ibid., pp. xii–xiii.

no Jewish authority would claim that if God would command rape that it would then become moral by definition of being commanded. On the other hand, no Jewish authority would take the SMU approach to mean that God has no relevance to morality whatsoever.[10] There are many Jewish scholars, Orthodox scholars among them, who are mistaken regarding the mechanics of SMU (or "Natural Law") and its limitations. In order to show where their folly lies, I will give a brief description of the concept of Natural Law (or SMU) in general and in Judaism, and then I will cite the sources used to bolster its precedent as the proper view. Finally, I will show how misunderstanding a fundamental aspect of "Natural Law" has led to an erroneous rejection of Divine Command Theory.

Thomas Aquinas, the Catholic theologian,[11] explained Natural Law as follows: "Natural law involves human participation in God's eternal law as regards the providential ordering of human life; the use of human reason to reflect on what our common human nature is; and what is required to respect that nature, as found in all human beings."[12] Professor Keith Ward gives a nice summary of Natural Law as it has been understood in the theological and philosophical world generally: "The moral law is rooted necessarily and eternally in the mind of God. Humans do not invent it, they discover it. They discover it by reasoning, by critical reflection on human nature and the conditions of its possible

---

10   For an example of a [non-Jewish] scholar who crossed this line, seventeenth century Dutch jurist Hugo Grotius said, "Even if there is no God, or if God is unreasonable or evil, Natural Law would still exist."

11   "The theory of natural law has the advantage of being open to both religious and philosophical perspectives: it emphasizes reason (philosophical) and allows for revelation and faith (religious)...A salient fact in this context is the recognition that Christian ethics has often been sympathetic to natural law theory. This is especially true among Catholic moral philosophers and theologians who respect Aquinas. But Protestant moral philosophers, such as Paul Ramsey, H. Richard Niebuhr, James M. Gustafson, and Paul Tillich, have also been receptive to natural law thinking...It is only fair to add that many Protestant ethicists have been critical of natural law ethics. Their opposition is largely based on the view that natural law theory relies on human reason, one of the human faculties susceptible to corruption and misuse" (Paul Diener, *Religion and Morality: An Introduction*, p. 89).

12   Prof. Father Joseph Koserski et al, *Natural Law and Human Nature* course guide book (The Teaching Company), p. 12c.

fulfillment in all human beings without exception. Insofar as humans reason correctly, they may discern what is in the mind of God. It seems right to say that there are true (and false) moral assertions. So, reason does not just prescribe moral recommendations. Reason tries to work out what the ultimate truths are."[13]

The Jewish concept that is similar to this is that God created humanity with an innate sense of right and wrong and basic morality. When we use our God-endowed logic to come up with basic morality to help society function, we arrive at objective and authoritative morality. There are a number of traditional sources that bring this out. The Talmud states that had the Torah not dictated its rational laws (*Mishpatim*), logic would have dictated that they be written.[14] Rabbi Nissim Gaon in his introduction to the tractate of *Berachos*, the first tractate in the Talmud, teaches: "All commandments that are rational and amendable to human understanding have been binding on everyone since the day God created man."[15] Along the same line, the *Ramban* wrote: "The reason why this sin sealed their fate over all others is because it is a law that is intuitively understood, and the people had no need for a prophet to warn them about it."[16] *Tosafos*, an indispensable commentary on the Talmud comments, "Each of us has the [inborn] ability to discern between good and evil."[17] Maimonides, the famous medieval scholar, also alludes to this concept: "...The judgments are those commandments whose motivating rational is openly revealed and the benefit of their observance in this world is known, e.g., the prohibitions against robbery and bloodshed, and honoring one's father and mother."[18] He also says: "And the intellect encompasses the human capacity to reason, speculate, acquire knowledge, and differentiate between good and bad

---

13   *Morality, Autonomy, and God*, p. 131.

14   Talmud, *Yoma* 67b.

15   He was answering the question of how could they have been punished for sins in the time of Noah. Because Noah preceded the giving of the Written Law though revelation, the question is asked as to how could a person be held responsible for sinning at that time?

16   *Ramban*, Genesis 6:13, explaining Talmud, *Sanhedrin* 108a.

17   *Berachos* 17a, *Tosafos*, s.v., *Ani*.

18   *Rambam, Mishneh Torah, Meilah* 8:8.

actions."[19] After seeing all of the sources for people being able to deduce morality from their innate sense of right and wrong and use reason to come up with a form of objective morality, one would not be out of line for asking the question: What need is there to have a Divine document given through revelation in the first place? Rabbi Spero gives us some insight into that question:

> *An important bit of evidence indicating that the rabbis believed in some kind of innate moral knowledge is to be found in their use of the concept of sevarah, by which they meant "self-evident reason" or "common sense." Often, they would accept this as a direct source of a particular halakhah [Jewish law] without any further recourse to a text. Frequently, the sevarah was quasi-moral in nature...by the middle of the fifteenth century, however, Joseph Albo had no difficulty in demonstrating the way in which Divine law based on prophetic revelation was superior to natural and conventional law based on human experience and was, therefore, essential if man was to reach human perfection. While Albo acknowledged that we find a general agreement among men that certain principles, such as justice and gratitude, are good, and others, such as injustice and violence, are evil, these principles are very general and do not provide adequate guidance in particular situations. This has already been suggested by Sa'adiah: "Man is fundamentally in need of the prophets, not only on account of the traditional law which had to be announced, but also on account of the rational laws...for the prophets must show us how to perform them...Reason disapproves of theft, but gives no definition of the way in which some objects of value become man's property." It is clear that when these thinkers speak of "reason" as a source of certain kinds of knowledge, they did not have in mind rational necessity but rather the evidence of*

---

common experience or those things which command general approval.[20]

In the introduction to the widely acclaimed ethical masterpiece, *Orchos Tzaddikim* (Ways of the Righteous), the author, who wrote the book anonymously, compared all of the character traits to pearls on a string and the string holding all of them in place as *yiras Shamayim*, fear of Heaven. He points out that if the string (i.e., fear of God) were to be broken, all of the pearls (i.e., character traits) would fall off, because nothing would be holding them together. From this insight, we can appreciate the lesson that morality still requires God to give our "naturally endowed" [by God] character traits solid direction. Furthermore, even if a person has an internal sense of right and wrong, they still have to contend with external factors that make it difficult not to try and justify or rationalize things that a person "naturally" knows are wrong. This is what the *Chovos Halevavos* had in mind when he wrote: "Man has internal stimulus (one enabled in the mind and implanted in his consciousness), but because bodily pleasures come first to man's soul, he needs external help (the Torah)."[21]

If this is the case, why did God wait so long to reveal the Torah? Rabbi Avidgor Miller explains:

> *Question: Is it possible to be a decent man without a Torah from Hashem? Answer: The answer is—absolutely, it's possible…You must know a teaching that is found especially in the Chovos Halevavos, but is indicated elsewhere in our ancient writings: that man is created with an inherent understanding of right and wrong (p. 55)…However, the Chovos Halevavos explains that, in the course of time, mankind adopted wrong precedents, and they became traditions. Now, even wicked things are commanded by parents to their children and teachers to their disciples—wrong ideals, sometimes foolish and sinful ideals. As the generations pass, these wrong ideals*

---

20   Shubert Spero, *Morality, Halakha, and the Jewish Tradition*, pp. 66–67.
21   See *Chovos Halevavos, Shaar Avodas Elokim*, chaps. 1–3.

become entrenched in men's minds. Therefore, it becomes difficult today for people to liberate themselves from the wrong traditions. Therefore, today, without a Torah, it's almost impossible to know good from bad...People have sunk to terrible depths today. How long can a man who is standing on a ladder kick the ladder from underfoot and say, "Well, I don't need that ladder. I am always standing on high." For a moment he may remain suspended, but sooner or later there will be a crash. And that crash is taking place today. We see on all fronts a breakdown of society...And, therefore, it's virtually impossible today without a Torah to remain decent for very long.[22]

The words of Rabbi Boruch Adler are also very pertinent to this situation regarding a change in society that lead to the necessity of a written revelation:

The Gemara [Talmud] (Bava Kama 46a, Kesubos 22b, Avodah Zarah 34b, Niddah 25a) sometimes discusses a certain issue and cites a particular pasuk [verse] to prove its point. The Gemara then asks: Why is it necessary to refer to a pasuk to prove a point? The conclusion it seems, can also be drawn from sevarah—common sense. The Gemara infers that common sense carries greater weight in its conclusiveness than even a pasuk. There are certain great truths stored in the human subconscious that rival even the legitimacy of the pasuk. The above Gemara could easily have asked the question in reverse: why would you use sevarah to prove a point, if this point can be sustained by a pasuk? Obviously, logic, a product of the human mind, contains profound truths that vie with the authority of the truths of the Torah. The Gemara (Niddah 30b) teaches that while a fetus is still in its mother's womb, it is taught the entire Torah. When the child is ready to enter this world,

---

22 *Rav Miller on Emunah and Bitachon*, collected and adapted by Rabbi Yaakov Astor, pp. 55–57.

a Malach [Angel] makes him forget what he was taught...The Torah taught to us by a Malach in the womb remains with us forever as part of our subconscious. In an absolute sense we do not really forget its teachings; that knowledge is just pushed to the deeper recesses of the mind. Our role in this world is to strive to reclaim the Torah. Rabbeinu Nissim Gaon (in his introduction to Berachos) asks why the early generations were punished for acts contrary to the Torah even before the Torah was given to man...By what standard were they punished? Rabbeinu Nissim Gaon suggests that man is required to follow the dictates of his conscience. Man's conscience is invested with Torah; Hashem created man with Torah as part of his mental composition (see Meshech Chochmah, Devarim 30:11–14)...When a human being claims to suffer from a guilty conscience, he is actually admitting to having rebelled against a precept of the Torah...We can now understand the Gemara's assertion in assuming that the use of logic holds equal validity with a pasuk. Logic is an expression of the human mind. It is one of the manifestations of the Torah that was stamped into man at the time of creation, and into each individual within the womb. How is the Torah of the conscience (or the subconscious) to be reconciled with the Torah given to Klal Yisrael at Har Sinai?...The Torah of the conscience built into Adam HaRishon, although less formal than the Torah of Sinai, nevertheless binds man to a standard of conduct. With each ensuing generation since creation, that conscience has become more clouded, and the ability of man to decipher Hashem's will through the use of logic has become weakened. The Chassidic Rebbe, Reb Tzvi Elimelech from Dinov, proposes that as far as halachah is concerned, the only barometer with which to understand the Torah is direct Torah interpretation, not the use of logic. He proves this with a Gemara in Eruvin (14b)...Why would Chazal turn to a pasuk to prove what can be deduced from a simple mathematical equation? In matters of halachah, the reliance on mere logic is not sufficient.

The Vilna Gaon offers an additional proof that reliance on logic in the explanation of mitzvos is not indicated. The Mishnah in Shabbos (11a) states that "one may not read by candlelight [on Shabbos]" without offering any reason for this injunction. Yet, the following Beraisa (ibid. 12b) explains: One must not read by candlelight on Shabbos, for fear that the reader might come to adjust the flame...The Vilna Gaon explains that once Rabbi Yishmael was given a reason for the law, he felt that he could take care to avoid coming to a transgression. Realizing his own near failure, he now acknowledged the brilliance of the Sages who offered no explanation for their ruling. It was only after Rabbi Yishmael heard the Beraisa's reason that he thought he could circumvent it. Hence, the Vilna Gaon concludes that halachically one may not rely on logic, but only on the absolute interpretation of the Torah...The Torah given at Sinai, through Moshe Rabbeinu, was a direct transmission from Hashem to man on a conscious level. Klal Yisrael relinquished control of their mental independence, and agreed to subjugate their conscious and subconscious to the will of Hashem...However, the Torah of Avraham Avinu was self-learned. Avraham gleaned Torah knowledge from his own intellect (Bereishis Rabbah 95:3), which seems contradictory to our established standard of mesorah—tradition. Mesorah implies the handing over of tradition from Hashem to man, from teacher to student (Maharal, Derech Chaim 1:1). What was Avraham's mesorah? What was it exactly that Hashem was so sure that Avraham would pass along?...However, once Hashem bestowed His Torah directly upon Klal Yisrael, it became the superior method of becoming familiar with Hashem (Shemos Rabbah 2:6)...The Torah was stamped into the consciousness of man to orient his behavior in conformation with Hashem's rules. Nature, man's environment, constantly serves to remind man of the power of Hashem. The fact that the Torah lives in our minds and totally surrounds our physical beings

should be enough for any rational man to embrace Hashem.
It is man's way, however, to take this world for granted, to
fail to recognize the subtle direction of Hashem behind our
moral conscience. Because of this, Hashem gave us the Torah
at Sinai, to ensure that errant man gets the message.[23]

Now that we have learned the place of Natural Law in Judaism,[24] I will explain where many people make the mistake regarding the idea that Natural Law is totally incompatible with Divine Command Theory. In a debate of God and Morality, Adam Lloyd Johnson explains well where the confusion often comes from: "The term 'Command' in the name 'Divine Command Theory' has led some to mistakenly think advocates for this theory believe people only have obligations if God gives them direct verbal instructions. Because of this confusion, it's important to note that many Divine command theorists, including Adams and Craig, are not using the term 'command' in this context to mean only direct verbal instructions. They maintain that God has communicated His will to us in many ways, including, but not limited to, direct verbal commands, moral intuition, and our consciences. Thus the term 'command' is used within most Divine Command Theories as a general term to encapsulate all the ways God makes us aware of His will for us, not merely direct verbal commands."[25]

The flaw lies in the misunderstanding of "innate natural disposition of right and wrong" being independent of God. In truth, the fact that God created and implanted this moral compass in us makes it as dependent on God as if it were written in the Torah. Descartes put it well when he said, regarding a verse in Genesis, "'And God saw everything He had made, and behold it was very good,'[26] as: 'The goodness' of Creation is not deduced in accordance with some independent criterion of the

---

23   Rabbi Boruch Adler, *Parsha Illuminations* (1998), pp. 68–78.
24   More specifically, the concept similar to it.
25   William Lane Craig, Erik Wielenberg, *A Debate on God and Morality, What is the best account of objective moral values and duties,* ed. Adam Lloyd Johnson, p. 21.
26   Genesis 1:31.

good, purportedly used to judge the quality of His Creation; instead, 'the reason for their goodness is the fact that He wished them so.'"[27]

The spiritual leader of the Yeshiva of Slobodka, Rabbi Avrohom Grodzinsky, pointed out in *Toras Avraham*: "Hashem only punishes people if they are warned first...All people (preceding the revelation of the written Torah) had the same judgment as people commanded from Hashem via the Written Torah...An act that is not in accord with what the *sechel* (inborn moral compass) dictates is treated with the same punishment as transgressing a written/explicit (revealed) command of God...The obligation of a person who was created in the Divine image, his wisdom (that he was endowed with) is the wisdom from above."[28]

Rabbi Samson Raphael Hirsch mentions this concept as well:

> It is on justice that God founded the universe. If you will raise your gaze to the heavens, if you perceive that there are laws by which the heavenly bodies move in their course, if you discern the law of creation which governs the earth, the plants, animals, and men, if you penetrate the inner working of all beings and analyze their composition—does it not become manifest even to your dull eyes that it is the hand of the Creator which everywhere has allotted to its creation matter, strength, and structure due weight and measure? The same hand which measured the earth and the sun and meted out matter to them in proportion to their pre-ordained courses, that same hand meted out mental power to man according to his spiritual destiny, prescribes the number of each being's members and size, allotted to all matter its ingredients, which make it what it is. In the same manner, the continued existence, development and activity of the universe is but justice...Add to this, above all, that God's will has been revealed to you, that He has implanted in your mind the general principles of truth and right—a spark of the law of His universal order—and that your mind echoes His voice which demands

---

27   Avi Sagi and Daniel Statman, *Morality and Religion*, p. 14.
28   Rabbi Avraham Grodzinsky, *Toras Avraham*, sect. "*Toras HaSeichel L'Enosh*," pp. 256–58.

truth and right everywhere and rebels against every injustice. Observe, then, that only that is truth which corresponds to the Divinely created reality of the external world or to the rules which God has implanted in your mind, and hence that God is your Source of truth. That is, you recognize as just that which satisfies your own sense of justice, which God has installed in you; thus God is also the Source of justice. And if you ask, why does this appear 'true,' as 'just' to me? You are unanswerably led to something for which there is no reason other than God's will, which has established both external reality and the internal reality of your mind and spirit. Thus truth and right are the first revelation of God in your mind. But the internal voice of justice can respond only to the general principle...The word of God which reveals your justice to you is His Torah. It is the warranty and message of your inner voice which demands justice; a warranty that this is God's voice and command that you do not disregard, despise, or misinterpret it; the message that you can thereby exercise that justice infallibly towards all creatures and towards yourself, for it is God Himself, by Whose word alone justice is what it is, Who has interpreted the claims of other creatures and of yourself against yourself.[29]

The main function of the "internal voice that demands justice" is in order to maintain a functioning society,[30] as well as to spur a person to search for a life of meaning. An inborn sense of morality does not mean that God is divorced from the picture. Regarding the episode in Genesis where Abraham responded to the inquiry of why he misled people to think that Sarah was his sister and not his wife, telling them he did so because, "There is no fear of God here,"[31] the *Malbim* comments that it

---

29   Rav Hirsch, *Horeb*, pp. 218–20.
30   "Refraining from stealing, murdering, etc. does not make you good. It just means you can function in society." Rabbi Yosef Albo, *Sefer Ha'ikarim*, 3:7...."The only obligations that mankind had before the giving of the Torah was only what was required to keep civilization going" (*Beis Elokim* 3:14).
31   Genesis 20:11.

was out of fear that reason and rational ethics alone would not restrain their passions.[32] As mentioned above, the *Orchos Tzaddikim* teaches that character traits without fear of God result in misplaced and incorrect morality.[33]

It is important to make a distinction between Ontology and Epistemology when it comes to ethics. Keith Ward defines Ontology as: "[A]n attempt to provide reasons that are not part of ethics for speaking of ethical statements as true and objective in a more trivial merely quasi-real sense."[34] Peter S. Williams, in his article, "Can Moral Objectivism Do without God?" comments:

> *Here McGinn exhibits a common confusion in that he conflates the argument for God as the ontological basis for objective moral values with the un-biblical epistemological claim that belief in God is a necessary condition of knowing the difference between right and wrong (cf. Romans 2:14–15). As J.P. Moreland and William Lane Craig caution: The question is not: Must we believe in God in order to live moral lives? There is no reason to think that atheists and theists alike may not live what we normally characterize as good and decent lives. Similarly, the question is not: Can we formulate a system of ethics without reference to God? If the non-theist grants that human beings do have objective value, then there is no reason to think that he cannot work out a system of ethics with which the theist would largely agree. Or again, the question is not: Can we recognize the existence of objective moral values without reference to God? The theist will typically maintain that a person need not believe in God in order to recognize, say, that we should love our children...Rather as Paul Copan explains, the moral argument urges that although "belief in God isn't a requirement for being moral...the existence of a personal God is crucial for a coherent*

---

32   See also *Radak* there.
33   As we will examine and illustrate in further sections.
34   *Morality, Autonomy, and God*, p. 79.

understanding of objective morality." In other words, although the non-theist can do the right thing because he knows what the objectively right thing to do is, his world view can't cogently provide an adequate ontological account of the objective moral values he knows and obeys.

Professor Keith Ward puts this in a different way: "It follows that created intellects are capable of knowing what is good without believing in God. They can know created goods without realizing that they are instantiations of the contents of God's mind, and without even believing that there is such a mind."[35] These scholars further argue that secular governments and people can recognize and execute good, but they lack a robust framework to understand why they recognize good.

Finally, I wanted to share another argument for the case that belief in God makes it easier and more compelling to lead a moral life. The following is from an article written by Rabbi Yitzchak Blau:

> *The following arguments offer practical reasons why a religious system leads to more successful performance. Hastings Rashdall argues that religion's advantage over secular morality consists of the personal relationship with a perfectly ethical being. "When God is conceived of as the realization of our highest moral ideals, love of God and love of duty become one and the same thing, with all the additional strength which love of a person can claim over the love of an abstract law." We often find greater motivation to perform duties we already know to be right when a person we respect encourages fulfillment of those duties. This motivation becomes magnified when the source of wisdom is God, the model of perfection. Thus, the presence of God adds both the force of a personal relationship and a model of perfect behavior to emulate. Iris Murdoch's writings inspire a different argument, although Murdoch herself does not argue for a religious position. She criticizes modern moral philosophy*

---

35   Ibid., p. 208.

*for emphasizing personal will at the moment of ethical choice
and ignoring the significant work done in between choices.
This work includes states of mind, dispositions and beliefs. The
moral life, on this view, is something that goes on continually,
not something that is switched off in between the occurrence of
explicit moral choices. What happens in between such choices
is indeed what is crucial.*

*Both Kantian and Utilitarian ethics tend to focus exclusively
on the moment of choice. Religion, on the other hand, includes
various ritual acts that demand attention to the inner life
even when not confronted with ethical choices. Prayer and
repentance represent the best two examples of such rituals,
and it is difficult to imagine an atheistic parallel...The recent
return to Aristotelian virtue ethics does blunt the distinction
somewhat, as this approach is an example of a non-religious
ethical theory that does emphasize the human personality
and not just the moment of choice. However, proponents of
virtue ethics do not have the ritual tradition of religion to rely
upon and it remains unclear whether or not such an approach
will successfully create virtue ethic rituals. In other words,
declaring the importance of the inner life does not mean one
has a mechanism for working on the inner life.[36]*

II: SCIENTIFIC NATURALISM / MATERIALISM

If a person is not getting their ethical grounding from religion, that
does not leave a wide variety of other options open for the secular
person. While some rely on different (atheistic) philosophies to ground
their morality, recently, a new contender on the world scene has put
itself on the open market, claiming to have possession of moral objectivity. This world view tends to be exclusively atheistic.[37] Scientific

---

36   Yitzchak Blau, "Ivan Karamazov Revisited: The Moral Argument for Religious Belief," *Torah
u-Madda Journal*, 11/2002–2003.

37   Liberal religions have adapted some of it into their vocabulary in an effort to be considered
properly "cultured" and "scientific."

Materialism, while not necessarily monolithic in the understandings of its adherents, is basically the opinion that the only reality that we exist in is a physical (natural) one, and science is the only method to arrive at truth.

This ideology gives many an illusionary and false sense of security in a moral system that is based on science alone, supposedly embracing people with the respect that they deserve while omitting the dangerous and divisive dogmas that are contained in religion. Followed to its logical conclusions, however, the dogma that this philosophy contains can lead to the dehumanization of humanity—quite the opposite effect that an ideal morality is capable of producing.

First, we consider the idea that, with naturalism, the possibility of a belief in racial superiority is impossible. Philosopher Erik Wielenberg says, "Naturalism is devoid of these dangerous ideas. As there is no God, there is no group of people who have been singled out for special attention."[38] Wielenberg's position does not clearly exclude such moral crimes as eugenics, since eugenics is not a religious doctrine and yet does endorse the superiority of one group. The United States has its own history of eugenics, but where it really was used for immense evil was Nazi Germany, a place that, before the war, was considered the pinnacle of civil society. Nazi Germany used their idea of naturalism to conclude that Jews (and others) were an inferior race. They didn't get this from a holy book; they got it from "science."

Along these lines, Rabbi Jonathan Sacks explains the moral impenitence that is natural to naturalism:

> *These—or so it seems—are the only alternatives: to deny the power or goodness of God or to deny the existence of unjustified evil. The first view, that of Karl Marx, says simply that there*

---

38   Erik J. Wielenberg, *Value and Virtue in a Godless Universe*, p. 150. The context of the quote was preceded by an example of (Islamic) suicide bombers (p. 149), and after the passage I quoted, he writes: "The naturalist rejects the divisive cry of 'no God but ours' (which always excludes more people than it includes) and replaces it with a cry of 'there is no God to help us; we're all in this together,' which applies to all human beings." Therefore, he was not only speaking in the abstract but also in application.

is no God. There is, therefore, no reason to expect that history will be anything other than the tyranny of the strong over the weak, of might over right, of "the will to power" over the will of the good. Justice is (as Plato's Thrasymachus argues in The Republic*) whatever serves the interests of the most powerful. This is a world of Darwinian natural selection. The strong survive. The weak perish. Homino homini lupus est, "Man is wolf to man." Nietzsche was its greatest exponent. For him, words like kindness, compassion, and sympathy were either disingenuous or naïve. There is nothing in nature nor in the untutored human heart to lead us to confer on others a moral dignity equal to our own. We do what is in our interest and what we can get away with. All else is an illusion, wishful thinking. There is no justice because there is no judge.*[39]

Second, if naturalism is the correct world view, then what is qualified to assign humanity a greater degree of value over animals or any other beings? If there is no God, there is no coherent answer to this question. In fact, we already see this ideology being played out when Peter Singer, Professor of Ethics at Princeton University, labeled the using of animals for the benefit of humanity "speciesist."[40] Furthermore, animal rights extremists[41] will also maintain that there is no difference between humans and animals.[42] This (naturalism—influencing and inflecting society) is why tragically, when many people are asked if in a situation where they could only save a human stranger or their dog, many say that they don't know which one (or worse, say they would save the dog)! The prophet Hosea alluded to this moral-inverted thinking when he wrote, "They say, 'Slaughter human beings; kiss calves.'"[43]

---

39   Rabbi Jonathan Sacks, *To Heal a Fractured World*, p. 21.
40   Peter Singer, *Practical Ethics*, p. 58.
41   Such as PETA, for example.
42   In fact, they are more likely to favor the animal than their meat-eating peers.
43   Hosea 13:2. "Some people (PETA) believe that eating animals is akin to the mass murder of people. Unless you have a religious basis to believe humans are made in God's image and animals are not, there is no reason to save people over dogs" (Dennis Prager, *Multiculturalism's*

Third, one of the severe, but not as damaging consequences of naturalism is the limitations on intellectual inquiry, limiting thought to merely considering the material. Professor John Haught articulates this problem well in his book, *Is Nature Enough*:

> *The promise of explaining all of the great "mysteries" of life in terms of the economical notion of reproductive success is hard to resist. It has led to the cult of "universal Darwinism" and the belief that natural selection is the bottommost foundation of all the manifestations of life. This exclusionary singleness of mind, however, may be compared to explaining the fire in my backyard by leaving out as completely irrelevant the fact that "I want marshmallows." If we can reach a simpler explanation at the level of the fire's chemistry, why bring up the fuzzy idea I would want something to eat? If one can explain why we have ears, eyes, and brains in terms of natural selection, why bring up the possibility that a transcendent creative principle of care wants the universe to become sensitive, conscious, and responsive? Would not such a proposal violate Occam's razor? Occam's razor, I must point out, was never intended to suppress layered explanation as such, even though this is exactly how naturalists often tend to slice up the world with it. If life were as simple as the evolutionary naturalists think it is, then of course Darwinian explanation would be adequate. Theological explanations of life would be superfluous. But William of Occam said explanations should not be multiplied unless they are necessary. Sometimes multiple layers of explanation are necessary for deep understanding. So there is no justification, either in Occam's maxim or in science itself, for arbitrary closing off of the road to explanatory depth.*[44]

---

war on Western values, SM40). Also see Rabbi Zalman Sorotzkin, *Insights into the Torah*, vol. 4 (*Bamidbar*), p. 23.

44   John Haught, *Is Nature Enough*, p. 19.

He writes furthermore regarding the absurdity of the certainty that nothing beyond the material exists: "Consequently, there is something immediately unseemly about the naturalist claim that nature is all there is. For how could one know that reality ends at the boundaries of nature unless the naturalist's own mind has also quietly extended beyond that of the limit? Can the mind know a limit as a limit, G.F. Hegel and others philosophers have asked, unless the same mind has already somehow—courageously—transcended that limit?"[45] His point is: "The naturalistic view of reality, if taken consistently, leads to the self-subverting of all truth claims, including those of science."[46] Toward the end of his book, Professor Haught deals the knockout blow to naturalism:

> *Is it possible in principle to give a fully naturalistic account of the mind's imperative to be responsible and at the same time declare in effect that the rest of us must adhere to the naturalist's rigid ethic of knowledge? Why is not the ethic of knowledge underlying the whole naturalistic project no less subject to naturalistic debunking than a religious ethic? The catch is that if the roots of the imperative to be responsible are ultimately biological, then the ethic of knowledge and the postulate of objectivity are themselves also exposed as purely adaptive, derived ultimately, for example from selective pressures on gene populations. If biology provides the deepest available justification for the postulate of objectivity and the naturalistic ethic of knowledge—and to the evolutionary naturalist why would it not?—then, once again, I want to know why I should pay any attention to it at all. The irony here is obvious, and it is fatal to the whole enterprise of naturalism. For why should anybody obey the postulate of objectivity if, like all other ethical postulates, science has figured out that the ultimate source of the imperative to be responsible is an*

---

45   Ibid., p. 42.
46   Ibid., p. 18

unconscious drive by our genes to get into the next generation, or if not precisely that, at least some other purely natural process?[47]

Finally, even though some people would like to think science and religion are in a mutually exclusive conflict,[48] the truth is that in the majority of cases, science does not conflict with religion; usually they are independent, different (not mutually exclusive) ways of explaining what is going on in the world in which we live. Certainly, there are conflicts that are irreconcilable regarding religion and science, but that does not mean all religion (or science for that matter) must be jettisoned due to the incompatibility of some issues. Furthermore, this does not mean that they are incapable of complimenting each other, as most often they do. Paul Diner points this out well in *Religion and Morality: an Introduction*:

> *Third, moral philosophers not totally enamored with reason point to the fact that reason is incapable of resolving conflicts between moral theories. MacIntyre's thesis that reason cannot bring different moral values into agreement may be right; rational principles do not resolve conflicts. Rationality does not remove partiality. Leslie Newbigin notes that we cannot rationally criticize a truth claim except on the basis of some truth claim totally accepted without question. He cites Michael Polanyi as one of the first scientists and philosophers to call attention to the inevitable subjective element in all knowing; pure objectivity or rationality is probably nonexistent, for all human knowledge involves the commitments of fallible*

---

47   Ibid., p. 153.

48   Take, for example, Sam Harris in *The Moral Landscape* (p. 10), where he says: "My goal is to convince you that human knowledge and human values can no longer be kept apart. The world of measurement and the world of meaning must eventually be reconciled. And science and religion—being antithetical ways of thinking about the same reality—will never come to terms. As with all matters of fact, differences of opinion on moral questions merely reveal the incompleteness of our knowledge; they do not oblige us to respect a diversity of values indefinitely."

human beings...Fifth, moral philosophers distrusting reason point out that reason seldom stands alone; reason depends on communities, traditions, and world views (metaphysics). A pure rationality without any presuppositions does not exist. As D.Z. Phillips says, "We do not have reason for our values, our values are our reasons."[49]

Regarding the desired "proof" of religious truth claims, C. Stephen Layman makes a good point in *Is Goodness without God Good Enough?*:

I shall employ a philosophical method that contrasts sharply with Descartes'. The alternative method, or something similar to it, has often been employed by philosophers. I think Aristotle typically employs it, so I'll call it the Aristotelian method. This method gives the benefit of the doubt to enduring widely held beliefs. It assumes that such beliefs are apt to have "something going for them." They should be rejected if they prove to be sufficiently problematic, but they are not to be jettisoned simply because they can be doubted. Nor should they be rejected simply because they cannot be proved. (Note that even the natural sciences presuppose some beliefs of this type—among them, the belief that the five senses are reliable.) Of course, under scrutiny, it might turn out that some enduring, widely held beliefs conflict logically with others, or with propositions that are firmly established even if not (or not yet) widely held (such as some well-established scientific theories). Then we will need to make adjustments in our belief system.[50]

In conclusion, I would like to point out a role of motivation that religion inspires and naturalism is not capable of embracing. In naturalism, a person is a victim of the biological hand dealt to him.[51] In religion

---

49 Paul Diner, *Religion and Morality: An Introduction*, pp. 37–38.

50 C. Stephen Layman in Robert K. Garcia & Nathan L. King (eds.), *Is Goodness without God Good Enough?*, p. 50.

51 Hence the ever-increasing lack of holding immoral people accountable for their actions; we will delve into this in the sections below.

(at least within monotheism), a person is able to transcend his nature with the help of appealing to a higher power. The *Sefas Emes* relates the Hebrew word *"neis,"* miracle, to the word *"nisayon,"* moral test, explaining that both involve a transcending of nature.[52] Rabbi Shubert Spero beautifully articulates how a religious perspective enhances one's ethical capabilities:

> *The teaching of Rabbi Akiva...now takes on an even greater significance: "Beloved is man, for he was created in the image (of God). An even greater sign of love is that it was made known to him that he was created in the image of God." If man has been given knowledge that he was created in the image of God, then it is indeed a sign of great love, for it inspires man to live morally, to redress injustice, to help the needy. In the words of Buber: "The fact that it has been revealed to us that we are made in his image gives us the incentive to unfold the image and in so doing imitate God."...What is the relationship between one's conception of the nature of man and one's moral code? The Humean contention that one cannot logically deduce an "ought" from an "is" statement would lead us to deny that there can be any beliefs about human existence B and any moral judgments M such that to affirm B and reject M, or vice versa, would result in a formal, albeit logical, connection of some sort...For what morality tells me is not merely that something must be done, but that I must do it. If morality, therefore, is the science of what men ought to do as men, then surely the question of "What is man" must be relevant to morality!...Another writer has suggested that the existential premises contributed by religion are not part of the reasoning processes that go within the realm of moral discourse. They may, however, be related to that realm on another level. Let us paraphrase an example offered by Toulmin:*

---

52   *Sefas Emes, Vayeira.*

Q. Why ought one to do what is right anyway?

A. That is a question which cannot arise, for it is to query the very definition of 'right' and 'ought.'

Q. But why ought one to?

A. Because it is God's will.

Q. And why ought one to do His will?

A. Because this is the way that we can realize ourselves as human beings created in the image of God and become more God-like.

The point is that after "the resources of ethical reasoning are exhausted," religious explanations may still be appropriate in that they "help us to embrace" moral duties and "feel like accepting them."...Yet, having said all this we can and must at the same time affirm the proposition that morality for Judaism is "nothing less than a three-term relationship involving man, his human neighbor, and God himself."...When I accept my duty, I do so with the awareness that I have an obligation. But who am I? I am man created in the image of God. When I respect my neighbor as a center of consciousness, creativity, and rationally, I do so because I realize that God is the ultimate ground of all value, I recognize in my neighbor a self likewise created in the image of God. And when I realize that my particular relationship to my fellow human being urges upon me a certain action that I recognize as morally right, I decide to do right because it is right but at the very same time joyously embrace it as the "way of God" and all that it entails. To conclude with a familiar metaphor: "Rules of life are the twigs; moral virtues are branches; the moral personality is the trunk; and the root is the Divine likeness which God set in the mind of man."[53]

---

53   Shubert Spero, *Morality, Halakha, and the Jewish Tradition*, pp. 88–91.

III: INDIVIDUAL (PERSONAL) ADVANTAGES
TO DIVINE MORALITY

In this section, I will discuss how a belief in God (hence God-based morality) is pragmatically (and philosophically) superior to the alternative of a secular morality. Before I begin this section, I want to reiterate that an individual atheist can be more moral than a person who is a theist. The ramifications of the ideology of secularism leaves its adherents, however, at an undeniable disadvantage. It is this disadvantage that I will be covering in this section and the sections to follow.

(1) Motivation

In *To Heal a Fractured World*, Rabbi Jonathan Sacks explains how, due to the rational consequence of atheism, hope would be illogical and non-existent:

> *The first difference is hope. The sociologist Peter Berger called hope a signal of transcendence...Where does hope come from? Unlike pleasure, pain, aggression, and fear, hope is not a mere feeling, something we share with non-human forms of life. Nor does it exist in every possible culture. It comes from a specific set of beliefs; that the universe is not blind to our dreams, deaf to our prayers; that we are not alone; that we are here because someone willed us to be and that our very existence is testament to the creative force of love...Hope and tragedy do not differ about facts but about interpretation and expectation. But they make a moral difference. Those who hope, strive. Those who are disillusioned, accept. In that respect, they are self-fulfilling prophecies. A morality of hope lives in the belief that we can change the world for the better, and without certain theological beliefs it is hard to see where hope could come from, if not from optimism. Optimism and hope are not the same. Optimism is the belief that the world is changing for the better; hope is the belief that, together, we can make the world better. Optimism is a passive virtue; hope is an active one. One needs no courage to be an optimist, but it takes a great deal of courage to hope.*

The Hebrew Bible is not an optimistic book. It is, however, one of the great literatures of hope.[54]

For an illustration about how relevant this is in molding behavior, Thomas D. Williams makes a stinging observation: "I'm sure you have known people who have turned their lives around, overcome vices, become better wives or husbands, and started taking their responsibilities seriously after a religious conversion. But how many people have you known that straightened out their lives because they discovered *atheism?*"[55]

(2) Structure for the Ethical Life

As mentioned above, one of the flaws of secularism is that it does not have a system in place to mold a person into a routine of ethical consistency. Rabbi Jonathan Sacks details this difference:

"Philosophy has tended—not always, but often—to present ethics as the problem of What and Why: What should we do, and why should we do it? Interesting though these are, they are not the major issue in the history of humankind. The real question is: What does it take to make people moral given all the distractions, temptations, and alternatives that our complex natures constantly throw in our path. If ethics were as simple as it is portrayed in some textbooks—empathy, sympathy, the disinterested spectator, doing your duty, obeying universal rules, or acting so as to maximize beneficial consequences—then how is it that for most of history, corruption, injustice, deceit, exploitation, violence, and war have been real and present dangers? If ethics are so easy, how does it turn out to be so hard? The short answer is that there is nothing inevitable about human virtue. Marx, Darwin, Freud, Rene Girard, and others remind us that there are other forces at work: conflicts of interest, competition for scarce resources, latent hostilities, and

---

54   *Fractured World*, pp. 165–66.
55   Thomas D. Williams, *Greater than You Think*, p. 19.

potential aggression. The moral sense is a flickering flame in a strong wind: hard to light, easy to extinguish. A philosophical treatise on ethics bears the same relationship to the ethical life as a medical textbook does to being healthy. Health is less a matter of what we know than how we live—what we eat, how we exercise, how we handle stress—and unless we develop healthful habits, practiced daily, all the medical knowledge in the world will not save us from ourselves...We become ethical not just by what we know, but also by what we do.[56]...

It is not the difficulty of divorce that gives marriage its power in Judaism, but the intricate and very often beautiful rules, customs, and traditions with which it is surrounded...Even the apparently non-rational laws known within Judaism as "statues"—commands, like the prohibition against eating milk with meat, wearing clothes made of mixed wool and linen, and not sowing a field with diverse kinds of seed—have a clear logic in terms of respecting the boundaries of nature, the ecology of creation...Far too little attention has been paid to the role of ritual in the moral life—in fact, I can't recall a single book on the philosophy of ethics that mentions it. Yet it makes a difference—sometimes all the difference—by turning abstract rules into living practices that, in turn, shape ethical character. The fact that each day I must pray, give money to charity, and make a blessing over all I eat and drink; that once a week, however busy I am, I must stop and spend time with my family and community; that once a year, during the High Holiday Days, I must atone for my sins and apologize to those I have offended; these things transform life. Would I apologize to those I wronged were it not a sacred duty? Without prayer, would I consciously recall, each day, that there are those to whom I am accountable—God, humanity, my ancestors who prayed the same prayers and entrusted their hopes to me?

---

56 *Fractured World*, pp. 168–69.

I don't know. All I can say is that ritual is to ethics what physical
exercise is to health. Medical knowledge alone will not make me
healthy. That requires a daily discipline, a ritual—and religion
is the matrix of ritual.[57]

On top of the ethical structure religion gives to one's lifestyle,
a religious society can also be a source that inspires, facilitating ethical behavior that one might not pursue otherwise. This observation
is made by Robert D. Putnam and David E. Campell: "In other words,
compared to nonreligious people, people involved in religious networks
behave more generously, in part because they are asked more often by
the people they meet in those religious networks to give and volunteer
for secular causes, as well as for religious causes."[58]

Finally, as pointed out by the *Nesivos Shalom*: "Secular education seeks
to ensure that one's ethical and moral training will remain with him
even when no one is looking and when he is beyond the reach of the law
and authorities. In short, the purported goal is to grant the intelligence
dominance over the threatening emotional drives. The underlying goal
of all of this, however, is not intrinsically related to character refine-
ment per se; it is no more than a means to an end."[59]

(3) Objectivity in Assessing Character

Rabbi Yisrael of Salant said, "People question God, but are certain
of themselves. They should rather be certain of God, and question
themselves." It is certainly and tragically true that people have (and
will) abuse religion for their perverse agendas and moral recklessness.
However, true as this is, it does not negate the fact that the objective set
of principles that religion offers dwarfs the option of a person assessing
his own character. This point is brought out well by Paul Johnson in
Intellectuals:

---

57   Ibid., pp. 170–71.
58   Robert D. Putnam and David E. Campell, *American Grace—How Religion Divides and Unites*
      Us, pp. 475–76.
59   *Nesivos Shalom, Nesivei Chinuch*, p. 106.

Over the past two hundred years, the influence of intellectuals has grown steadily. Indeed, the rise of the secular intellectual has been a key factor in shaping the modern world. Seen against the long perspective of history, it is in many ways a new phenomenon. It is true that in their earlier incarnations as priests, scribes, and soothsayers, intellectuals have laid claim to guide society from the very beginning. But as guardians of cultures, whether primitive or sophisticated, their moral and ideological innovations were limited by the cannons of external authority and by the inheritance of tradition. They were not, and could not be, free spirits, adventurers of the mind. With the decline of clerical power in the eighteenth century, a new kind of mentor emerged to fill the vacuum and capture the ear of society. The secular intellectual might be deist, sceptic, or atheist. But he was just as ready as any pontiff or presbyter to tell mankind how to conduct its affairs. He proclaimed, from the start, a special devotion to the interests of humanity and an evangelical duty to advance them by his teaching. He brought to this self-appointed task a far more radical approach than his clerical predecessors. He felt himself bound by no corpus of revealed religion. The collective wisdom of the past, the legacy of tradition, and the prescriptive codes of ancestral experience existed to be selectively followed or wholly rejected entirely as his own good sense might decide. For the first time in human history, and with growing confidence and audacity, men arose to assert that they could diagnose the ills of society and cure them with their own unaided intellects; more, that they could devise formulae whereby not merely the stricter of society, but the fundamental habits of human beings could be transformed for the better. Unlike their sacerdotal predecessors, they were not servants and interpreters of the gods, but substitutes. Their hero was Prometheus, who stole the celestial fire and brought it down to earth.[60]

---

60   Paul Johnson, *Intellectuals*, pp. 1–2.

(4) Ethical Responsibility
and the Ramifications of Determinism

One of the most distinctive disadvantages of the atheistic world view is the scientific naturalism/materialism that it implies. It is difficult, on the one hand, to hold us up to a higher standard than animals, while at the same time preaching that we are no different from them. One of the great rabbis of this past century, Rabbi Yitzchak Hutner, said the great heresy of his day[61] was the behavioral psychology of determinism.[62] He said the reason he was so opposed to it was because it sought (quite effectively) to take away a person's free will, thus eliminating his responsibility for his actions.

John G. West, in *Darwin Day in America*, lays out numerous examples of what Rabbi Hunter was referring to:

> *Freudians who applied psychoanalysis to crime were explicit about the material nature of the drives that determined human behavior and ruled out free will. "The source of the instincts is our physical condition, the chemical-physical state of our body," wrote Freudian physician David Abrahamsen in Who Are the Guilty? published in 1952. Abrahamsen demonstrated how the psychoanalytical approach to crime could be just as reductionist as a strictly biological approach. Offering up story after story to show that criminals are largely the victims of their unconscious drives, Abrahamsen argued that "the criminal very rarely knows completely the reason for his conduct. Only when he has learned about himself (specifically through psychoanalysis) will he become aware of his motivations." Discussing the case of a teenage boy who repeatedly stole cars ostensibly "to get even with people," Abrahamsen shared*

---

61   Which has continued into ours. For a current example: "All of our behavior can be traced to biological events, about which we have no conscious knowledge: this has always suggested that free will is an illusion...Many scientists and philosophers realized long ago that free will could not be squared with our growing understanding of the physical world. Nevertheless, many still deny this fact" (Sam Harris, *The Moral Landscape*, p. 103).

62   Rav Shlomo Wolbe also writes this in *Alei Shor*, vol. 2, pp. 437–38.

how psychoanalysis revealed the real cause of the boy's crime. Under the professional guidance of Abrahamsen, the boy came to understand that he stole cars so that he could search for the mother he never knew. At an even deeper level, Abrahamsen came to believe that "a car in itself had a meaning" for the boy because "in a symbolic way it represented his mother. Since he could not get her, he had to have a substitute, and a car was that substitute. Hence, his thrill every time he drove the car; hence, his continuous stealing."

While Abrahamsen acknowledged that "to the average reader such an explanation may seem farfetched," he assured his readers that "clinical experience shows that a car often stands for a woman." His evidence for this claim? "In daily language, we often call a car 'she,'" and, "when we have the tank filled with gasoline we say, 'Fill her up!'"[63]...Behavioral psychology made no apologies for describing human beings as completely determined by their heredity in conjunction with environmental conditioning.[64]..."Nearly all psychologists believe that behavior is completely determined by heredity and environment," noted John Staddon, professor of psychology at Duke University during the 1990s. "A substantial majority agree with Skinner that determinism rules out the concept of personal responsibility. This opposition between determinism and responsibility is now widely accepted, not just by behaviorists but by every category of mental-health professional."[65]...Debate over Powell displayed with peculiar clarity the tension between the traditional legal system and the modern philosophy of scientific materialism. The traditional legal system was based on the assumption that most people had some ability to choose whether or not to commit crimes; thus, those who committed crimes were regarded as morally

---

63   John G. West, *Darwin Day in America*, p. 56.
64   Ibid., p. 57.
65   Ibid.

blameworthy and deserving of punishment. Scientific materialism, by contrast, presumed that all behaviors could be reduced to material causes, rather than free choices of the individual; according to this view, it was unclear whether anyone could ever be considered "morally blameworthy" in the classical sense.[66]

Rabbi Jonathan Sacks poetically identifies Abraham[67] as an archetype example of how to overcome the determinism that is so pervasive today:

The call to Abraham is a counter-commentary to the three great determinisms of the modern world. Karl Marx held that behavior is determined by structures of power in society, among them the ownership of land. Therefore, God said to Abraham, "Leave your land." Spinoza believed the human conduct is given by the instincts we acquire at birth (genetic determination). Therefore, God said, "Leave your place of birth." Freud held that we are shaped by early experiences in childhood. Therefore, God said, "Leave your father's house." Abraham is the refutation of determinism. There are structures of power, but we can stand outside them. There are genetic influences on our behavior, but we can master them. We are shaped by our parents, but we can go beyond them. Abraham's journey is as much psychological as geographical. Like the Israelites in Moses' day, he is travelling to freedom.[68]

Finally, Professor Keith Ward addresses how this materialism is not limited to the domain of action, but thought as well:

In asking what might give, we might point to what are probably the weakest points of the reductionist theory—the claim that I am wholly determined to believe whatever I do believe, and that new information or thought can make no difference, as

---

66 Ibid., pp. 72–73.
67 Beloved by the three major monotheistic religions.
68 *Fractured World*, p. 145.

meaningful information or logical thought, to what I believe. It seems more plausible to think that I may have genetically based predispositions to form certain sorts of beliefs, but that new sensory information, consciously considered, can modify or direct these predispositions in various ways.[69]

IV: SOCIETAL ADVANTAGES TO DIVINE MORALITY

In this section, I discuss how having a morality based on the Divine is more advantageous for society than a secular based one. Even though this is a separate section, there will be some overlap between the point made for the individual and the society at large.

(1) Divinity—the Best Safeguard for Justice

Rabbi Jonathan Sacks explains how justice is best served to humanity:

The existence of a covenant with God means that all human sovereignty is delegated, conditional, and constitutional. This gives rise to the principles of crimes against humanity and justified civil disobedience. If there is a conflict between the laws of humans and the law of God, the latter take priority. This is the greatest single safeguard against tyranny, totalitarianism, and the rule of might over right. It is also the principle that brought into being one of the great moral institutions of humankind: the prophet, the world's first social critic. The man or woman who "speaks truth to power" does so on the specific mandate of God Himself. Plato wanted to ban poets from his ideal republic because they were subversive of the established order. The Israelite prophets took as their mission to be subversive of the established order, whenever they saw the corruption of power…God alters the equation without Himself being changed. Divine ownership of the world means that the worldly goods we enjoy, we do not own, we merely hold in trust. Hence the concept of tzedakah, charity-as-justice,

---

69   *Morality, Autonomy, and God,* pp. 7–8.

becomes possible in a way it would not if there were absolute human ownership.[70]

Finally, he frames his point succinctly and concisely: "A world without a Judge is one in which there is no reason to expect justice. The human condition becomes a tragic script in which ideals prove to be illusions, revolution a mere change in places in the seats of power, and the ship of hope destined to be wreaked by the cold iceberg of reality."[71]

(2) The Value of Human Life

One of the great advantages to a God-based morality is that it lacks the devastating disadvantage of a culture of scientific materialism and naturalism. Basil Mitchell brings the potency of the difference to light in *Morality: Religious and Secular*: "The first question is best answered in relation to particular examples, and the obvious one to take first is the one selected by Hampshire, respect for human life. Hampshire uses the expression 'sanctity of human life' and asks how its use can be justified: 'The question cannot be evaded: What is the rational basis for acting as if human life has a peculiar value, quite beyond the value of any other natural things.'"[72] He writes further:

> *Some people might, of course, think otherwise; they might, for example, attach more importance to pleasure and avoidance of pain than to self-determination, and this would reflect fairly fundamental differences in their philosophy of life. Perhaps one can concern a complete difference of approach in relation to abortion. Those who regard the fetus as entirely at the disposal of the mother seem to be committed to denying it any share in human status, and this might be because, for them, experiences are more important than persons. If you attach importance primarily to the person as such you will be impressed by the continuity between the fetus and the person it is to become*

---

70 *Fractured World*, p. 167.
71 Ibid., p. 173.
72 Basil Mitchell, *Morality: Religious and Secular*, p. 122.

(if, that is, you do not regard it as a person already). If you attach importance to the person chiefly as the subject of experiences and could always be replaced by another potential bearer of experiences. Thus a woman whose ethic is experience-oriented will feel justified in terminating an inconvenient pregnancy and having a child at a more convenient time, whereas one whose ethic is person-oriented will not.[73]

A frightening example of where scientific/naturalistic materialism can lead is perhaps best highlighted by an article written in the *Journal of Medical Ethics* published by a couple of Italian philosophers questioning the legitimacy of opposition to "after-birth abortion" (read: infanticide). The crown jewel was the comment made by the editor of the publication in response to the response of indignation by much of the readership regarding the article (he of course defended it):

As Editor of the Journal, I would like to defend its publication. The arguments presented, in fact, are largely not new and have been presented repeatedly in the academic literature and public fora by the most eminent philosophers and bioethicists in the world, including Peter Singer, Michael Tooley, and John Harris in defense of infanticide, which the authors call after-birth abortion...What the response to this article reveals, through the microscope of the web, is the deep disorder of the modern world. Not that people would give arguments in favor of infanticide, but the deep opposition that exists now to liberal values and fanatical opposition to any kind of reasoned engagement.[74]

Along the same lines, but in a slightly different format: If there is no God, how can one condemn the ethical positions of Peter Singer,

---

73   Ibid., p. 131.
74   "Liberals Are Disgusting": In Defense of the Publication of "After-Birth Abortion," February 28, 2012, by Julian Savulescu (ed.), BMJ Group, responding to Alberto Giubilini and Francesca Minerva, "After-birth abortion: why should the baby live?" *Journal of Medical Ethics*, published online February 23, 2012.

who has expressed righteous indignation over the U.S. military using dolphins to clear mines rather than expose the actual soldiers to the destructive devices?[75] After all, that's just plain speciesist!

(3) Motivation for a Caring and Compassionate Society

One of the advantages to a society based on religion is that it is more conducive to giving charity and looking after other people. As Robert Putnam and David Campell explain: "In other words, compared to non-religious people, people involved in religious networks behave more generously, in part because they are asked more often by the people they meet in those religious networks to give and volunteer for secular causes, as well as for religious causes."[76] If you look at the hospitals, soup kitchens, and volunteer organizations helping out the less fortunate at home and abroad, you will notice that there are some secular people who help out, but the founding and maintaining of such operations is primarily the domain of the faithful. The undeniable truth is that while there are certainly secular people who are involved in charity and civic welfare, the structure of inculcating these values to the next generation has a distinct advantage via a religious framework.

(4) The Society of Rights or the Society of Responsibility

While it is true that a secular society based on responsibility is possible, it is predominantly the ideology of religion-based systems that focus on responsibility (i.e., obligations) rather than rights. What do I mean by responsibility over rights? In practice, they accomplish the same result. However, the mentality that focuses on responsibility over rights is immeasurably superior to the lifestyle that focuses on rights rather than responsibility.

In general, a society that is based on secularism is more interested in the rights of the individual than the obligation of its citizens. On the flip side, in general, religious societies are prone to focus more on

---

75   Peter Singer, "Dolphins have no part in this dispute with Iran," *The Guardian*, January 19, 2012.

76   Putnam and Campell, *American Grace*, pp. 475–76.

obligations than rights.[77] Rabbi Jonathan Sacks explains the difference that the focus makes on society:

> *Rights are passive. Responsibilities are active. Rights are the demands we make on others; responsibilities are demands others make on us. A responsibility-based culture exists in the active mode. It emphasizes giving over receiving, doing not complaining. What is wrong with what Mary Ann Glendon calls "rights-talk" is that it draws on resources that only exist if we recognize responsibilities. It puts the cart before the horse. It neglects the moral commitments we need to create if rights are to be honored at all. Rights are the result of responsibilities; they are secondary, not primary. A society that does not train its citizens to be responsible will be one in which, too often, rights-talk will be mere rhetoric, honoured in the breach, not the observance.[78]*

Even the United States—where rights are given a major premium—appeals to God's authority and providence in order to counteract the flaws of a purely rights-based system. Dennis Prager quotes Thomas Kidd: "Thomas Kidd summarized Alexis de Tocqueville, the great nineteenth-century French observer of America, on this matter: 'The partnership of religion and liberty lay at the heart of America's political success...Freedom by itself would inexorably degenerate into rabid selfishness, but religion nurtured the purposefulness of freedom.'"[79]

V: HOLINESS—BEYOND ETHICS

Despite the fairly recent attempt by academia and animal-rights activists to minimize the unique role humanity has been dealt, most people would admit there is something unique and elevated about

---

77 Keep in mind, when people are following their obligations, by nature the rights of others are enforced.

78 *Fractured World*, p. 183.

79 Dennis Prager, *Still the Best Hope*, p. 323; Thomas Kidd, *God of liberty: A Religious History of the American Revolution*, pp. 245–46.

the human condition. In fact, even most secularists expect a distinct behavior difference between humanity and the animal kingdom.[80] The question is, if scientific materialism is true, other than intelligence, what does distinguish us from animals? The religious answer is that a human has a soul and was created for and with a purpose. One of the primary ways of achieving this goal is to separate ourselves[81] from our animal instincts and utilize our free will to become closer to God.

The following is primarily taken from a Dennis Prager lecture on how holiness elevates humanity.[82] His material is taken from Jewish law and practice, but certainly similar themes can be found in the other monotheistic religions:

> *Ethics and holiness are not the same thing. An act can be ethical, but not holy; it cannot, however, be holy, but unethical. During the 60s, ethics came to be represented by the idea: "As long as it does not hurt anyone, it is acceptable." A person can eat like a pig at the dinner table, burying his head in his food; he is not hurting anyone, but this is still not considered civilized behavior. If a person goes to the bathroom in a public park, it is not hurting anyone, but it is still widely regarded as unacceptable. There are a plethora of possibilities where a person can engage in behavior suitable to an animal, not hurt anyone, and still be regarded as disgusting. If we are just animals, what is so wrong about acting like one so long as no one gets hurt? The truth is, even for (most) people who consider humanity to be animals with two legs instead of four, there are certain expectations, and we expect humans to act with dignity.*
>
> *Holy means different, separate, distinctive. Modern life has warred against the idea of separateness. [Dennis Prager expressed that] the older he gets, he realizes that morality,*

---

80   Despite the pervasive language of grouping humans with "other animals."

81   The Hebrew word for "holy" is "*kadosh*," which means "separate," i.e., to separate from.

82   "The Case of Holiness: Why Ethics Is Not Enough," R61.

decency, and democracy are all predicated upon the idea of separateness; and the opposite of democracy is when you end all separateness. In Jewish life, you see one of the manifestations of distinction in the separation of life and death: the kosher law of not eating meat (representing death) with milk (representing life); Kohanim[83] are not allowed to be within proximity of the dead (with certain exceptions); niddah, the separation of a couple after the woman has a period (blood = death, intercourse = life); the kosher law about not having a blood spot (death) on an egg (life). Judaism[84] affirms that there are differences between men and women.[85] These differences, however, do not mean that one is better than the other but serve to complement each other—the one's strengths filling in for the other's weaknesses and vice versa. When these differences are maintained, there is unity in male-female relationships. It is important to recognize the distinction (i.e., separation) between the Creator and the created.

Finally, the differences and distinctions between people and animals are being obliterated. When people say, "people and other animals," it serves to lump people with animals. Whatever we share with the animals (e.g., eating, procreating), Judaism has the most laws concerning [them].[86] The purpose of many of Judaism's laws is to raise us from the animal to the Divine.[87] God does not say, "Be good because I, Hashem, am good." He calls humanity to a higher standard: "Be holy for the Lord your God is holy."

---

83   Priests in the Biblical sense, not the modern conception of pastor or minister (though there are some similarities).

84   As well as other monotheistic religions.

85   Actually, until fairly recently, this was common knowledge for non-monotheists as well.

86   Eating, for example: what, when, and how we eat; also marital relations.

87   As Dennis Prager has mentioned in numerous lectures and on the radio: Religion teaches we are "made in the image of God." Now (because of secular societal teachings), we make man in the image of the animal.

On top of this, even regarding the actions that secular society condemns, Jewish law goes further to elevate morality beyond what directly harms people. Rabbi Shubert Spero, Irving Bunim, and Dennis Prager, to name a few, give telling descriptions of how Jewish law (insert morality) transcends the basic ethical code:

We know that both Torah law and secular, civil law often deal with the same areas that prohibit the same crimes. Torah law, however, follows the concept of a crime down to its roots and through all of its possible manifestations. In secular law, we have first-degree murder, second-degree murder, manslaughter, involuntary manslaughter, and so forth. But only in Torah do we find the Rabbinic teaching that insulting or shaming a man in public is also [akin to] murder. When you make him blush or blanch in embarrassment and mortification, you have, in effect, "spilled blood." You have "assassinated" character. This, too, is murder. In secular law, cases of stealing are classified as grand larceny, or petty larceny, according to the value of stolen goods. In Torah's ethic, the prohibition "You shall not steal"[88] also forbids a theft call[ed] geneivas daas, lit., "stealing someone's mind," which means creating a false impression. If, for example, you ask a shopkeeper for the price of something you have no intention of buying, you are also guilty of stealing, in a sense, for you create in the shopkeeper the false impression that you wish to buy the object in question. As a result, he treats you with a certain deference and esteem and gives you information to none of which you are entitled. You have "stolen" something intangible from him.[89]

But over and above the devastating social consequence of evil speech, there is another reason why the rabbis view this vice with such horror. Judaism believes the power of speech and the capacity to form language to be a uniquely human

---

88   Exodus 20:13.

89   Irving M. Bunim, *Ethics from Sinai*, vol. 1, pp. 26–27.

property related to man's having been created in the image of God. If the spark of divinity in man is associated with something in his spiritual makeup (mind, self-consciousness, ego, personality, freedom of will), then speech must be seen as that wondrous tool by which man can break out of his isolation, express his thoughts and feelings, and communicate with others. Even God is described as breaking forth into creativity and ultimately into revelation by means of the word: "And the Lord said…" What is so heinous about evil speech is that a person takes a priceless and unique gift—the Divine-like power of verbal conceptual expression that can be used to build authentic relationships between man and man, and between man and God—and abuses it.[90]

Speech is another example. In our increasingly secular world, fewer and fewer attempts are made by people to elevate their speech. That is why public cursing is now much more prevalent. In most ballparks and stadiums, one hears language shouted out that would have been unimaginable a generation ago. Sanctifying speech is another religious value; it is not a secular value. Whenever I see a vehicle with an obscene bumper sticker, I am sure of only one thing: The owner of that vehicle does not regularly attend religious services.[91]

VI: RELIGIOUS MOTIVATION FOR ETHICS

One of the things criticized almost as often as the Bible is the motivations of the people who try to live up to what the Bible expects of them. The primary reason for this is the secular effort to mitigate the contributions religion plays in engendering religious communities' stellar achievements in kindness. Not only is being ethical with less than admirable motivations not a reason to discount the ethics of such

---

90   Shubert Spero, *Morality, Halakha, and the Jewish Tradition*, p. 146.
91   Dennis Prager, "We are not just animals: Judeo-Christian values part XV,"…dennisprager. com, Prager's Column, Tuesday, June 14, 2005.

people, but the very critics who level this argument are guilty of also being ethical for ulterior motives.[92] "What reason can religious moralists give to be moral? Hell, they've got lots of reasons. Eternal bliss for being moral, and eternal damnation for not being immoral."[93]

Even if people stay in line ethically due to a desire for Heavenly reward or fear of Divine punishment, their lifestyles are still ethical. Spiritually, they may need some further development in their maturity, but pragmatically they are still following the rules and contributing to a better world. If you were starving (not just hungry, literally starving), and the person offering you food and drink is doing it to score brownie points in Heaven, would you really care? In fact, in a certain way, it could be better. As a motivating factor, there is certainly stronger incentive once a person considers Divine reward.

Secular people are just as capable of being ethical for less than pure motivations. How many stories are we aware of where a boy joins a charity cause to impress his female target? How many people have we heard of who give substantial donations to worthy causes as a method of trying to gain a better social image? How many people have there been who have joined charities as a means toward financial gain (connections and the like)? The domain of ulterior motives is not relegated to the religious by any means.

Another reason to be moral is...reason. Professor Keith Ward articulates this point well: "Belief in the objectivity of reason does make a difference to our perception of what morality is. If there is a supremely rational creator of the universe, who embodies in himself all the perfections of truth, beauty, and goodness, and invites us to share in these perfections to the extent that we can, then—even without consideration of rewards and punishments hereafter—we shall have the strongest motivation for committing ourselves to the rule of reason, which will be the rule of God, in our lives."[94]

---

92   Albeit different ones, and ones to which religious people are also vulnerable.
93   Walter Sinnott-Armstrong, *Morality without God*, p. 119.
94   Keith Ward, *Morality, Autonomy, and God*, p. 27.

Still, some further points need to be addressed regarding this subject: Walter Sinnott-Armstrong delivers the criticism of invalid religious motivation with the following parable:

> *Several religious traditions require tithing.[95] When tithing is commanded as a strict duty, whose fulfillment is rewarded by Heaven and whose violation is punished by Hell, then it should not be surprising that many believers tithe and that their motive is often (though not always) their own self-interest. Forced gifts, however, bring no moral credit. Imagine that an employee gives a donation to his boss's favorite charity only because his boss told him that he would be promoted if he donated and fired if he didn't. Does this donation show that the employee is morally good? Of course not, partly because he would have donated even if he despised the beneficiaries. This employee might have donated to that charity even without the boss's promises and threats, but that is hard to tell after the promises and threats are made. More generally, we cannot be sure who deserves moral credit when donations are forced. The same goes for religious people. If they donate to charities after they have been promised Heaven for donating and threatened with Hell for failing to donate, then it is not clear whether they deserve moral credit for donating, because their motives are clouded. Probably most religious believers would donate to the same charities without the promises and threats, but which ones would do so is hard to tell once they believe in such extreme promises and threats.[96]*

In any relationship, there is a possibility of self-interest. If a husband does not give his wife an anniversary present, will he be in the dog house? Yes. If he gives her a gift that far exceeds her expectations, will he be "in Heaven"? Yes, he will. Does the fact that there are possible positive and negative consequences for his actions negate his desire to

---

95   Leviticus 27:30.
96   *Morality without God*, p. 46.

do something for his wife because it is the right thing to do? No, it does not. Self-interest and doing the right thing for the right reasons are not mutually exclusive. How about the morality of children? If a child is punished for wrongdoing and rewarded for correct behavior, does this automatically render the child incapable of acting morally without ulterior motives? The answer is clear that it does not. Divine reward and punishment function in much the same way;[97] the intention of reward and punishment is to be used as a tool to give us extra incentive for proper behavior. Finally, it is not hard to tell what motivates a person (religious or secular) once you get to know him, no matter how extreme the consequences are for his actions.

Another objection to religious-based ulterior motives is raised by Dan Barker: "Mother Teresa added, 'I think the world is much helped by the suffering of the poor people.' So much for theistic compassion!"[98]

His claim is essentially that many religious people want human suffering in order to accumulate brownie points. Besides being vile, this character assassination of Mother Teresa (and others) is also ridiculous. The sad fact is that currently human suffering is a part of this world. As unfortunate as that is, her observation was that the opportunity for the world to try to relieve suffering is a positive benefit of there being poor people. Mother Teresa was saying that the world becomes a better place and people become better people when we help the poor. Did Barker really think that Mother Teresa was so sadistic as to desire the suffering of people because it gives people the opportunity to improve themselves by helping others? If this shallow accusation was true, why would she be trying to make things better?

Sam Harris is convinced that obedience to God and supernatural reward prevent the faithful from trying to improve this world: "Because most religions conceive of morality as a matter of being obedient to the word of God (generally for the sake of receiving a supernatural reward),

---

97   Obviously on a different scale.
98   Dan Barker, *Godless*, p. 215.

their precepts often have nothing to do with maximizing well-being in this world."[99]

This clumsy and baseless accusation of Harris reveals that his ignorance of Scripture is sublime, and his lack of awareness of religious communities' devotion to wellbeing in this world is on par with his Biblical impairment. For one who is even tangentially familiar with the Bible, it is common knowledge that the prophets of Scripture demanded social justice in many different facets. If one would merely listen to a conservative radio station for one day, the ample evidence contrary to Harris' claims would be enough to make his statement laughable.[100]

Though this is consistent with the previous mentioned fallacies, because of the slight variation, I wanted to give it separate treatment. Walter Sinnott-Armstrong says: "The conflict arises only because infiniphiles (or infiniphiliacs?) love the infinite so much that they deny that finite goods, harms, and lives have any meaning at all in the face of eternity. The problem with infiniphilia is that it robs us of any incentive to improve this finite world."[101]

It is a clear and observable fact that most of the faithful who are "obsessed" with the infinite are not less prone to have incentive to improve this finite world. The reason is that while they think about and look forward to their eternal reward, they still live in this finite world, and their Infinite God has told them of the Divine expectation to improve this world! Perhaps a person will find a few exceptions that deviate from the norm of their religious community and accept inauthentic religious teachings or pervert the interpretation of Scripture beyond recognition. However, just as many (if not more) people have perverted secular philosophy[102] as justification for living a nihilistic and selfish lifestyle. The argument for the damage done by people obsessed with the finite, material world could certainly be made much stronger.

---

99   Sam Harris, *The Moral Landscape*, p. 63.
100   If not for his animosity, and the sad fact that some people will be in agreement with it.
101   *Morality without God*, p. 128.
102   According to ethical secularists.

Finally, I can't speak for Christianity or Islam, but I assume that both religions teach and encourage doing moral actions for reasons other than receiving Divine reward and punishment. However, I can speak for Judaism, which teaches that keeping commandments for the ulterior motives of reward and punishment is considered a substandard outlook, and the person with that outlook is encouraged to change. The Jewish texts teach that a person must serve God primarily for His (God's) sake, i.e., out of gratitude for all God has done,[103] and not for any reward.[104] The critic may then proceed and object that being moral because it is God's command is also a form of ulterior motive for doing the right thing.[105] However, this objection also fails for the simple reason that, for a religious person, morality for its own sake and because God commanded it are interchangeable. Therefore, it is not self-interest.

The argument of the critic that religious people only are moral for their own self-interest, and are, therefore, immoral, ultimately fails on three counts. First, even if it were true that religious people were motivated by pure self-interest, it is still desirable[106] because society benefits greatly from it. Second, even if a person has personal gain for being moral, that does not mean it is the only motivation for his behavior. Being moral for altruistic reasons and personal gain are not mutually exclusive. Third, there are a number[107] of authoritative sources that teach the ultimate expectation of the elevated spiritual person is being ethical "*lishmah*," for its own sake.[108]

VII: CONCLUSION

Professor Keith Ward sums up the essence of this chapter well: "There is a morality that may be founded on human sympathy together with cool self-love, and recognition of the necessity of a cohesive society for

---

103 *Chovos Halevavos, shaar Avodas Elokim.*
104 *Avodah Zarah* 19a; *Pirkei Avos* 1:3; *Rambam, Mishneh Torah, Teshuvah* 10:4.
105 See Harris' comment quoted above.
106 Albeit not the highest level of morality.
107 At least within the Jewish tradition.
108 For an excellent lecture on this topic, listen to: Rabbi Dr. Dovid Gottlieb, "Religious Motivation and Altruism 1," Jerusalem Echoes, tape G42, www.DovidGottlieb.com.

the secure pursuit of most of our interests. Yet, we may be left feeling that this rather comfortable morality lacks the resources for passionate resistance to injustice or for real self-sacrifice for the sake of others. At least for many people, including some of the great moral heroes of history, morality has an objectivity and seriousness that such a morality cannot encompass, which requires a more transcendent source if it is to be truly compelling. That is a good reason for seeking a view of morality that is more than hypothetical and naturalistic, that commands rather than serves our natural desires, and that centers on an ideal that is worthy of human devotion and commitment."[109]

While I know there are many who disagree,[110] there is a lot of truth to the words of James Boylan Shaw: "Morality without religion is a tree without roots; a stream without any spring to feed it; a house built on the sand; a pleasant place to live in till the heavens grow dark and the storm begins to beat."

While it is certainly true that there are ethical secularists, it is equally true that the path ahead for an exclusively secular society is not a pretty one. Although people can be motivated to be ethical without religion, can we really expect the same steadfastness without the support of an ethical system that transcends humanity when the storm of human weakness will test it? Even without the threat of the storm, I have demonstrated that a moral system based on religion is superior to that of secularism both philosophically and pragmatically. As Professor Ward says: "A non-theistic morality need not be less obligatory than a theistic one. But theism provides a metaphysical context that gives moral claims a different character, a clearer objectivity and authority, and a distinctive form of motivation (love for the supreme perfection of a personal God) that is rarely found in non-theistic views. Theism, in other words, will support and complement, but not replace the normativity of moral obligation and the objectivity of moral goodness."[111]

---

109 *Morality, Autonomy, and God*, p. 45.
110 Take for example, Dan Barker: "Humanism is not just better than the Bible—the Bad Book—it is the only way we could be moral," *Godless*, p. 202.
111 *Morality, Autonomy, and God*, p. 112.

I have attempted to balance this chapter with solid philosophical depth and a user-friendly format. This is a very formidable challenge. On the one hand, I want to give an in-depth treatment to very important issues, but at the same time I limited some of the discussion for the sake of the reader. I am not naïve enough to think I have exhausted the topic and covered all the details in the religion vs. secularism debate in one chapter—something that can't even be done in one book. What I do hope to achieve, however, is to make a persuasive argument and give food for thought on how a central belief in God is imperative for a healthy society and for the good of individuals as well. In *To Heal a Fractured World*, Rabbi Jonathan Sacks points out that there is a lot of literature debating whether or not a person has to be religious to be moral. "They fail, however, to touch on a real issue, namely: What difference does religion make to the moral life even if we concede that you don't have to be religious to be moral?"[112]

Professor Keith Ward, regarding the purpose of his book, *Morality, Autonomy, and God*,[113] nicely sums up the purpose of this chapter: "I conclude with the claim that theism gives objectivity, authority, effectiveness, and hope to morality that no secular view can match. Nevertheless, humans can know what is good without believing in God, and morality can exist without religion. My claim is not just that there is one thing, morality agreed by all, to which some would add peripheral religious beliefs. Rather, theistic morality is in principle different to secular morality, and may reasonably claim to incorporate a peculiarly penetrating view of human nature and its ills."

It is no secret that great atrocities have been committed in the name of religion. One of my major motivations for the undertaking of this work is the perspective of many people that the Bible is the primary force causing evil and violence in the world. Yet, religion (and the Bible) has been exploited by unholy people for unholy purposes. While it is tragic that this has and does occur, it still does not invalidate the truth or the value of Scripture. Science and politics also share with religion

---

112 *Fractured World*, p. 165.
113 *Morality, Autonomy, and God*, p. xvi.

different instances where noble goals were hijacked by wicked people who abused the system in order to serve their own goals—goals that were achieved at the expense of others, including others' lives.[114] And, yet, we haven't seen a call to forsake science or political structure of any kind. David B. Hart articulates this point well when he observed:

> *Does religious conviction provide a powerful reason for killing? Undeniably it often does. It also often provides the sole compelling reason for refusing to kill, or for being merciful, or for seeking peace; only the profoundest ignorance of history could prevent one from recognizing this. For the truth is that religion and irreligion are cultural variables, but killing is a human constant...I maintain only that to speak of the evil of religion or desire its abolition is, again, as simpleminded as condemning and wanting to abolish politics.*[115]

This should ring as self-evident, but I feel that I need to point out that religion has also been a force that has been utilized to transform the world for the good in unparalleled ways. One has only to reflect on how many orphanages, alms houses, hospitals, schools, shelters, relief organizations, soup kitchens, medical missions, and charitable aid societies owe their founding and preservation to a group of people whose religious convictions compelled them to build and maintain such institutions. While it is true that secular and humanist people also perform these charitable acts, the fact remains that an overwhelming majority of the organizations in which they participate, if not currently faith-based, likely stem from religious roots.[116]

---

114 The following quote from Professor Howard Ellens, Biblical Interpretation at Auburn Theological Seminary, would be comical if it were not for the fact that he is actually serious: "Until modern times, virtually all warfare was explicitly religious. Even in modern secular societies, wars of national interest are given a patina of religious justification. No one, it seems, wishes to kill others and risk being killed themselves without justification by the highest authority in the universe" (J.H. Ellens [ed.], *The Destructive Power of Religion*, vol. 3, p. 265).

115 David Bentley Hart, *Atheist Delusions*, p. 13.

116 In addition to all this, the number of religious people who are involved in these charitable

May our children live in a time when the Bible and religion are never abused. Until this utopia is achieved, however, it is important to keep the words of Keith Ward in mind: "There is no conceivable system of religion or political thought that has no potential dangers. The most we can do is to find the most adequate internal checks against those dangers being realized. But when economic and social affairs are in crisis, nothing on earth can prevent humans from misusing any system whatsoever."[117]

SUMMARY

While it may not have the label "Natural Law," there is such a concept found in the teaching of the Bible. However, this concept is nuanced and different from the traditional understanding of the philosophical term "Natural Law." Scientific naturalism (or materialism) is very limiting of human potential and negates the uniqueness of the human condition. We also debunked the theory that scientific ideology makes a person immune to elitist positions. We further mentioned that a purely materialist worldview puts a limit on intellectual inquiry. We discussed how science and religion may have some conflicts, but they certainly are not mutually exclusive, and often they complement each other very well.

We covered the general topic of individual (personal) advantages to Divine Morality, offering some specifics that show where the advantages are to be found. First, we covered motivation, explaining how a purely materialistic universe does not have the capability to produce hope. Next, we moved onto structure for an ethical life. We discovered that secularism does not have a system in place to mold people's ethical behavior. After that, we covered objectivity in assessing character; we learned that, without a Divine, objective set of standards, it is very difficult for people to overcome their biases and interests.

In the final sub-section for Section III, the idea of ethical responsibility and the ramifications of determinism were covered. We saw that

---

deeds **likely** dwarfs the number of people who are secular or humanist who are involved in such things.

117 Keith Ward, *Is Religion Dangerous?*, p. 64.

the logical follow-through of scientific naturalism is that we are just advanced animals and that we, in essence, have no free will. How this is problematic for stable ethics is self-evident.

Next, we delved into another general topic of our discussion: the advantages of Divine morality on a societal level. First, in this section, we argued that Divinity is the best safeguard for justice. We learned that a world without a judge is a world very susceptible to shaky justice. Next, we spoke out some of the concerns that a society that does not believe human life is special is a society that has very little regard to the value for human life, and considered some of the nasty ramifications that such a view entails. In the last sub-section of this section, we showed how a society based on monotheistic values produces a unique motivation for caring and compassion, whereas in a scientific/naturalism worldview, one is compassionate despite his ideology, not because of it.

In the next section, we discussed how holiness is something unique to religion that secularism does not provide. We learned that we don't just expect people not to "not act bad" but to also live in a dignified and elevated manner.

In the final section in the chapter, we analyzed the accusation leveled at religious people that they only act morally for the ulterior motive of fear of Divine punishment and desire for Divine reward. In the final analysis, we came to the conclusion that this accusation is flawed on a number of premises. First, even if it were true that religious people were motivated by pure self-interest, it is still desirable because society benefits greatly from it. Second, even if a person has personal gain for being moral, that does not mean it is the only motivation for his behavior. We also covered that acting moral for altruistic reasons and personal gain are not mutually exclusive. Third, there are a number of authoritative sources that teach the ultimate expectation of the elevated spiritual person is being ethical "*lishmah*," for its own sake.

EPILOGUE

n the introduction to this book, I presented a methodology for learning Scripture in the most authentic fashion. I then supported my contention that the approach of Orthodox Judaism to understanding the *Tanach* (Bible) is the most accurate method. I also laid out a foundation for how to follow the rest of the material in the book, and provided a background to appreciate the style of the structure that followed.

In Chapters One through Three, I covered a myriad of topics germane to different contemporary issues that are rooted in the Bible. I often found patterns within different verses containing a common thread by which to understand why such drastic measures were put into place. I also provided historic and textual context to address the moral accusations leveled against different parts of the Bible. In some cases, I showed there were no issues at all; rather, the indictment was based on a misreading of the text. In other instances, I was able to mitigate the severity of perceived extremism with the proper understanding of the episodes through the teachings of the Sages. In many cases, I was not only able to show that the commandment was not immoral but that it was actually practical and preferable.

In Chapter Four, I made the argument that morality independent of God is not only a subjective morality at best but is also detrimental to the moral roots of the individual as well as society in general. The moral framework provided by God's expectations of humanity as practiced by the monotheistic religions enhances not only society but the individual as well. Furthermore, I demonstrated the negative effects of a secular-based morality, both on society and the individual as well (not to mention the philosophical weakness of the secular worldview). Finally, with parts of this chapter combined with Appendix B, I was able to refute the philosophical attacks on a God-based morality as well as expose the philosophical weaknesses of the alternative.

To sum it all up, I am not naïve enough to expect that people will read my book and change their world view overnight. I also appreciate many will read my book and will still maintain that the Bible is morally outdated and archaic. What then did I hope to achieve by writing this book? For the skeptics, I would certainly love for them to be completely persuaded by my arguments; however, I would be very content if what I wrote in this book would at least give such people serious pause. I would hope that they would, in the very least, come away with the understanding that the Bible cannot be addressed in a superficial fashion and that honest dialogue about the Biblical texts requires one to approach the text with more open-minded analysis. For the believers, I would hope that they gain a deeper understand of the Bible, and, through this understanding, a deeper relationship with the one who gave it—God Almighty!

A CRITICAL EXAMINATION OF ARGUMENTS OFFERED BY GAY ACTIVISTS

W hen considering the arguments of gay activists, it is, on the one hand, important not to judge gays for having a homosexual orientation, and yet, on the other hand, essential that we must understand that tolerance for the agenda and arguments of the activists is unwarranted both within the realm of Biblical morality and logically consistent application. The reason I bothered adding this appendix is that, although many gay people (take Dave Rubin or Douglas Murray, to name a couple of well-known personalities) are for gay marriage but are opposed to activists pushing acceptance of gay lifestyles as normative on people who don't wish to see it (gay lifestyles) mainstreamed. Many activists are not satisfied with equal rights but also push for others to be forced to respect their lifestyles. I address the arguments given for the forced mainstreaming of the gay lifestyle.

From the standpoint of Biblical law, the prohibition of homosexuality is not relegated to desires but rather the person acting on those desires.[1] Rabbi Aharon Feldman writes about this eloquently:

---

1   See *Rambam, Mishneh Torah, Issurei Biah* 1:14 and *Sanhedrin* 54. Under this prohibition,

Judaism looks negatively at homosexual activity, but not at the homosexual. Whatever the source of his nature, whether it is genetic (the Torah does not express any view on the matter), is immaterial. The nature in no way diminishes or affects the Jewishness of a homosexual. He is as beloved in God's eyes as any other Jew, and is as responsible as any Jew in all the mitzvos (commandments). He is obligated to achieve life's goals by directing his life towards spiritual growth, sanctity, and perfection in his character no less than any other Jew.[2]

Although this letter was directed to a Jew, the truth is that the idea that it is the homosexual activity that is taboo, and not the person who has such desires, includes gentiles as well. Rabbi J. David Bleich echoes the words of Rabbi Feldman when he says: "The homosexual act is a matter quite distinct from the state of homosexuality. The former is an act governed by free will, while the latter is a state of being. The former can be proscribed; the latter may well be beyond a person's control. It is the act, rather than the psychological state, which is the subject of the Torah's admonition."[3]

Before I go into the arguments, another point that needs to be taken into consideration is that the homosexual individual has the additional challenge of remaining loyal to God and abstaining from acting on his sexual desires. In the words of Rabbi Aharon Feldman: "In his [the homosexual person's] specific case, God has given him a special obligation: he must refrain from sexual activity and direct his life towards Divine service. If he does so, he will be rewarded with a life filled with joy, holiness, and happiness, perhaps even more than what his heterosexual neighbor might achieve. For our joy and fulfillment

---

there is also a ban on willfully engaging in homosexual fantasy, though, of course, prohibited fantasies are not limited to homosexual ones.

2   Rabbi Aharon Feldman, *Jewish Action* 58/3 (Spring 5758/1998), p. 69. This excerpt should not be taken as evidence that Rabbi Feldman accepts the theory that homosexuality is genetic; he does not. We see this from his book, *The Eye of the Storm*, p. 233, where he writes: "Common sense as well as many case histories of individuals who have converted to heterosexuality give evidence to the contrary..."

3   Rabbi J. David Bleich, *Judaism and Healing: Halakhic Perspectives*, p. 71.

are the products of our triumph of the spirit over fleshly challenges. The challenge is greater for the homosexual, but the potential reward is commensurately greater."[4] Therefore, before I start my critique, I want to be unequivocally clear that a person who is not trying to change the Torah's expectations, but rather is earnestly struggling with fulfilling those expectations deserves not only our respect but also our admiration for his intellectual honesty and his desire to strive for a goal that is very difficult to achieve.

The arguments presented below are mainly taken from an excellent lecture by Rabbi Dr. Dovid Gottlieb dealing with the subject of gay liberation.[5]

Argument #1: The American Psychological Association voted by majority (in 1974) that homosexuality is not a disease, hence not undesirable, and hence equally valid.

Response: The question of whether homosexuality is a desired condition is a moral judgment. The American Psychological Association (APA) does not have the training or certification to make a moral judgment. Another point to ponder is that if the APA would have come to a majority vote on the other side of the issue,[6] would gay activists accept that decision? They most likely would respond by saying that personal biases, political convenience, etc., played a role in the decision, hence making the findings not objective. It should be noted that people who consider homosexuality to be an unfavorable condition are entitled to the same defense of their position.

---

4   *The Eye of the Storm*, p. 232.
5   Rabbi Dovid Gottlieb, "Homosexuals and Homosexuality," audio tape, G62. The same topic can be found at www.dovidgottlieb.com. I recommend listening to the tape if possible, because after Rabbi Gottlieb presents his material, he is challenged by a proponent of gay liberation, and his response to the man's criticism of his lecture is recorded on the tape.
6   That was the case prior to the 1970s. See Elan Karten, "Sexual Orientation Change Efforts, A Clinical Perspective," *Dialogue* (For Torah Issues and Ideas), Fall 5773/2012, no. 3: 40–41.

Argument #2: Homosexuality is a genetic condition, hence there is no responsibility, and hence homosexuality is an equally valid lifestyle.

Response: The claim that homosexuality is a genetic condition has not been verified by the scientific community.[7] However, let us assume for the sake of argument that it is conclusive that homosexuality is genetically determined. Two problems still remain:

1. Even if it is a genetic condition, that does not mean people are unable to control themselves from turning desire into action. As Rabbi Dovid Orlofsky has mentioned in numerous lectures, people are attracted to other people's spouses. Are we then to say they are morally justified to pursue extramarital relationships because they are attracted to the person in question? Not likely.

   Rabbi J. David Bleich put it more eloquently: "The validity or non-validity of the claim that homosexuality is natural rather than aberrant, or a normal state rather than an illness, is irrelevant to Jewish teaching regarding the matter. Not everything that is normal and is natural is also licit and morally acceptable. Monogamy, for example, is probably not natural to the human species...yet Western Society has commonly maintained that...monogamy represents a moral value despite the fact that a monogamous lifestyle is not dictated by emotional, physiological, or sexual impulses. Divine commandments, by their

---

7   "Scholars are not likely to come to an agreement anytime soon about the causes of sexual orientation or its nature. Various disciplines look at sexuality in different ways and rarely confront each other's ideas. In many cases, they seem to be altogether unaware of them. Biologists who review most traits as inherited, and psychologists who think sexual preferences are largely determined in early childhood, may pay little attention to the finding that many gay people have had extensive heterosexual experience, and that a fair number of straights have had some homosexual experiences. Sociologists are just as unlikely to know about, or take seriously, research on hormones or family structure. Often, they are not even cognizant of the journals in which such research is published...Short of definitive evidence, which no theory has thus far received, the disagreement is likely to continue" (Prof. David Greenberg, *The Construction of Homosexuality*, pp. 480–81).

very nature, are designed to curb and channel human desires. They are not necessarily reflective of that which comes naturally to man."[8]

2. Color blindness and Down syndrome are also genetic conditions, but no one is suggesting that they should not be regarded as undesirable because they are genetic. The fact that the medical community is actively and aggressively seeking ways to eliminate these genetic conditions illustrates the fact that their genetic cause does not mean it follows that these circumstances should be accepted.

Furthermore, Rabbi Chaim Rapoport articulates a response to another variation of this argument: "Even if we are to accept the notion that homosexuality is biologically or genetically determined, and, consequently, one could argue that 'it is God Almighty Who has made a certain percentage of people naturally homosexual,' this would not constitute reason for avoiding change. Whatever the reason may be, many of us were created with natural 'imperfections' and—given the chance—it is our responsibility to become 'partners in the dynamics of creation' by working towards perfection. By way of analogy, a person may be created with biological infertility. Yet it would not be considered wrong for such a person to endeavor, through medical procedures, to become fertile. Far from being an intrusion into God's domain, those who attempt to mend nature's deficiencies are actually responding to the Divine calling on mankind. We are enjoined by the Creator to bring 'perfection' (or *tikkun*) to those elements of creation which we find 'wanting.'"[9]

Argument #3: Homosexuality is unchangeable; therefore, we should accept it.

---

8   Bleich, *Bioethical Dilemmas*, p. 134.
9   Rabbi Chaim Rapoport, *Judaism and Homosexuality*, p. 23.

Response: There are two fundamental flaws with this line of reasoning.

1. Even though Down syndrome is considered "unchangeable," has that prevented the medical and scientific community from trying to find a cure? No, because there is still hope that eventually a cure will be discovered. (I am not comparing having Down syndrome to having homosexual desires. My only point of connection is to refute the suggestion that because something is [perceived as] unchangeable, we would, therefore, neglect to try and change it.)

2. Homosexuality may be a condition that could be changed, and science cannot verify otherwise. There are too many variables of possibilities to invalidate the possibility that homosexuality can be changed, especially if the resources of the medical and scientific community were directed appropriately by people motivated to help a homosexual change his sexual inclination.

Argument #4: Because homosexuality has gained social acceptance, it is wrong to regard it is an undesirable condition.

Response: When homosexuality was considered an undesirable condition on a wide social scale, would that have made it (then) an undesirable condition according to the gay activists? Of course not! The entire motivation for their movement is founded on the premise that the previous social understanding was flawed. It should be quite clear that "social acceptance" is a relative litmus test and should not be used to determine what is, in reality, a good or a bad thing.

Argument #5: Homosexuality is not an undesirable condition because it is an isolated condition. That is to say, it does not cause societal dysfunctions like murder, robbery, etc.

Response: Not everyone agrees that homosexuality does not create societal dysfunction (they are not suggesting that the dysfunction is crime; the suggestion is that it does have a negative impact on others). The experts have not come to a unified conclusion on the issue. Therefore, to pretend that no respectable experts in the field claim that homosexuality creates societal dysfunctions is intellectually dishonest. Second, even if it were true that homosexuality creates no societal dysfunction in its condition, this ignores the point that homosexuality is, in and of itself, considered an undesirable condition (by those who think it is—so the argument is circular). Dennis Prager often makes an interesting point on his radio show and in his lectures: All things being equal (yes, clearly a hypothetical situation, for the purpose of making a point), is it preferable for children to have a mother and a father instead of two mothers or two fathers, or does it make any difference at all? For most people receptive to having a two-way conversation, this point would give a person pause.

In conclusion of this section, it is noteworthy to understand that one of the facets that make the discussion of the topic of homosexuality so potentially volatile is that many gays identify their same-sex attraction as an inherent part of their personality. Therefore, it should not come as a surprise that they are very sensitive and sometimes have reactions perceived as an overreaction with regards to legitimate criticism of homosexuality. Nevertheless, it is also important to keep in mind that, before the nineteenth century, most cultures looked at homosexuality as something one could do, not something one could be. The Bible does not subscribe to the ideology of "you are what you are; be proud of it," rather the Torah commands us to constantly try to transcend our nature and become better. To label a person a "homosexual" is inappropriate because you are identifying a person only according to his sexual desires and (perhaps) activities. Homosexual should not be a noun but rather an adjective that describes a person's sexual activity. (For the sake of convenience, I have labeled people with homosexual desires as "homosexuals," though I strongly feel it is important to be cognizant of the point just mentioned.)

This appendix is necessary because gay activists (by and large) are not asking for compassion or even acceptance, but are instead demanding that society accept their view of homosexuality as a normal kind of human sexuality. Even with all of the sensitivity and consideration that we must apply toward individuals, the actual acceptance of homosexuality as a valid lifestyle is an impossibility for a person who embraces the Divinity of the Bible. As Dr. Benzion Sorotzkin put it, "One component of compassion is being non-judgmental. It is unfortunate, though, that many people equate refraining from being judgmental with avoiding forming a judgment."[10]

In summary, if a person's reference to himself as homosexual is a term limited to his sexual desires and actions, then that person remains an undifferentiated member of society, and, if Jewish, part of a Jewish community. Such a person need not feel excluded from the community any more than anyone else struggling with other aspects of Torah observance who feels at home in the community while individually dealing with his personal struggles with Torah observance. The clash should only arise if a person flaunts and advocates his (homosexual) lifestyle choice with the intention, expectation, or goal that Jewish religious institutions will change their ideological position and conform to a set of moral standards that are not only outside of the Torah, but entirely against its teaching, in order to appease this person and his agenda.

---

10   Benzion Sorotzkin, "Same-Sex Attraction: Beyond the Rhetoric," *Dialogue* (For Torah Issues and Ideas), Fall 5774/2013, no. 4: 225.

PHILOSOPHICAL ADVANTAGES TO DIVINE-BASED MORALITY

THE EUTHYPHRO DILEMMA

will start with the most-often invoked argument against Divine Command Theory (belief that what God decrees is moral by definition) known as the Euthyphro argument. It is noteworthy that philosophers of religion, both theist and atheist, always cover this fundamental topic on the issue of morality and religion,[1] even the atheist philosopher Erik J. Wielenberg said in his book, *Value and Virtue in a Godless Universe*, "I have yet to encounter a discussion of the relationship between God and ethics that does not at least allude to the Platonic dialogue *Euthyphro*."[2] Yet, in the books of the "professional atheists" (aka, New Atheists), their moral criticisms of religion never even mention the Euthyphro argument.[3]

---

1   See Brian Davies (ed.), *Philosophy of Religion—A Guide and Anthology*, p. 635; Eleanor Stump and Michael J. Murray (eds.), *Philosophy of Religion: The Big Questions*, pp. 417–27 ; Norman Kretzmann, "Abraham, Isaac, and Euthypro: God and the Basis of Morality," pp. 417–27; William J. Wainwright, *Religion and Morality*, p. 65; Erik J. Wielenberg, *Value and Virtue in a Godless Universe*, p. 65.

2   *Value and Virtue*, p. 65.

3   See Christopher Hitchens, *God Is Not Great*; Richard Dawkins, *The God Delusion*; Dan Barker,

The Euthyphro Dilemma is one of the main arguments used to argue against Divine Command Theory.[4] Wikipedia gives a good summary of this issue:

> *The Euthyphro dilemma is found in Plato's dialogue Euthyphro, in which Socrates asks Euthyphro: "Is the pious...loved by the gods because it is pious, or is it pious because it is loved by the gods?" As Leibniz presents this version of the dilemma: "It is generally agreed that whatever God wills is good and just. But there remains the question whether it is good and just because God wills it or whether God wills it because it is good and just; in other words, whether justice and goodness are arbitrary or whether they belong to the necessary and eternal truths about the nature of things."[5]*

There are two "horns" to the dilemma: The first one is that which is right is commanded by God *because it is right*, and the second horn is that which is right is right *because it is commanded by God*. Rabbi Jonathan Sacks has some insight on the dilemma in general worth quoting in whole:

> *Plato's dilemma is elegant because it forces us to make a choice between two invidious possibilities: religion is either opposed to ethics or superfluous to it. In fact, however, Plato's dilemma belongs to a particular time and place, Athens in the fourth century BCE. The culture of Plato's day was mythic and polytheistic. The gods fought and committed appalling crimes. Kronos castrates his father Uranus, only to be murdered by*

Godless; Sam Harris, *End of Faith* and *The Moral Landscape* [a book about ethics!]; Daniel Dennet, *Breaking the Spell*; and R.D. Gold, *Bondage of the Mind*.

4   Even so, it is not popular with all critics of Divine Command Theory. Erik Wielenberg said of it [Euthyphro Dilemma]: "I hope to distinguish myself from many of Craig's atheist opponents by not triumphantly advancing the moldy Euthyphro problem as a deathblow for Divine command theory!" William Lane Craig, Erik Wielenberg, "A Debate on God and Morality: What is the best account of objective moral values and duties?" Adam Lloyd Johnson (ed.), p. 44, fn. 22.

5   See http://en.wikipedia.org/wiki/Euthyphro_dilemma.

his son Zeus in return. Greek myth is amoral or pre-moral, and what Plato represents is one of the earliest attempts to think morally by breaking free from the mythological past. Looking back with the hindsight of history, we can see that for Plato, to be moral was to liberate yourself from the world of myth—much as Abraham, in Jewish tradition, could only arrive at truth by breaking his father's idols. In their different ways, Abraham and Plato were both iconoclasts. In Judaism, the Euthyphro dilemma does not exist. God commands good because it is good. Without this assumption, Abraham's challenge over the fate of Sodom—'Shall not the Judge of all the earth do justice?'—would be incomprehensible. God and humans are equally answerable to the claims of justice. But the good is what God commands because God-the-lawgiver is also God-the-creator-and-redeemer. Morality mirrors the deep structure of the universe that God made and called good. Plato's challenge arises because the Greek gods were not creators. Material was eternal. The gods had no special authority except for the fact that they were held to be powerful. Plato was therefore correct to challenge the popular cults of his day by, in effect, drawing a principled distinction between might and right. The gods may be strong, but that is no reason to invest them with moral authority. For the Bible, however, God who teaches us how to act in the world is also the maker of the world in which we act. This means that in monotheism, morality means going with, not against, the grain of the cosmos and history. God Himself empowers His prophets to challenge kings—even Himself—in the name of justice and mercy. To be sure, there are occasions—most famously, the binding of Isaac—in which God seems to demand pure obedience; but this itself suggests that the story must be more subtle than it seems. Taken as a whole, Judaism embodies Divine faith in the moral capacity and literacy of humankind.[6]

---

6   Rabbi Jonathan Sacks, *To Heal a Fractured World*, p. 164.

We will return to some of the points Rabbi Sacks brought up further on. First, I would like to explain why, in his view, the Euthyphro Dilemma is not a challenge to Judaism (or monotheism in general).

"That Which Is Right Is Commanded by God Because It Is Right"

(1) **The acceptance of Divine commands as the criterion of what we ought to do requires a prior moral standard.** This line of attack has been taken by Kai Nielsen, P.H. Nowell-Smith, Keith Campbell, and A.C. Ewing, and is mentioned as well by Robert Merrihew Adams. It carries the implication that morality cannot be fundamentally dependent on God and his commands, as Divine-Command Morality claims.[7]

There is a concept that God created humanity with an inborn knowledge of right and wrong (to a certain extent, some would call this "Natural Law"; it is discussed in the first part of Chapter Four). This being the case, following written commands does not require a non-Divine command to precede it. In other words, another possible response is that God's moral views are logically prior to any other ethical system. Theists who contend that God created everything conclude that God is therefore responsible for all possible sources of ethics as well. So, if a secular ethic (the first horn above) exists, it is secondary to religion because God created the conditions necessary for that source of ethics.[8] As Professor John M. Frame explains:

> Remember that God's Word is his self-expression. God's goodness is a goodness which is exhaustively self-expressed; and God's self-expression is his entire self-expressed character, his goodness. So, contrary to Euthyphro, neither Word nor goodness comes before the other; the two are correlative. There is nothing in God's nature which His Word does not express; and there is nothing in His Word which lacks truth. So, God's

---

7   Janine Marie Idziak (ed.), *Divine Command Morality*, pp. 13–14.

8   "Euthyphro Dilemma," Wikipedia.

goodness determines God's revelation, and God's revelation determines His goodness.[9]

(2) Sovereignty. If there are moral standards independent of God's will, then "[t]here is something over which God is not sovereign. God is bound by the laws of morality instead of being their establisher."[10]

As we learned in the section dealing with Natural Law (beginning of Chapter Four), morality predating the Written Command is not independent of God-based morality (hence Divine Command).

(3) Omnipotence. These moral standards would limit God's power; not even God could oppose them by commanding what is evil and thereby making it good.[11]

To make something evil into something good would be an internal contradiction. It would be akin to claiming God not being able to make a "square circle" is a limitation to His power. Just as the second case is a contradiction in terms, and is clearly no threat to God's power, so too the first case fails to challenge God's Omnipotence.

(4) Freedom of the will. Moreover, these moral standards would limit God's freedom of will; God could not command anything opposed to them, and perhaps would have no choice, but to command in accordance with them.[12]

This would only be true if one accepted the limitation of this horn, i.e., that God is limited by an external morality. In truth, most traditional forms of modern philosophy reject both horns as they are conceptualized.[13]

(5) Morality without God. If there are moral standards independent of God, then morality would retain its authority even if God did not exist. This conclusion was explicitly (and notoriously) drawn by early-modern political theorist Hugo Grotius: "What we have been

---

9   John M. Frame, *Euthyphro, Hume, and the Biblical God*, accessed October 3, 2012, https://bit.ly/3mvPDFK. I should note that I don't agree with everything Professor Frame says in his article; I only agree with what I quote (primarily the first two-thirds of the piece).

10   "Euthyphro argument," Wikipedia.

11   Ibid.

12   Ibid.

13   See Anselm, Augustine, Aquinas, Rabbi Jonathan Sacks, Avi Sagi, and Daniel Statman.

saying [about the natural law] would have a degree of validity even if we should concede that which cannot be conceded without the utmost wickedness, that there is no God, or that the affairs of men are of no concern to him." On such a view, God is no longer a "law-giver" but, at most, a "law-transmitter" who plays no vital role in the foundations of morality. Non-theists have capitalized on this point, largely as a way of disarming moral arguments for God's existence: If morality does not depend on God in the first place, such arguments stumble at the starting gate.[14]

The argument from the theist is that there is an inborn ability to rationally know what is right or wrong (to a certain extent) that preceded the Written Command (i.e., the giving of the Law). However, the theist never claimed that there are moral standards independent of God. The theist believes that the "intuitive morality" also comes from God; it is merely a different vehicle for God to express His morality.

The Second Horn: That Which Is Right Is Right Because It Is Commanded by God

(1) **Divine command ethics makes morality dependent on a Divine choice that is arbitrary.** A.C. Ewing has recently argued this point for the metaethical variety of Divine-Command Morality; this criticism has also been mentioned by the twentieth century theologian Carl F.H. Henry.[15]

One response, as pointed out by Professor Idziak, is: "Patterson Brown has developed a response based on the fact that 'God is…defined as perfect in knowledge, justice, and love.' Thus, Brown claims that God would 'by definition will in accord with these several attributes' so that 'the result would be anything but arbitrary.'"[16] As we have previously mentioned a point brought up by Rabbi Sacks (Prof. John M. Frame and other philosophers make the same point), Plato's argument was based on the assumption that the "Divine" was the gods. The Greek

---

14   Wikipedia, accessed October 3, 2012.
15   Idziak, "Divine Command Morality," pp. 14–15.
16   Ibid.

gods that Plato was critiquing were as fallible and morally subjective as the Greeks themselves were; hence the problem of possible arbitrary morality. However, in our context, the God of Israel (i.e., the monotheistic Deity) is not subject to the possibility of arbitrary morality because of His unique nature.

(2) Anything goes. This arbitrariness would also mean that *anything* could become good, and *anything* could become bad merely upon God's command.[17] God could command actions to be performed which are abhorrent and obviously immoral in character, such as murder and pointless acts of cruelty. If Divine command morality were correct, such actions would be regarded as right. This line of argument against Divine command ethics, which has a foundation in the Divine command moralist William of Occam, is mentioned by Graeme de Graff, A.C. Ewing, Ralph Cudworth, William K. Frankena, Philip L. Quinn, and Eric D'Arcy.[18]

The response to this is that morality has an objective definition. Therefore, the suggestion that God can create an illogical definition by commanding it is a logical contradiction. It is not possible for God to command something that is a contradiction in terms.

(3) Moral contingency. In other words, no action has its moral status necessarily; any right action could have easily been wrong, if God had so decided, and an action which is right today could easily become wrong tomorrow, if God so decides. Indeed, some have argued that Divine command theory is incompatible with ordinary conceptions of moral supervenience.[19]

As I mentioned previously, a lot of the "arbitrary arguments"[20] are not applicable to the monotheistic conception of God. Therefore, there is no possibility of God breaking with His Essence, meaning it is not possible to make something that is inherently morally wrong into something virtuous.

---

17   Ibid.

18   "Divine Command Morality," p. 16.

19   Wikipedia, accessed October 3, 2012.

20   They are at root the same, but with variant points based on the false premise of the nature of God being susceptible to arbitrariness.

(4) Why do God's commands obligate? So, in order for God's commands to obligate us, He must derive commanding authority from some source other than His own will...To avoid circular reasoning, one might say our obligation comes from gratitude to God for creating us. But this presupposes some sort of independent moral standard obligating us to be grateful to our benefactors. As eighteenth-century philosopher Francis Hutcheson writes: "Is the Reason exciting to concur with the Deity thus, 'The Deity is our Benefactor?' Then what Reason excites to concur with Benefactors?"[21]

The principle that God is to be loved is "known from its own terms." But to love God is to obey God. So, we know without further justification that God is to be obeyed.[22]

(5) No morality without God. Divine command theorists disagree over whether this is a problem for their view or a virtue of their view. Many would argue that morality does indeed require God's existence, and that this is, in fact, a problem for atheism. But Divine command theorist Robert Merrihew Adams contends that this idea ("that no actions would be ethically wrong if there were not a loving God") is one that "will seem (at least initially) implausible to many," and that his theory must "dispel [an] air of paradox."[23]

There can be a kind of "morality" without God.[24] For a secular person, this is a bitter pill to swallow, nevertheless, even if it may seem implausible to many,[25] that does not detract from its truth. While many secularists will fight this tooth and nail,[26] a number of prominent atheist

---

21   Wikipedia, accessed October 3, 2012.
22   This answer was given to the author via e-mail from Dr. John Hare. He based it off of a teaching of Duns Scotus. The answer to this question both within Judaism and Christianity is that God created us. This certainly is theologically a sound answer to the question. However, I am working with the premise that most of my target audience needs a more philosophically fulfilling answer; one that answers what rule, reason, or principle am I going on that would give a reason to obey our Creator.
23   Wikipedia, accessed October 3, 2012.
24   As we have mentioned at the outset, there are moral atheists.
25   We will explain why this could be in the next section.
26   In this section, I suggest why this is a hopeless fight.

philosophers have swallowed that bitter pill,[27] such as Dr. Jonathan Glover,[28] Dr. Steven Stewart-Williams,[29] Dr. Richard Rorty,[30] Jean-Paul Sartre,[31] Dr. Paul Kurtz,[32] Kai Nielsen and J.P. Moreland.[33] Even the militant atheist Richard Dawkins[34] goes as far to say, "It is pretty hard to defend absolutist morals other than religious ones."[35] To be fair, there are some religious thinkers who think an atheist is entitled to objective morality. In the rest of this section and the following one, I will demonstrate why they are mistaken.

(6) The is-ought problem and the naturalistic fallacy. According to David Hume, it is hard to see how moral propositions featuring the relation "ought" could ever be deduced from ordinary propositions, such as "the being of a God." Divine command theory is thus guilty of deducing moral "ought"s from ordinary "is"s about God's commands. In a similar vein, G.E. Moore argued (with his open-question argument) that the notion of good is indefinable, and any attempts to analyze it in naturalistic or metaphysical terms are guilty of the so-called "naturalistic fallacy." This would block any theory which analyzes morality in terms of God's will and, indeed, in a later discussion of Divine command theory, Moore concluded that "when we assert any action to be right or wrong, we are not merely making an assertion about the attitude of mind towards it of any being or set of beings whatever."[36]

By now, I am sure it will not come as a surprise that I am going to quote from Professor Frame's article:

---

27   At least part of it, some of them use the Euthyphro argument and other arguments against DCT to suggest that theists are also left without moral objectivity, i.e., "We may not have it, but neither do you!"

28   Cited from Dennis Prager, "Can we be good without God?" The Oxford Debate, CD #58b.

29   Cited from Dennis Prager, *Still the Best Hope*, pp. 345–46.

30   Dr. Richard Rorty, *Contingency, Irony, and Solidarity*, p. xv.

31   Jean-Paul Sartre, *Existentialism Is a Humanism*, p. 28.

32   Dr. Paul Kurtz, *Forbidden Fruit*, p. 65.

33   Kai Nielsen and J.P. Moreland, *Does God Exist*, pp. 97–135.

34   Richard Dawkins, "God's Utility Function," *Scientific American*, Nov. 1995: 85.

35   Dawkins, *The God Delusion*, p. 232.

36   Wikipedia, accessed May 21, 2013.

Hume's argument, you may recall, was that "you cannot deduce 'ought' from 'is.' That is, you cannot derive normative conclusions from merely descriptive premises. G.E. Moore used the phrase "naturalistic fallacy" to describe that kind of error...At the same time, Hume is right in that one may not proceed from a merely descriptive premise to a normative conclusion. That is what non-Christian ethics often does, in trying to find morality in a godless world. The attempt to derive obligation from premises about matter, motion, time, and chance is truly a "naturalistic fallacy." And that is, of course, the hopeless task which is faced by all ethical systems which reject biblical revelation....You should be prepared to answer that challenge. In other words: it is always legitimate, in ethical debate, to ask, "Where do you get your norm?" "Why ought we to do as you say?" Indeed, that is often the most important question that can be asked. It is a question that unbelieving ethics is fundamentally unable to answer. For this reason, Christians may often seem to be reasoning from description to norm. "God commanded x, therefore I must do x." Is that a naturalistic fallacy? No, because we are not passing from a merely descriptive premise to a normative conclusion. Because God's commands are supremely normative, the self-expression of God's supremely normative nature, they entail normative conclusions.[37]

Dr. David Novak gives us more insight into this discussion:

Indeed, the world of things that Hume and so many others have constituted as primary, be these things natural entities or human-made artifacts, is always within the context of interpersonal interactions. As such, we can never stop evaluating things in one way or another. It is not that "is"

---

37   Dr. John Frame, *Euthyphro, Hume, and the Biblical God*, accessed October 3, 2012, https://bit. ly/3mvPDFK. While Dr. Frame was addressing his article to Christians, this portion of his article is applicable for all three monotheistic religions.

functions independently of "ought" is constituted after "is,"
so that it must be derived from a higher state of being that
functions as a transcendental base for deduction of duties.
Instead, every "is" functions within a prior world of "oughts,"
which are personal claims. Things are found; persons claim.
Things themselves are constituted within what Husserl called
the "lived world" (Lebenswelt). This world can best be seen
as the domain of interpersonal transactions. Things that are
human artifacts or potential human artifacts ("raw materials")
are included in this realm by technology. They are useful; hence,
they are to be taken up into our place. Things that are natural
entities, which are seen as limits on human praxis to be placed
beyond human use, are included in this interpersonal realm by
pure science (theoria). They are beautiful, hence to be left to
exist in their own place. Science itself begins as an aesthetic
quest. And works of fine art (poiesis) are also inviolable
because they are imitations of this natural beauty. But the
realm of interpersonal transactions is more than technology or
pure science or fine art, or even than any combination of all
three. It always surrounds them all inclusively. No things are
ever beyond the human capacity for categorical description,
beyond the capacity for giving common names. Humans
themselves, however, receive their proper names as a call from
other persons. Only God names himself.[38]

OTHER PHILOSOPHICAL OBJECTIONS
TO DIVINE COMMAND THEORY (DCT)

(1) In Divine command morality, to determine what we ought to do, it is necessary to resort to some other ethical principle to know what it is that God commands; thus Divine command morality is in effect useless as an ethical standard. This criticism of Divine command ethics was made by Jeremy Bentham.[39]

---

38   David Novak, *Covenantal Rights: A Study in Jewish Political Theory*, pp. 23–24.
39   Idziak, p. 14.

As we discussed in the Natural Law section of Chapter Four, this objection does not account for the possibility that God "programmed" us with certain inclinations and rational capabilities to realize that following the Divine will is in our best interest. Also, this criticism makes the mistake of assuming DCT is relegated to the written expression of God's will. I will argue it is not.

(2) Divine command morality reduces ethics to a matter of power. This objection has been most forcefully argued by D. Goldstick, and is mentioned as well by Anthony Flew and A.C. Ewing.[40]

While it is certainly true that God's power could be a more compelling reason to "stay in line" than that of secular morality, I have never seen it argued from a religious perspective that the argument from God's power is the reason for Divine moral objectivity. Why would it be? It is a formidable challenge to see if someone can come up with a prominent theologian who suggests God gets His moral objectivity from His power. The "because God said so" comes from the objectivity, not some theory of "might makes right."

(3) Divine command ethics represents an infinite form of morality in that it is deontological and heteronomous in character. This criticism of Divine command morality has been offered by P.H. Nowell-Smith. The apparently heteronomous character of Divine command ethics has also been discussed by W.D. Falk, Graeme de Graaff, and Phillip L. Quinn.[41]

"Deontological" means a form of ethics that focuses on obligations rather than ends or goals to be achieved. God's commands were certainly given for the benefit of man, not God. The point of DCT is an understanding of where we get our obligations from, not what they accomplish. Therefore, DCT does not deny that commandments have a benefit beyond just doing what you are told. (However, the ultimate point of commandments is to establish a relationship with God to the person who follows them. So, it could be argued that the

---

40   Ibid., p. 16. See also Kai Nielson, "Morality does not imply the existence of God," in Brian Davies (ed.), *Philosophy of Religion—a Guide and Anthology*, p. 670; Professor Patrick Nowell-Smith, "Morality: Religion and Secular," in Eleonore Stump and Michael J. Murray (eds.), *Philosophy of Religion: The Big Questions*," p. 404.

41   Idziak, pp. 16–17.

"deontological argument" fails here as well. This is the case because keeping the commandments because you are told to fulfills the "ends" or "goal" of connecting to God.) "Heteronomy" (lit. "other-law") means that man does not legislate for himself but accepts another's authority. Heteronomy is a term invented by the German philosopher Immanuel Kant. He felt this was an issue because it conflicted with his version of morality. However, a typical, traditional theist may ask: "What's wrong with being accountable to God?"[42]

(4) Divine command morality is theologically unacceptable because it does not permit a coherent account of the moral attributes of God to be formulated. This objection has been constructed by William K. Frankena, but most extensively studied by Robert Merrihew Adams and Phillip L. Quinn.[43]

Adams formulates the problem in this way: It is doubted that God, as an agent, can properly be called "good" in the moral sense if He is not subject to a moral law that is not of His own making...Adams responds to this criticism by suggesting a meaning for the statement "God is good" that he believes to be compatible with Divine command morality.

(5) Morality cannot depend solely on Divine commands, since nothing can be good, just, or the like without possessing the nature (i.e., defining properties) of goodness, justice, etc.[44]

The underlying premise of this argument is going on the assumption that goodness, justice, etc., was always there; therefore, the nature of justice is what it is. The critic argues, therefore, that it did not come about because of anyone's will or choosing. This has the common flaw that many arguments against DCT have, in that it is referring to the gods of Greece, not the God of Abraham, Isaac, and Jacob.

(6) Professor Jonathan Gluber makes the argument that even if we go with the assumption that God created us, why does it then follow that we must follow God's commands? He uses the example of supposing

---

42   Many thanks to Rabbi Dr. Shalom Carmy and Dr. Phillip Cary for their insights into this argument via e-mail with the author.

43   Idziak, pp. 17–18.

44   Ibid.

he wanted to build his own English football team by having a lot of children. Just because he created them, does that mean they are obligated to fulfill his "dream" of having his own football team?[45]

The argument could be made that because God is the "fundamental Being" that sustains the universe, He is in a better position to know what is "good and best" for humanity, hence, following His will is objectively what is best for us.[46] Furthermore, God created us for our own good. A conceptual point worth adding from Dr. Phillip Cary is: "...that God could not have created us for selfish purposes (like creating a soccer team!). He could not have done this because there is nothing He needs from us. The inescapable fact is that He has nothing to gain by creating us. It follows that He could not have created us for His own good, but only for our good."[47] Finally, from a theistic perspective, God gave us the gift of life. It is clearly within His moral domain to tell us how to use it. Many of the objections to DCT are projections of human nature/limitations onto the Divine. However, when we examine these objections with an understanding of the difference between human frailty and the traditional monotheistic conception of God, the arguments often refute themselves.

(7) The appeal to skepticism: that there is no logically sound theory for ontologically objective morality without God, is not competent to enforce the conclusion that there will never be one.

The idea that one can never "prove" that a satisfactory answer will ever be given is itself a weak argument. On the same note, a person could say the atrocities of the Nazi's "may someday be morally justified." You may not be able to refute that, but at present, you have a lot of precedent to think a valid justification will never be offered.

(8) The theist claims that God's will "creates morality." Before He says something, there is no morality? Also, before He reveals His will, we are still calling Him good.

---

45   Dennis Prager, "Can We Be Good without God," The Oxford Debate, CD #58a.

46   Credit for this point goes to Dr. Joshua Golding, in an e-mail discussion with the author.

47   In an email with the author, June 18, 2013.

This is really a rephrasing of the questions above. (I have chosen to respond to them in all their forms so that their slight change of angle or wording does not make one think it is a different and perhaps legitimate possibility.) The typical, traditional concept of God is that when He created the world, He created the system of justice that was to accompany it. Therefore, before He created the world, there was no morality; once the world was created, it was established with justice as part of the "blueprint." (Therefore, "before He says something" is a false dichotomy.) Before God reveals His will in the written word, His (moral) will was still established as part of the Creation. We are calling His will "good" even before He reveals it because the very nature of God is good.[48]

(9) If I can make a hypothetical judgment of God's actions, that indicates independent moral concepts and standards by which to judge God. For example: "One of the seventeenth-century Cambridge Platonists, Benjamin Whichcote, pointed out that when Abraham questioned God (in his pleading against the destruction of Sodom), 'Shall not the Judge of all the earth deal justly?'[49] this implied that there is a standard of justice to which God, *ke'vayachol*, can be held accountable."[50]

As we covered in our section on Natural Law (beginning of Chapter Four), God implanted in us a certain capability to come up with rational moral concepts, independent of the written command of God. I am in disagreement with the author of this article and the Cambridge Platonist (who was also opposed to DTC) on the understanding of this Biblical passage. Professor David Novak gives us wonderful insight into what is going on in this portion of the Bible.[51] The thrust of his argument is that Abraham was telling God, "If I am to imitate your justice, I need to be able to perceive it on human terms." He writes:

> Yet even here, as we shall see, these human procedures need a Divine exemplar to imitate so that they be consistent with

---

48 Even prior to us knowing His will.
49 Genesis 18:25.
50 "Being Frum and Being Good," Lecture #6, accessed October 3, 2012, http://vbm-torah.org/archive/develop/06develop.htm
51 David Novak, "Divine Command," *Studies in Christian Ethics*, vol. 23 [2010]: pp. 6–20.

the way God legislates his own just law and adjudicates accordingly to it, the law whose application to human affairs has been revealed to humans...[52]

It would seem that the way Abraham (and his descendants thereafter) is meant to know God's law and properly apply it is to understand how God applies it when judging cases that come before God because the rights that law is enacted to respect have been violated. This understanding is not just intellectual; it is meant to be intelligently practical. It is to be mimesis. This people are to act by comparing their action with the Divine exemplar rather than being mere passive spectators looking at a drama that makes no active claims upon them. They are to imitate, but not emulate, God's execution of justice whenever they can do so with at least some positive effect...[53]

When it comes to actually learning from God's practice of justice in the world and to thereby imitate it, Abraham runs into a profound dilemma: it seems that God's justice might be indiscriminate, blind revenge that makes no distinction between the guilty and the innocent. Thus, with much trepidation, Abraham confronts God, asserting: "It is unworthy of you [chalilah lecha] to do such a thing: to put to death the innocent [tzaddik] along with the guilty [rasha]! That the innocent and the guilty be alike, that is unworthy of you! Shall the judge [ha'shofet] of all the earth himself not do justice [mishpat]?!"[54] Now we must ask two questions. One, why must God's practice of judgment in the human world be of such concern to Abraham? Two, what is the real meaning of Abraham's challenge to God?...As to the first question, Abraham's concern with God's practice of justice in the human world is because Abraham's ability to command his clan to "keep the way of the

---

52   Ibid., p. 8.
53   Ibid., pp. 12–13.
54   Genesis 18:25.

Lord"[55] depends on "doing it" the way God does it. Thus to keep the way "of the Lord [derech Hashem] to do what is right and just" refers to both God's doing and man's doing. Since human action as the action of those unique creatures created in the image of God is to imitate Divine action, Divine action must be imitable, and it must be performed intelligently by God and be intelligible to man.[56]

Nevertheless, illogical action is not imitable, and it is clear God wants Abraham to imitate his judgmental action in the world whenever and wherever Abraham can do so. Indeed, why else would God have revealed to Abraham what he proposes to do?...It is "the impossibility of illogical thought," and much more the impossibility of illogical commands, that is at issue here. One cannot be asked to imitate the inimitable. However, if God's concern for his unique human creatures entails an ongoing intelligent and purposeful relationship with us humans, then God must act in a way that is intelligible to us as the kind of coherent action we humans could possibly imitate.[57]

We should look upon Abraham's challenge to God as a logical rather than an ontological challenge, for an ontological challenge would presume that Abraham really has a ground upon which to stand against God to accuse God from which Abraham would be self-sufficient enough to face God as an equal. Yet too many moderns have presumed that when Abraham says: "Shall the judge of the earth not himself do justice [mishpat]?" He is holding God up to a standard above God himself, a standard by which Abraham could judge God...But, contrary to Plato and the Stoics, and even more so contrary to the modern "evaluators," God can only be asked to conform to God's own autonomous standard. God is only answerable to himself. In the context of God's covenant with

---

55   Ibid., v. 19.
56   Novak, p. 14.
57   Ibid., p. 15.

Abraham and his community, God is answerable to God's own promise, which is, as the Psalmist puts it, "to judge the earth, judging the world with justice [b'tzedek] and the peoples rightly [be'meisharim]";[58] and as the prophet Isaiah says to Israel: "I the Lord have called you with justice [b'tzedek]...and I have made you a covenanted people to enlighten nations [l'ohr goyim]."[59]..."It is important to remember that when Abraham holds God up to "justice" [mishpat], he is not holding God up to an independent, superior, abstract, metaphysical entity called "justice." Abraham is not Socrates, who gets the pious Euthyphro to admit that justice is to be loved because of what it is per se rather than being loveable because the gods love it. And Abraham is not Plato who saw his creator god being answerable to a Form higher than himself when creating the cosmos out of primordial chaos.[60]

We also see from a different Biblical passage (Jeremiah 12:1) of "challenging God" that questioning is a form of trying to understand the Divine method. The classical Jewish Biblical commentators, *Rashi* and the *Radak*, are in agreement (see their commentary on this verse) that even though we know God is correct, the questioning is done out of a desire to understand the Divine will, not challenge it.

(10) Why do we (i.e., *Tanach*, Talmud, Rishonim [early Jewish Biblical commentaries], and Acharonim [later Jewish Biblical commentaries]) need to "justify" God's actions if His will is automatically good?[61]

There are two primary, different explanations of why the commentators would explain, or "justify," God's actions in the Bible even if they accepted the premise that whatever God does is good by definition.

---

58   Psalms 98:9.

59   Isaiah 42:6.

60   Novak, p. 17.

61   Rabbi Yehudah Geller gave Rabbi Dr. Dovid Gottlieb this observation about who needs explanations for parts of *Tanach* where God, "does something immoral" if by definition what God does is good? Rabbi Dovid Gottlieb, "Absolute values and conscience," Jerusalem Echoes G30, tape #2.

First, the *Palgei Mayim* comments on a verse in Lamentations: "It is not from the mouth of the Most High that evil and good emanate."[62] He comments on the fact that, in the Hebrew, "evil" (*ha'raos*) is in the plural, while the "good" (*ha'tov*) is in the singular. He explains there are four basic elements involved in God's judgment: commandment, reward, transgression, and punishment. He says that commandment (mitzvah) is in the realm of people (to keep), reward (*s'char*) is in the realm of God (to give out), transgression (*averiah*) is in the hands of humanity (to break the law), however punishment (*onesh*) is in the hands of man. Hence, three things do not come from God, and so the verse writes "evil" in the plural.

This requires explanation. The *Palgei Mayim* explains that when it comes to transgression and punishment, the system is more of a cause-and-effect set-up. That means that ultimately when a person sins, he is, in reality, inflicting himself with what will be the outcome (punishment) of his transgression. As it were, God takes a passive role and does not directly inflict the person; rather, God's "active" role is that He does not intercede (unless a person repents) on behalf of the person who is about to receive the effect of their cause. Therefore, to return to our topic at hand, in many cases the Sages appear to be "justifying" God's actions, while really they are explaining why a person's actions warranted the results that he received.[63]

Another approach is based on the explanation that Professor David Novak laid out regarding the occasion of Abraham "challenging" God. If we are to implement God's justice, we need to be able to understand it on our level. Therefore, when the Bible or the Sages go "out of the way to justify God's actions," we can understand it as a tool that is used to help us understand how to imitate Divine justice, rather than a way of holding God up to an independent ethical standard.

---

62   Lamentations 3:38.
63   Thanks to Rabbi Moshe Heigh of Cincinnati for pointing out this source to the author.

(11) If by definition God's will is good, why does Psalms (34:9) say: "Taste and see that Hashem is good"? Why taste? We already "know" that God is good by definition.[64]

There is a difference between the knowledge we experience and the knowledge that we know. This is the difference between *daas*, knowledge, and *chochmah*, wisdom. Not only does our knowledge-base grow when we learn new things, but also it increases the depth of the knowledge of what we know already. It means sensory perception, not just abstract information. The transformation of abstract information to sensory perception happens through experience—"taste and see."[65]

Rabbi Avigdor Miller, in his commentary to Exodus (14:31), writes:

> "And they believed in Hashem, and Moshe his servant." But "the people believed" already, when they had witnessed the signs which Moshe and Aharon had performed.[66] After seeing such convincing miracles, would any doubt have been possible? We see, therefore, that Emunah (faith) is not mere conviction, but rather a state of Perfection of the mind which has unlimited potential development. Every additional degree of this quality, which we shall call Awareness, is a great gift from Hashem. The episode of the sea of Suf was a grand opportunity whereby Israel gained a higher degree of Emunah, and for this superlative gift they sang their song of thanks to Hashem.[67] But even this degree of Awareness which they now received was a preface to a still higher degree of Emunah which was yet to come...[68]

The more we "taste," i.e., know, the more (depth) we attain in knowledge.

---

64 Rabbi Dr. Dovid Gottlieb, "Religion and Morality: the Sacrifice of Isaac," G2 Jerusalem Echoes, tape 2.

65 The author is indebted to Rabbi Yaakov Shapiro for this explanation.

66 Exodus 4:31.

67 Ibid., 15:1.

68 Rabbi Avigdor Miller, *A Nation Is Born*, p. 178.

SECULAR ATTEMPTS AT OBJECTIVE MORALITY INDEPENDENT OF GOD

The following are popular secular attempts to ground moral objectivity in a godless universe. I am not going to bother addressing non-moral realist theories because, as the philosopher Iris Murdoch points out, "The ordinary person does not, unless corrupted by philosophy, believe that he creates values by his choices. He thinks that some things really are better than others and he is capable of getting it wrong."[69] Some are known and espoused by the population in general, and some are prominent in academia but unknown to the general population. It is impossible to list every attempt to have morality without God due to the fact that an individual who has his own perspective technically has his own philosophy. Also, the concepts I am mentioning have had books written on them specifically, and to cover each one in-depth is beyond the scope of this work. My hope is that by citing the general premise of a number of commonly held philosophical positions and giving critical points of refutation, it will be an impetus for the reader to pursue further investigation and challenge some commonly held assumptions.

Plato: Virtue and Knowledge

Plato opts for a standard of morality independent of God and he finds this in the Forms. Plato was a moral realist, as he held that moral statements were true or false as far as they correspond to an absolute moral order.[70] Plato considered that if words like beauty, justice, or good were applied in so many different situations, they must all have something in common. He argued that everything we see in the world that we call beautiful in some way participates in or resembles the perfect Form of Beauty. The Form of Beauty (as of Justice, the Good, etc.) exists timelessly and spacelessly; the Forms are neither created, nor do they create. Beautiful, just, or good things or persons in some way, albeit imperfectly, resemble these Forms. The Forms represent

---

69 Iris Murdoch, *The Sovereignty of the Good*, p. 95.
70 Peter Vardy and Paul Grosch, *The Puzzle of Ethics*, pp. 8–9.

Absolute Reality as opposed to the particular things that in some small way resemble them.[71]

One problem with Plato's approach is that it is elitist; most people are in the shadow of ignorance, and it is the philosopher who, after much study, can pierce through the shadows as see this world "rightly."[72] Since, according to Plato, virtue is knowledge, he did not think it was possible for a person to do something wrong if he knew it was wrong. Vardy and Gorsch highlight this point:

> *However, this does not take into consideration the weakness of a person's will. Knowledge does not lead to virtue, and the whole of Plato's moral philosophy relies on the claim that it does...One of the gravest problems in Plato's approach is that individuals can never be sure that they have arrived at a correct understanding of virtue and the nature of the good—how does one know that one has emerged from the cave and is not still in the shadow?...The second problem is that Plato's approach is far from particular and gives no guidance as to how to act in the day-to-day situations which individuals face.[73]*

Aristotle and Virtue Theory

The Nicomachen Ethics, generally regarded as the most detailed and coherent of Aristotle's works on moral philosophy, is a collection of lectures compiled and edited by his son, also called Nicomachus, after his grandfather. It concludes that contemplation of the Good (that is, the life of philosophic reflection) is the highest form of happiness. In Book 1 of *The Ethics*, Aristotle makes a number of points concerning the true object or purpose of life. First, he makes the seemingly obvious point that everything a person or a group does is directed toward some kind of aim.[74] This is also known as "telos." The first sentence in *The*

---

71   Ibid., p. 11.
72   Ibid., p. 16.
73   Ibid., pp. 16–17.
74   Ibid., p. 21.

Nicomachen Ethics says: "Every craft and every inquiry, and similarly every action and project, seems to aim at something good; hence the good has been well defined as that at which everything aims."

As Alasdair MacIntyre writes in *Short History of Ethics*: "Good is defined at the outset in terms of the goal, purpose, or aim to which something or someone moves. To call something good is to say that it is under certain conditions sought or aimed at."[75] Alasdair MacIntyre explains why this philosophy is not suitable for the general populace:

> *Aristotle's audience, then, is an explicitly leisured minority. We are no longer faced with a telos for human life as such, but with a telos for one kind of life which presupposes a certain kind of hierarchical social order and which presupposes also a view of the universe in which the realm of timeless truth is metaphysically superior to the human world of change and sense experience and ordinary rationality. All Aristotle's conceptual brilliance in the course of the argument declines at the end to an apology for this extraordinarily parochial form of human existence. At once, the objection will be made: this is to judge Aristotle against the background of our values, not of his. It is to be guilty of anachronism. But this is not true. Socrates had already presented an alternative set of values in both his teaching and his life; Greek tragedy presents other, different possibilities; Aristotle did not choose what he chose for lack of knowledge of alternative views of human life.*[76]

Furthermore, Aristotle looks for the primary function of human beings, but why assume that there is a primary function? And how does one know what the unique function is? Finally, Martha Nussbaum levels another blow to the Aristotelian ethic:

> *Aristotelian dialectic...makes several controversial assumptions about the nature of the ordinary person's ethical beliefs.*

---

75   Alasdair MacIntyre, *Short History of Ethics*, pp. 57–58.
76   Ibid., p. 83.

It assumes that these beliefs are essentially healthy: truth is in there, along with whatever is false, and in such a way that, in the process of scrutiny, the true beliefs will turn out to be the "greatest in number and the most basic." Since the beliefs in question are for the most part socially taught, the procedure also assumes the relative health of the surrounding society.[77]

Kant and the Moral Law

Kant said that his aim in *The Groundwork* was to establish a completely isolated metaphysic of morals that is not mixed with any theology or physics or metaphysics.[78] Unlike Plato, Aristotle, or Aquinas, he is not concerned with some "good for human beings." Kant was concerned with the fundamental principles that form the basis for our moral choices. He considered moral principles to be an *a priori* given and therefore to be arrived at independent of experience.[79] Peter Vardy and Paul Gorsch explain Kant's moral formulation as follows:

Kant distinguishes between two types of imperatives or commands under which human beings act:

- *Hypothetical imperatives are imperatives that are based on an "if," for instance: "If you want to stay healthy, then exercise," or "If you want your wife to love you, remember her birthday." We can reject the command (to take exercise or to remember birthdays) if we are willing to reject the "if" on which the command rests. These imperatives bid us to do things which are a means to some end. They are arrived at by the exercise of pure reason.*
- *Categorical imperatives, by contrast, are not based on any "if"; they do not depend on a particular end, and Kant considers they would be followed by any rational agent.*

---

77   Martha Nussbaum, *The Therapy of Desire*, pp. 102–3, cited in Bruce W. Hauptli, "Selected Criticisms of Aristotle's Ethics," online.

78   *The Puzzle of Ethics*, p. 53.

79   Ibid., p. 54.

Categorical imperatives are arrived at through practical reason, and they are understood as a basis for action.

Kant has a problem at the heart of his whole enterprise which is often not recognized and which he did not fully resolve. Kant considered that human beings should aim to act wholly in accordance with the Categorical Imperative—the maximum of their action would then be good. However, he recognized that many people would fail to do this and they would become corrupt as they acted from evil, false or irrational maxims. Once a person's life had become dominated by such general principles, he would then be in bondage. The difficulty Kant had was how to explain moral regeneration or a turnaround from evil to good when he also considered that human beings could bind themselves by their corrupt maxims.[80]

Another problem with the theory is that it cannot resolve conflicts between duties: between two perfect duties, and between a perfect and an imperfect duty.[81] Alasdair MacIntyre comments on the Categorical Imperative:

It follows that, in practice, the test of the categorical imperative imposes restrictions only on those insufficiently equipped with ingenuity. And this surely is scarcely what Kant intended. The logical emptiness of the test of the categorical imperative is itself of social importance. Because the Kantian notion of duty is so formal that it can be given almost any content, it becomes available to provide a sanction and a motive for the specific duties which any particular social and moral tradition may propose. Because it detaches the notion of duty from the notions of ends, purposes, wants, and needs, it suggests that, given a purposed course of action, I may only ask whether, in doing it, I can consistently will that it shall be universally done,

---

80   *The Puzzle of Ethics*, pp. 59–60.
81   Stephan O Sullivan and Phillip A. Pecorino, online Ethics textbook.

and not ask what ends or purposes it serves. Anyone educated into the Kantian notion of duty will, so far, have been educated into easy conformism with authority. Nothing, of course, could be further from the intentions or from the spirit of Kant himself.[82]

G.E. Moore, *Principia Ethica*

In the introduction to his *Principia Ethica*, G.E. Moore proclaims that he is able to make the distinction regarding objective morality in ethical philosophy that all of those that preceded him were not able to make.[83] Alasdair MacIntyre explains:

> *Moore takes it that the things which ought to exist for their own sake are those which we call intrinsically good. How do we know what is intrinsically good? The answer is that we cannot fail to recognize the property of the intrinsic goodness when confronted with it.*[84]*...Moore's one genuine argument is used to show that good cannot be the name of any complex whole. Of any such whole, however defined, we can always significantly ask whether it is itself good. This argument can be deployed not only against the attempt to define good as the name of a complex, but also against the attempt to define it at all. Suppose that I identify good with pleasant. My mistake can be exhibited by showing that I can always significantly ask of pleasure or of anything pleasant, is it good? But if good names the same property that pleasure names, to ask, is what is pleasant, good? [It w]ould be equivalent to asking, is what is pleasant—pleasant?—that is, it would be seriously tautologous.*[85]

---

82   Alasdair MacIntyre, *A Short History of Ethics*, p. 198.
83   Ibid., p. 249.
84   Ibid.
85   Ibid., pp. 250–51.

Next, MacIntyre levels two more objections to Moore's theory:

Is good, then, the name of a simple, unanalyzable property? To doctrine that it is, there are at least two conclusive objections. The first is that we can only use the name of a simple property intelligibly where we are acquainted with some standard example of the property by reference to which we are to recognize whether it is present or absent in other cases. In the case of a simple property like yellow we can use standard examples of the color to recognize other cases of yellow. But how could learning how to recognize a good friend help us to recognize a good watch? Yet if Moore is right, the same example property is present in both cases. To this, a disciple of Moore might reply that we are confusing the question by our example. A good watch is not 'intrinsically' good. But how, then, do we recognize the intrinsically good? The only answer Moore offers is that we just do. Or to put this point another way: Moore's account could only reach the level of intelligibility if it were supplemented by an account of the relation between learning it in connection with some cases, and knowing how to apply others. The second objection is that Moore's account leaves it entirely unexplained and inexplicable why something's being good should ever furnish us with a reason for action. The analogy with yellow is as much of a difficulty for his thesis at this point as it is an aid to him elsewhere. One can imagine a connoisseur with a special taste for yellow objects to whom something's being yellow would furnish him with a reason for acquiring it; but something's being 'good' can hardly be supposed to furnish a reason for action only to those with a connoisseur's interest in goodness. Any account of good that is to be adequate must connect it intimately with action, and explain why to call something good is always to provide a reason for acting in respect of it in one way rather than another.[86]

---

86   Ibid., pp. 252–53.

Finally, to quote Peter Vardy and Paul Grosch in *The Puzzle of Ethics*: "He dispenses with Moore's intuitionism with the comment: Twentieth-century moral philosophers have sometimes appealed to their and our intuitions; one of the things we ought to have learned from the history of moral philosophy is that the introduction of the word 'intuition' by a moral philosopher is always a signal that something has gone badly wrong with an argument."[87]

Bentham and Mill: Utilitarianism

Utilitarianism is often labeled as the moral philosophy that teaches that morality is the greatest happiness for the greatest number. Jeremy Bentham measured the greatest good as a measure of quantity. John S. Mill, who was a follower and admirer of Bentham's theory, understood the qualifier (of goodness/pleasure) should be measured in quality.[88] Professor Peter Kraft, in his lecture at Prager University, "If good and evil exist, God exists," gives a strong objection to Utilitarianism: If 90% of the people in the world get great benefit from enslaving the other 10%, would that make slavery right?[89] Peter Vardy and Paul Grosch explain the further difficulties of the philosophy in *The Puzzle of Ethics*:

> *One of the problem's [sic] with Bentham's theory and his hedonic calculus was that its results were based on a quantitative measure. That is, how much sheer quantity of pleasure can be gained from an action...The second problem is that utilitarianism relies strictly on its predictive value. But who can predict that the child will grow up happy and productive, that the old man will soon die anyway, and that the sum total of pleasure to be gained by the young family is going to be greater than the old man's? The child may grow up to be a mass murderer, the family may then lead a collective life of guilt and misery, and the old man may, like Bertrand Russell,*

---

87   *The Puzzle of Ethics*, p. 103, cited in Alasdair MacIntyre, *After Virtue*, p. 69.
88   *The Puzzle of Ethics*, p. 68.
89   His lecture can be found at www.prageruniversity.com.

have been destined to make his major mark on political life in his eighties and nineties.[90]

...The second problem is perhaps greater than the first. The philosopher D.W. Ross (1877–1971) pointed to the inherent difficulties of what one might call a "single-factor" moral theory. We cannot simply rely on a single principle of equation such as the greatest good or the greatest happiness or the greatest pleasure for the greatest number. Life's ethical dilemmas cannot be reduced to a prepackaged, predictive calculus which balances outcomes. We experience internal conflicts between what our reason tells us, what duties we feel we ought to perform, and the need, obviously, to bring about the greatest good. Suppose, for example, you and your young son were seated next to a brilliant young doctor who, through your conversation, you learn is close to finding a cure for the AIDS virus. The bus is suddenly involved in an accident and catches fire. You have just enough time to save one person before you are engulfed in the flames. Who do you save: your son or the doctor? Application of the simple greatest happiness principle would undoubtedly lead you to having to save the doctor because of the number of lives ultimately he will save. The strict dictates of reason would lead to the same conclusion. However, your personal duty coupled with the moral bond of affection which ties you to your son, plus an over-riding instinct, would lead you to save your son. The saving of one's son would, using the concept introduced by Ross, be a prima-facie duty, that is, the most important duty and therefore the one that should rightly be put first.[91]

Reason

This is the position that, based on human reason alone, we should be able to acquire objective morality. Reason may be a good tool for

---

90   *The Puzzle of Ethics*, p. 67.
91   Ibid., pp. 69–70.

morality but not a source. People use reason to plan out nefarious plots, so the act of reasoning itself is not a deterrent to wrong behavior. Also, there are noble actions people do that fly in the face of reason; it is not logical to risk your own life to save someone else's. In the book, *The Nine Questions People Ask About Judaism*, Dennis Prager and Joseph Telushkin point out: "The use of reason to justify what is wrong is so common that we have a special word for it—rationalization.[92]...Reason is amoral, education is amoral, and human nature is amoral. Yet these constitute the basis of the secular humanist's prescription for a moral world."[93]

In *After Virtue*, Alasdair MacIntyre exposes the flaw of using reason alone to determine objective morality:

> *...It is very much to the point that such writers cannot agree among themselves either on what the character of moral rationality is or on the substance of the morality which is to be founded on rationality. The diversity of contemporary moral debate and its interminability are indeed mirrored in the controversies of analytical moral philosophers. But if those who claim to be able to formulate principles on which rational moral agents ought to agree cannot secure agreement on the formulation of those principles from their colleagues who share their basic philosophical purpose and method, there is once again prima facie evidence that their project has failed, even before we have examined their particular contentions and conclusions. Each of them in his criticism offers testimony to the failure of his colleagues' constructions.[94]*

Finally, in the words of Professor Keith Ward:

> *However, the understanding of the mind is not the assent of the will. While Clarke said that reason is the natural and authoritative guide of a rational being, we are not wholly*

---

92   Dennis Prager and Joseph Telushkin, *The Nine Questions People Ask about Judaism*, p. 23.

93   Ibid., p. 104.

94   *After Virtue*, p. 26.

rational beings, and this is not a rational world. Reason is perhaps a reliable guide only for passionless beings in a world of similarly passionate beings. For the rest of us, members of a violent species in a nature "red in tooth and claw," it would be the height of foolishness to pretend to be reasonable in the midst of universal terror. Our business is survival and dominance. To appeal to "eternal and immutable laws of reason" if we find ourselves trapped in a violent and radically unjust world will be ineffective and, paradoxically, irrational.[95]

Conscience

Conscience is an aptitude, faculty, intuition, or judgment of the intellect that distinguishes right from wrong. It is often suggested that if people follow their intuition, then they will be able to objectively know what is right and wrong. If this is the case, what about people who do evil in the name of what their conscience dictates is right? Clearly conscience alone is not a source of morality. Rather, conscience is the intuition to keep us up to par with the morality that we are already aware of. Furthermore, similar to the case of humanism, it has the drawback of not having a system for implementation. Morality is not the mere absence of killing and stealing, rather it is a system that is supposed to elevate our existence.

Finally, the whole section below is an in-depth explanation of the incompleteness of conscience and a refutation of the idea that it is all we need to be moral agents.

Iris Murdoch: The Sovereignty of the Good:

Iris Murdoch is a neo-Platonist who is well known in the philosophical world of ethics for her conception of objective morality known as "the sovereignty of the good." Though an atheist, she challenged many atheistic approaches aimed at a morality independent of God. In "The Sovereignty of God's Goodness," William Schweiker writes: "In presenting this moral vision, Murdoch, unlike most contemporary thinkers,

---

95   Keith Ward, *Morality, Autonomy, and God*, p. 26.

does not believe that we ought to expunge religious concerns from ethics. However, she does insist that we can and must replace God with Good as the central concept in ethics."[96]

In *God's Call*, Professor John E. Hare writes of Murdoch:

> *I want to isolate one concession she makes, which takes her some distance from the position of G.E. Moore. The concession is that human beings are by nature selfish...It is a concession to subjectivity in that she recognizes and indeed stresses that accurate moral perception needs obedience, a selfless attention, a pure heart; but our moral thinking is in fact usually characterized by the opposite of these—by root inclination to favor ourselves unjustly. She is a Platonist about value, but with an Augustinian rather than Platonist view of the heart. Moore agrees that humans are capable of great evil. But he has no equivalent to what Murdoch calls "the fat relentless ego," which corrupts our nature at its root.*[97]

This falls very nicely in line with the teaching of the Bible: "The inclination of man's heart is evil from his youth."[98] If we take the above into consideration, it is not hard to see why many theist ethical philosophers are quite fond of Murdoch. Nevertheless, it behooves us to heed the words of Professor Stanley Hauerwas in his essay, "Murdochian Muddles": "I will suggest that Murdoch's account of the moral life cannot be appropriated uncritically by Christian theologians for the simple reason that her account of the 'muddles' that constitute our lives is correlative to a metaphysics we cannot accept...Yet I hope to show that we are not simply left with 'So you believe this and I believe that.' Instead, we are left with the very character of our lives which, I would argue,

---

96   Willam Schweiker, "The Sovereignty of God's Goodness," in Maria Antonaccio and William Schweiker (eds.), *Iris Murdoch and the Search for Human Goodness*, p. 209. Also see there Franklin I. Gamwell, "On the Loss of Theism," where he concludes: "Thereby, I have sought to recommend that her friendship with theistic religion need not be reserved and in truth may become an embrace."

97   John E. Hare, *God's Call*, pp. 11–12.

98   Genesis 8:21.

gives us a basis for thinking that we might be creatures with purposes we did not create."[99]

David Tracy, in "The Many Faces of Platonism," gives further reason for theists to take Murdoch with a grain of salt:

> *Her problem with Jewish, Christian, or Muslim under-*
> *standings of God seem to me to have less to do with familiar*
> *metaphysical difficulties than with what can be called a prob-*
> *lem of sensibility or even spirituality. She fears that any*
> *acceptance of a personal God, unlike the impersonal Good, will*
> *eventually console us in a way that allows us to escape once*
> *again—facing reality—reality as what must be endured,*
> *which breaks though our egotism and fantasizing imagination*
> *by its unrelenting necessity. For her, a belief in God can func-*
> *tion as another veil created by our anxiety to hide away what*
> *is terrible and absurd in life and reality.[100]*

According to Murdoch, a fundamental idea of her thesis is based on no external point (telos) to life: "First, however, I wish to mention very briefly two fundamental assumptions of my argument. If either is denied, what follows will be less convincing. I assume that human beings are naturally selfish, and that human life has no external point or telos."[101] A major question on her premises can be asked: If there is no external point to life, on what grounds is there a major issue with being selfish? Professor Keith Ward frames this difficulty well:

> *For us to regard ourselves as free rational agents, morally*
> *obliged to realize our potentialities in creative, just, and*
> *compassionate ways, may come to seem an almost irrational*
> *option if we also regard ourselves as accidental by-products of*
> *a morally indifferent and directionless cosmic mechanism. It*

---

99 Stanley Hauerwas, "Murdochian Muddles," in Maria Antonaccio and William Schweiker (eds.), *Iris Murdoch and the Search for Human Goodness*, p. 194.

100 David Tracy, "The Many Faces of Platonism," in Maria Antonaccio and William Schweiker (eds.), *Iris Murdoch and the Search for Human Goodness*, p. 74.

101 Iris Murdoch, *The Sovereignty of the Good*, p. 78.

may come to seem a matter of taste or subjective preference
whether or not we give moral endeavor a central place in our
personal lives. If our lives have no objective meaning and
significance, why should morality have some sort of ultimate
and decisive importance?[102]

Professor John Hare gives further thought to Murdoch and her concept of "the good" and telos (purpose):

The Good, Murdoch says, unifies all these fragmentary
experiences of value into a whole that transcends us. It is
a "magnetic center," to which we feel the attraction but which
we never reach. There is an aspect of Murdoch's thought which
is hard to fit with her talk of a "magnetic center." She holds
that human life holds no external point or telos. She thinks
Christianity panders to us by claiming to give us a guarantee
that the good will in the end prevail. But the effect of her denial
is to make the Good completely inert, contrary to Plato, for
whom the human world is neither aimless nor self-contained.
The Forms for him, and especially the Form of the Good, have
a causal role as well as an epistemological one. I do not myself
see how to reconcile Murdoch's talk about aimlessness with the
talk about a magnetic center.[103]

Professor Keith Ward challenges Murdoch's implementation of following "The Good" further:

The question arises whether there is anything that is supremely
good and beautiful, or whether this is a mythological projection
of human dreams of perfection, which does not correspond
to anything in reality. Might the sort of "just attention" to
reality that Murdoch recommends not lead to despair rather
than reverence for a good which is so transient, flawed, and

---

102   Keith Ward, *Morality, Autonomy, and God*, p. 213.
103   *God's Call*, p. 13.

doomed to extinction? She admits, indeed stresses, that human life is bedeviled by the "fat relentless ego," and that evil is so apparent and prevalent that it rules out the existence of any sort of "finality" or objective purpose in reality—which rules out God. Yet there does seem to be something about achieved excellence in both art and in human living (and in scientific understanding too) that strikes us with admiration and awe. She writes, "There is...something in the serious attempt to look compassionately at human things which automatically suggests that 'there is more than this'" (1970, p. 73). Hovering between compassion and despair, she finds herself strangely compelled to opt, as Existentialists such as Camus and Sartre did, for "the higher ground," absurd though it may be.[104]

...If we believed in the objective existence of goodness, would that provide the emotional purchase we need to transform our self-centered passions into passionate that is truly worthwhile?[105]

After all, as John Hare observes: "This concession [the fat relentless ego] has far-reaching consequences for Murdoch's views. It means that our access to the good is always precarious and incomplete, and we are always fatally prone to self-deception."[106] This being the case, it should be taken into consideration that, according to her own views, Murdoch is very hard pressed to find an effective way to overcome human selfishness with regards to reaching the objective good. The words of Stanley Hauerwas shed light on the magnitude of her problem: "We are no doubt possessed and blinded by the 'fat relentless ego' so wonderfully depicted by Murdoch. That we are so afflicted, moreover, results in muddles from which we cannot will to be free. The problem with Murdoch's muddles is not simply that we lack the resources to be free from them if God does not exist, but that the full reality of such muddles

---

104   *Morality, Autonomy, and God*, pp. 60–61.
105   Ibid., p. 61.
106   *God's Call*, p. 12.

remains unarticulated in a world without God."[107] William Schweiker boils it down: "If her argument is to hold, she must show that the Good is implicit in all acts of consciousness and that it is necessarily real."[108]

We have to ask: Did she accomplish this? How does she learn out objective morality from "the good?" Professor Ward crystallizes her position very nicely: "Murdoch believes that great art, or music, or literature, opens the mind to depths of reality, aspects of the natural world that are not captured by the analytic procedures of natural science, but that show us what is truly there. This is a sort of 'moral sensibility' that is not shared by everyone. But it is a way of seeing the world of human experience as disclosing commanding values that call for dispassionate attention and the sacrifice of self."[109]

Stanley Hauerwas explains Murdoch's attachment to art as a tool for finding the objective good: "For the great enemy of the moral life is 'personal fantasy: the tissue of self-aggrandizing and consoling wishes and dreams which prevents one from seeing what is there outside one' (Sovereignty, 59). That is why art is so crucial. For by experiencing the transcendence of the beautiful, we are called out of our fantasies (Sovereignty, 60). Art can be the occasion for training us to see this or that rock or this or that person free from fantasies of who they should be for 'us.'"[110] Professor Ward also explains Murdoch's interest in art, and explains why it fails as a litmus test for the objective:

> *It is not surprising that she seems more confident in speaking of Beauty and of art than of love and goodness. Her view of art seems to me almost desperately (I fear I would also say often falsely) romantic, seeing it as implying "love and detachment," as "without any point beyond itself," as "totally opposed to selfish obsession," and as affording "a pure delight*

---

107   John E. Hare, "Murdochian Muddles," in Maria Antonaccio and William Schweiker (eds.), *Iris Murdoch and the Search for Human Goodness*, p. 206.

108   William Schweiker, "The Sovereignty of God's Goodness," in Maria Antonaccio and William Schweiker (eds.), *Iris Murdoch and the Search for Human Goodness*, p. 222.

109   *Morality, Autonomy, and God*, p. 92.

110   John E. Hare, "Murdochian Muddles" in Maria Antonaccio and William Schweiker (eds.), *Iris Murdoch and the Search for Human Goodness*, p. 198

in the independent existence of what is excellent" (Murdoch, 1970, p. 85). The good artist is "brave, truthful, patient, and humble." Art is "a sacrament." Art "shows us the only sense in which the permanent and incorruptible is compatible with the transient...pierces the veil and gives sense to the notion of a reality which lies beyond appearance" (ibid., p. 88). "The enjoyment of art is a training in the love of virtue," enabling one to forget self and see justly. The fact is, however, that great artists are not usually known for their moral heroism, much less for their patience and humility. Wagner with his arrogance, and his obviously racist views, seems to me to be a great musician, but a rather poor example of a saint. His music is sublime, but some aspects of his libretti were morally ambiguous enough to be loved by Hitler and the Nazis. If you walk into a gallery of modern art, you will find irony, satire, the desire to shock and offend and to express personal visions of life that are often disturbing and despairing. Murdoch's view of art is very idiosyncratic, and much contemporary art is not concerned with the idea of Beauty with a capital letter, at all...So it is odd that Murdoch, who sounds rather like Plato at times, turns art into such a sacrament of reality and truth. It is not. It is the expression of the artist's vision. It may reveal much that we had not perceived, but what it reveals may not be beauty or goodness at all.[111]

Furthermore, regarding this matter, Professor Ward asks a follow up-question: "If we believed in the objective existence of goodness, would that provide the emotional purchase we need to transform our self-centered passions into a passionate love of what is truly worth-while[?]"[112] Later in his book, he makes the argument stronger: "So, even if there is a conceptual realm of values—and it is easy to dismiss it as imaginative fiction—why should it have any effect on my conduct? It

---

111   *Morality, Autonomy, and God*, pp. 94–95.

112   Ibid., p. 63.

certainly provides a good reason for moral action, and it articulates our natural belief that such things as the contemplation of beauty and personal affection are intrinsic goods. But such considerations may seem as relevant to this largely ugly and violent world as dreams of Utopia are in a military dictatorship."[113] William Schweiker also offers another shortcoming of Murdoch's conception of "the good" and consciousness: "In other words, if consciousness were in fact value-conferring, then moral attention would be directed to what individuals share rather than the particularity of their existence. Idealism, like existentialism, ends by denying the complexity of individuals."[114]

While there is more to be said, I wish to limit the arguments against Murdoch to one more. Specifically, I am referring to the disadvantage that "the good" is put in from an atheistic point of view. William Schweiker sums up how Murdoch replaced God with the "Good" well:

> *Murdoch's replacement of God with Good rests on a series of interrelated claims. First, she contends that "God" is the name of a supernatural person and that confusion arises if we try to extend the word "God" to cover any or all ideas of spiritual reality. She believes, second, that nothing is lost spiritually or morally by forgoing the idea of a supernatural person in favor of the Good. In fact, the ontological proof works to this end by showing that the concept of an existing personal being cannot meet the demands of necessary existence. Third, Murdoch insists that the Good is what the old God symbolized, especially the absolute, necessary moral claim upon humanity manifest in every experience of distinguishing degrees of perfection. And therefore, Murdoch, finally, frees religion from theism and defines it as "a mode of belief in the unique sovereign place of goodness or virtue in human life" (p. 426). This completes Murdoch's response to the problem of the loss*

---

113 Ibid., p. 95.

114 William Schweiker, "The Sovereignty of God's Goodness," in Maria Antonaccio and William Schweiker (eds.), *Iris Murdoch and the Search for Human Goodness*, p. 226.

of value as metaphysically basic and her proposal for a theology without God. She has shown the ubiquity of value in human consciousnesses and also the reality of Good.[115]

After explaining Murdoch's position, Schweiker proceeds to ask some important questions:

> *The question focuses on the object of moral concern, that is, the individual, and then forces us to consider the ground of morality in order to make sense of that object of concern. And as we have seen, Murdoch insists that the focus of morality is love and knowledge of individuals. The "central concept of morality," she writes, "is 'the individual' thought of as knowledge by love, thought of in the light of the command, 'Be ye therefore perfect'" (Sovereignty, 30). This, then, is our question: What is the ground for this claim about the centrality of the individual? More pointedly, why ought the individual be an object of love and moral attention when any real, actual individual is always less than perfect[?] Was it not precisely the fact of contingency and imperfection that led Murdoch to reject a personal God in the favor of the impersonal Good? Why does the same argument fall on actual, existing human beings? In a word, the question is about what confers value on individuals.*[116]

> *...Murdoch rejects existentialist and idealist positions on precisely this point. Consciousness is directed towards the real, and human freedom only makes sense in that context. But then the question returns. What confers value on individuals? Murdoch has established the reality of the Good, but what is the goodness of reality of individuals? This is the point, I judge, that a residue of the Christian insistence of the created worth of individuals plays its role in Murdoch's thought. Simply in virtue of being created, persons are worthy of respect and love.*

---

115   Ibid., p. 224.
116   Ibid, pp. 224–25.

> *In the light of creation, one affirms that esse qua esseestbonum, to cite Augustine. But can we make sense of that claim without a creator, without God?...For if I am right, a realist ethics which holds to the dignity of the individual on grounds other than an act of power within the self—be that the will or consciousness—is only possible by appeal to some idea of creation and thus also a creator. But that would mean that we cannot replace God with Good. It would mean, in other words, that the Good is not all that God symbolizes.*[117]

In highlighting the other effect of a morality independent of God (i.e., The Good), Schweiker says:

> *An ethics of the Good, as Murdoch presents it, finally does not have the conceptual resources to make this argument. This is so because of the symbolism of the Good itself. What do I mean? Murdoch insists that the Good is that which the "light of truth is seen; it reveals the world, hitherto invisible, and is also a source of life." But it is absolutely important to note that as the source of life the Good does not recognize or respond to what is other than itself. In other words, the Good does not symbolize the transformation of value creating power so that power respects and enhances finite life. And this is why, I believe, it is difficult for Murdoch to specify the ground for the value of the individual. In grasping this point, we have isolated the inner limits of the Good as a symbol of the real...*[118] *Claims about God designate than a valuation of power, of the Divine reality which enables things—like persons, moral values, the world—to come to be and to continue to exist in complexes of interaction and thus the very source of value. This is why God is irreducible and primary in understanding the world and human life. A theological ethics articulates the meaning and truth of the sovereignty of God's goodness, that is, the*

---

117   Ibid, p. 227.
118   Ibid., pp. 229–30.

authority of value creating power to constitute our sense of what is unconditionally good. To direct one's attention towards God has the effect of transforming self-consciousness, one's construal of the world, and one's assessment of other persons. This is the claim, I take it, of Christian and Jewish faith. It is the center of these particular ways of human life.[119]

Franklin I. Gamwell, in his essay, "On the Loss of Theism," also sheds light on this final point quite nicely:

The difference between God and the Good is that the latter may be loved, but is not loving, while the former means a supreme person or Thou who is responsive to us. "God is love" is, perhaps the identifying conviction of theistic religion.[120] *...If "God is love" is the identifying convection of theistic religion, its central affirmation is that we ought to love God because all of our lives in all of their detail make an abiding difference to the Divine reality. In contrast, the Good, as an Idea rather than an individual, is always to be loved, but is never loving.*[121]

To end the coverage of this philosophy,[122] in the words of Professor Keith Ward: "In this way, the doctrine of one God who actively creates and loves the cosmos develops considerably beyond the Platonic concept of the Good, which neither acts nor loves, but is simply an unchanging ideal."[123]

---

119 Ibid., p. 231.
120 Franklin I Gamwell, "On the Loss of Theism," in Maria Antonaccio and William Schweiker (eds.), *Iris Murdoch and the Search for Human Goodness*, p. 177.
121 Ibid., p. 182.
122 As I said above, there is much more to be said on the topic. While I quoted extensively from, *The Sovereignty of God's Goodness*," the truth is there is much more valuable content in his essay. For those interested in this topic, I cannot recommend highly enough that you read it in its entirety.
123 *Morality, Autonomy, and God*, p. 199.

Erik Wielenberg and Godless Normative Realism

Erik Wielenberg, like Iris Murdoch, is a moral Platonist. However, Wielenberg is currently the most well-known philosopher pushing Godless Normative Realism—namely, the idea one can be an atheist and still believe in objective morality. Even though Wielenberg has written two books on his moral philosophy (*Value and Virtue in a Godless Universe* and *Robust Ethics*), I feel the most compelling arguments he made against Divine command theory (DCT) can be found in an article he wrote for *Faith and Philosophy*.[124] I will mention the arguments in the piece that I feel really deserve attention and why nevertheless I think his arguments in the end are not devastating to DCT.

I divided up his points into four basic points that may overlap but I think deserve specific attention of their own. I think these four points are what is most relevant regarding his material.

1. Wielenberg thinks that just like theists believe that God just exists, the same can be said of ethical brute facts.
2. Wielenberg says: Objective morality requires a foundation external to itself. Why accept such an assumption?
3. God's ability to impose obligation by way of His commandments depends on the truth of certain ethical facts that are not themselves grounded in God.
4. Neither the theist nor the non-theistic moral realist can satisfy the demand of grounding moral claims.

(1) Wielenberg thinks that just like theists believe that God just exists, the same can be said of ethical brute facts.

Response: This may be true. However, what makes us obligated to follow the moral laws still needs an accounting for. Also, as Dr. William Weinwright says: "I agree with Wielenberg that not every value fact cries

---

124   Erik Wielenberg, "In Defense of Non-Natural Non-Theistic Moral Realism," *Faith and Philosophy*, vol. 26, no. 1, January 2009: 23–41.

out for an explanation and terms of something distinct from it. The fact remains that Wielenberg thinks pet statements of basic moral obligation stand in no need of explanation and I do. The question expressed by 'I agree that truth telling is prima facie good but why is it obligatory?' is neither confused nor misguided. Second (and I'm sure Wielenberg would agree), metaphysical questions should be distinguished from epistemic questions. That statements of basic moral obligation like 'one has a prima facie duty to assist those in distress' are obviously true and stand in no need of justification doesn't entail that they don't stand in need of explanation."[125]

(2) Wielenberg says: People claim objective morality requires a foundation external to itself. Why accept such an assumption?

Response: That the laws themselves exist and do not require a foundation external to themselves for existence is true. However, it is more likely that the laws were designed than they just appeared, as J. Beckswith and Greg Koukl say: "A command only make[s] sense when there are two minds involved, one giving the command and the one receiving it."

Dr. Paul Copan points out in *Ethics Needs God*:

> *Theism offers a more plausible context than atheism/non theism for affirming a cluster of features related to human dignity and moral duties...The worldview favoring a robust moral world is theism, in which a good, rational, supremely aware Creator makes human beings in His image. God's existence secures the existence of genuine value and rights in the contingent world, easily accounting for human dignity, rights, moral responsibility (which includes rationality and free will), and duties. On naturalism, however, why think that morally responsible, valuable beings would be the product of mindless, non rational, physical, valueless, non conscious processes? Unlike*

---

125   William Weinwright, "In defense of non-natural theistic realism: a response to Wielenberg."

theism, naturalism's context can't anticipate the emergence of value...A personal Creator, who makes human persons in the Creator's image, serves as the ontological basis for the existence of objective moral values, moral obligation, human dignity, and rights. Consider: (1) Without the existence of a personal God, no persons would exist at all. God is the sufficient reason for the existence of anything (rather than nothing) at all. And (2) if no persons would exist, then no moral properties would be instantiated or realized in our world. Without this personal God and Creator of other persons, why think moral properties would be instantiated? Moral values—the instantiation of moral properties—and personhood are intertwined: moral properties are instantiated through personhood, which is ontologically rooted in God's personhood...Surely intellectual honesty forces us to admit that human rights and universal benevolence more naturally or fittingly flow from a theistic universe than a naturalistic one... Second, the naturalistic moral scenario is indeed a shocking coincidence, unlike the natural connection between a personal, good God's existence and that of morally valuable creatures. Let's assume that moral facts are necessarily part of the universe's furniture and that the beings luckily evolved via a torturous, profoundly contingent series of unguided physical events to be morally constituted and thus obligated to those pre-existing facts. It is strange in excelsis and staggeringly coincidental that these moral facts should (a) "just exist" and (b) perfectly correspond to intrinsically valuable beings that happen to emerge so late on the cosmic scene...Theism, by contrast, does not lean on such a weak metaphysical reed; rather, it brings together unproblematically two otherwise unconnected features—moral facts (rooted in a Divine necessary being's personhood) and moral creatures in whose image they have been made.[126]

---

126   *In Debating Christian Theism*, J.P. Moreland, Chad V/ Meister, and Khaldoun Sweis (eds.) (Oxford: Oxford University Press, 2013), pp. 85–100.

Furthermore, accountability is certainly more compelling with a Divine lawgiver. To quote Peter S. Williams: "Logic can't tell us that we have a categorical moral obligation to 'be reasonable' or to value truth over falsehood."

To further quote Copan: "So naturalism's context doesn't inspire confidence in (a) the emergence of objective moral values; (b) the actual existence of human dignity, duty, and rights (however strongly we are wired to believe in their existence); or (c) in the trustworthiness of our belief-forming structures since naturalistic evolution is interested in survival not truth... Value cannot emerge because self-consciousness, rationality, and free will cannot emerge in a naturalistic universe... A universe of electrons and selfish genes has no metaphysical wherewithal to produce beings possessing intrinsic dignity and worth (and thus certain inviolable rights)."

(3) God's ability to impose obligation by way of His commandments depends on the truth of certain ethical facts that are not themselves grounded in God.

Response: Dr. Steven Evens points out (to me via email): "This is correct but harmless. The Divine command theorist (such as Robert Adams and myself) holds that there must be facts about the good that are independent of God's commands. In that way God can be guided by the good, and it can also be true that it is good to obey God. The part of morality grounded in God's commands are obligations. Wielenberg thinks a moral obligation is this; what you have good reason to do when you have no reason to do anything else. That is a weak view of obligations."

(4) Neither the theist nor non-theistic moral realist can satisfy the demand of grounding moral claims.

Response: Again, Dr. Steven Evens (said to me via email): "Obligations are grounded in God's commands. The good is grounded in God's nature. Finite things are good to the extent they resemble God or participate in God. Theistic Platonism makes much more sense than non-theistic Platonism."

I also found some of the points made on the blog quoted below worthwhile and relevant to the topic of non-theistic moral Platonism.[127]

Moral values are not abstractions: How could moral values exist as abstractions apart from minds? Think of justice. It makes sense to understand some*one* as being just, but it doesn't make much sense to think that justice can exist as an entity in itself. The concept of justice itself is not just, in the same way that quickness is not quick, nor laziness lazy. To be meaningful, these abstractions must be mind-dependent.

Cannot ground moral duties: Even if it could be shown how certain abstract objects are invested with the property of having moral value, the Platonist still cannot explain why we are morally obliged to obey them. Why think they apply to us? Why not ignore them if we choose? Are the abstract objects going to enforce themselves? Clearly not.

Abstract objects, particularly moral objects, require thinkers: Abstract objects are objects of thought. It makes no sense to think of objects of thought existing for eternity without thinkers to know them. Indeed, what applicability would abstract objects like love, justice, fairness, tolerance, and the like have apart from personal minds? These sorts of objects require the existence of minds to even be meaningful. Human thinkers have not existed for eternity, so the existence of these abstract moral objects would require an eternal mind, which we would identify as God. As Alvin Plantinga writes:

> How could there be truths totally independent of minds or persons? Truths are the sort of things persons know; and the idea that there are or could be truths quite beyond the best methods of apprehension seems peculiar and outré and somehow outrageous. What would account for such truths?

---

127   See https://bit.ly/2ZIRaiz.

How would they get there? Where would they come from? How could the things that are in fact true or false propositions, let's say, exist in serene and majestic independence of persons and their means of apprehension? How could there be propositions no one has ever so much as grasped or thought of? It can seem just crazy to suppose that propositions could exist independent of minds or persons or judging begins. That there should just be these truths, independent of persons and their noetic activities can, in certain moods and from certain perspectives, seem wildly counterintuitive. How could there be truths, or for that matter, falsehoods, if there weren't any person to think or believe or judge them?

If God must exist to ground abstract moral objects, then it makes better sense to ground moral values in God rather than abstract objects.

Human Nature / Humanism

While somewhat related to conscience, Human Nature/Humanism differs from it in that it proposes that humanity is decent enough, we are generally good people, and we want to see the human race flourish. The problem, however, is that human nature is the reason we need objective morality so it can confine and shape it. Not many people would want to live in a world where the majority of the populace (not to mention everyone!) indulged in whatever "felt natural." The (atheist) philosopher Iris Murdoch felt that humanism does not have much to offer either: "I shall argue that existentialism is not, and cannot by tinkering be made, the philosophy we need. Although it is indeed the heir of the past, it is (it seems to me) an unrealistic and over-optimistic doctrine and the purveyor of certain false values. This is more obviously true of flimsier creeds, such as 'humanism,' with which people might now attempt to fill the philosophical void."[128]

---

128 Iris Murdoch, *The Sovereignty of the Good*, p. 46.

"The problem is: Humanism has ideas, but no legal system of implementation."[129] In *The Persistence of Faith*, Rabbi Jonathan Sacks says: "Stuart Hampshire put it well when he wrote that 'human nature, conceived in terms of common human needs and capacities, always undermines a way of life.'"[130] Finally, Professor Keith Ward lays out an unpleasant truth that destroys Humanism as a viable moral system at its foundations: "The 'natural' world is a darker place than humanist and liberal morality pretends. It is this fact that makes morality not a matter of the human and dispassionate calculation of maximization of compatible interests, but a matter or relentless and passionate battle of the moral will against the insistent pressures of lust, hatred, aggression, and arrogance that dominate human lives."[131]

The Dictates of Society

Some people suggest that a way to reach moral objectivity is to follow the standard of the collective society and that people will keep in line because of mutual self-interest. A quick look at history debunks this assertion quite easily. The Nazi party was voted in, and a majority of Germany's citizens agreed with their evil platform. If a person would say, relative to the world, the Nazi's position was not held by the majority of the world, we can just as easily find other examples. For the majority of its history, the majority of the world had no qualms with slavery. The majority of human history has been dominated by the concept of might makes right; hence the near-universal practice of the strong taking advantage of the weak. Human history attests to the sad but obviously clear truth that just as individual people have faults that interfere with moral objectivity (greed, etc.), societies also are inflicted with the imperfect human condition, and hence are capable of evil.

Another aspect of the appeal to society is the concept of a "social contract," where the members of the society follow a set of morals out of self-interest. Professor Keith Ward explains the difficulty with this:

---

129   Dennis Prager and Joseph Telushkin, *The Nine Questions People Ask about Judaism*, p. 108; see there for context.
130   Stuart Hampshire, *Morality and Conflict*, p. 155, in Sacks, *The Persistence of Faith*, p. 47, fn. 14.
131   Ward, *Morality, Autonomy, and God*, p. 63.

People do not have to be moral or reasonable in their actions. I can justify moral principles as principles calculated to sustain a safe and healthy human society, and to support individual well-being on the whole. I can see that these are wholly reasonable foundations for morality. But, at the same time, I can opt to be a "freeloader" who takes advantage of the morality of others to procure my own interests. This is a risky gamble, which social sanctions will seek to bring ruin. But in many societies and for many people it may succeed. Moral principles, principles rationally calculated for the public good and for the personal good of many, may carry little sway with me, especially if I am beyond their reach.[132]

...But what if their view on morality as founded on natural sentiments is adopted by a society of racist and elitist thugs, whose natural sentiments are of hatred of foreigners and contempt for the weak? What right will we have to condemn them, except that we have different feelings, a fact that, used as an argument, seems lamentably weak and pitifully arbitrary?[133]

It is clear that society itself is not an appropriate litmus test for objective morality.

---

132   Ibid., p. 33.
133   Ibid., p. 43.

Appendix C

LOOSE ENDS

WHY NON-BIBLICAL JUSTIFICATIONS FOR VIOLENCE ARE IRRELEVANT IN THIS BOOK

The entire structure of this book is based on the premise that the contents of Scripture are morally justified if one understands them in the context of the totality and reality of the Biblical picture. Therefore, the arguments of philosophical/ideological systems that address the contents of the Bible based on their value system are immaterial. To understand the text of Scripture, it is imperative to assess its contents using the structure of the system that it was transmitted through by the people of the book who have studied and preserved its understanding for thousands of years.

On a related note, the point that many people who believe in the totality and reality of their doctrine, while using it to justify immoral actions, is also irrelevant to this book. The point is an important one, but because the focus of this book is limited exclusivity on the moral accusations leveled against Scripture (what is recorded to have happened there), I have omitted this point due to its not being related specifically to morality of the Bible itself. In other words, it is a post-Biblical issue, not an issue pertaining directly to the contents of the Bible.

A JUSTIFICATION FOR BIBLICAL VIOLENCE, NOT A PROMOTION FOR POST-BIBLICAL VIOLENCE

This book is an effort to explain the reasoning and justification for the violence contained in the Bible, not a source for condoning current violence done with the claim of Scriptural support. As I mentioned in the first chapter, one does not have to be concerned with adherents of Orthodox Judaism using the Bible as a reference and support for violence. As Chief Rabbi Jonathan Sacks put it:

> *Three thinkers, Jan Assmann, the Jewish scholar Henri Atlan, and the Christian theologian Miroslav Volf, have something deeply insightful to say about Divine vengeance. Assmann points out a fundamental difference between the Hebrew Bible and other ancient civilizations. In the others, the human king takes on the attributes of a god. The anger of the king is the anger of the god; the latter legitimates the former. In avenging himself against his enemies, the king is doing god's work. Violence receives a religious sanction. In the Hebrew Bible, by contrast, there is a profound and unbridgeable distance between the human king and God. Anger is "theologized" and thus "transferred...from earth to heaven." Atlan argues, likewise, suggesting that "the best way to rid the world of the violent sacred is to reject it onto a transcendence." The "transcendence of violence" results in "its being expelled from the normal horizon of things." In other words—vengeance is removed from human calculation. It is God, not man, who is entitled to exercise it. To be sure, there are times when God commands human beings to act on His behalf—the battles against the Midianites and the Amalekites are two obvious examples. But once prophecy ceases, as it has done since early Second Temple times, so too does violence in the name of God.*[1]

That being said, I want to reiterate that the material contained in this book must be taken in the proper context of very specific situations and timeframes. The contents of this book are meant to serve as an understanding of the Biblical justice system, not as an incitement to create and enforce some perceived Biblical justice in our current day

---

1   Rabbi Jonathan Sacks, *Haazinu* 5770, "Vengeance."

and age. As Paul Copan wrote of Divinely initiated wars: "…They were never intended for non-prophet organizations!"[2]

MANY INTERPRETATIONS TO CHOOSE FROM, BUT WHO HAS THE ADVANTAGE?

When it comes to objective interpretation of the Bible, there are really only two potential paths to follow.[3] One can either rely on an established tradition on the meaning of the Bible, or he can try to extrapolate extra-Biblical sources and use various scientific, archeological, and linguistic methods to obtain insights that allow them to arrive at their conclusions.

One has to keep in mind the clear truth that when it comes to making an assessment of various Biblical narratives, there is very little available to go on using the tools in the shed of the academics (i.e., extra-Biblical sources, archeology,[4] and linguistics).[5] Therefore, when it comes to knowing about most wars and incidents in the Bible, the academic community is, at best, on the same playing field as the traditionalists who take the Bible at face value.

However, I suggest that the Orthodox Jewish tradition has an advantage over all others. The Orthodox Jewish tradition is a living system, an unbroken chain of understanding that has been in use for thousands of years. If I want to learn the best interpretation of Scripture, does it

---

2   Paul Copan, *Is God a Moral Monster?*, p. 161.

3   Some coming from certain Christian perspectives may offer another, "What their heart inspired by God tells them it means." Being that this is at best a clearly subjective path, I will omit it from being a contender in Biblical interpretation.

4   For example, Professor Robert Eisen of George Washington University wrote of the war against the Canaanites: "Archeological findings also raise questions about the historicity of the genocide in that no evidence has been found to support it" (*The Peace and Violence of Judaism*, p. 26).

5   Evidence of this truth is found in the words of a vehement opponent of the Bible, Steven Pinker. In *The Better Angels of Our Nature*, he writes: "The good news, of course, is that most of it {Michoel: Stories in the Bible} never happened. Not only is there no evidence that Ya-eh inundated the planet and incinerated its cities, but the patriarchs, exodus, conquest, and Jewish empire are almost certainly fictions" (p. 10). If he felt there was sufficient ammo to level more severe charges against the Bible, surely he would fire away. Alas, he has to limit himself to: "Whether or not the Israelites engaged in genocide, they certainly thought it was a good idea" (ibid., p. 11).

not make sense that the people who live by it and dedicate their lives to it would be the most pristine source for the understanding of the document that is in question? The academic/secular criticism of the Bible is rarely based on the tools that give them their supposed advantage. The undeniable advantage to understanding Biblical events is to accept the authentic methodology that was passed on and preserved by the people of the Book themselves, i.e., Orthodox Jews.

Rejecting the traditional nature and context of Scripture to use a system from outside of the Biblical system to then, in turn, understand the Biblical system is illogical and a dishonest fantasy.

IS BELIEF IN GOD ESCAPISM?

In *The Great Partnership*, Rabbi Jonathan Sacks encapsulated what I believe to be a very effective short response to this accusation:

> *I never understood why it should be considered more courageous to despair than to hope. Freud said that religious faith was the comforting illusion that there is a father figure. A religious believer might say that atheism is the comforting illusion that there is no father figure, so that we can do what we like and can get away with it: an adolescent's dream. Why should one be considered escapist and not the other? Why should God's call to responsibility be considered an easy option? Why should the belief, held by some on the basis of scientific determinism, that we have no free will and therefore no moral responsibility, not be considered the greatest escapism of them all?[6]*

---

6   Rabbi Jonathan Sacks, *The Great Partnership*, p. 27.

ABOUT THE AUTHOR

Michoel Stern spent over a decade learning in yeshiva and *kollel*, and has been involved in various teaching, outreach, and community leadership roles ever since. His articles on the intersection of Jewish thought and contemporary questions have appeared in numerous Jewish publications around the United States and have achieved wide acclaim. He specializes in the works of scholars of philosophy and religion, a longtime passion, and corresponds regularly with the scholars themselves.

Michoel Stern currently lives in Cincinnati, Ohio, with his wife and children. Visit him at www.michoelstern.com.